Misogynous
Economies

Misogynous Economies

The Business of Literature in
Eighteenth-Century Britain

Laura Mandell

THE UNIVERSITY PRESS OF KENTUCKY

Publication of this volume was made possible in part
by a grant from the National Endowment for the Humanities.

Editorial and Sales Offices: The University Press of Kentucky
663 South Limestone Street, Lexington, Kentucky 40508–4008

03 02 01 00 99   5 4 3 2 1

Library of Congress Cataloging-in-Publication Data

Mandell, Laura.
    Misogynous economies: the business of literature in eighteenth-century
Britain / Laura Mandell.
        p.   cm.
    Includes bibliographical references (p.   ) and index.
    ISBN 0-8131-2116-7 (cloth : alk. paper)
    1. English literature—18th century—History and criticism. 2. Miso-
gyny in literature. 3. Capitalism and literature—Great Britain—History
—18th century. 4. Women and literature—Great Britain—History—18th
century. 5. English literature—Women authors—History and criticism.
6. Capitalists and financiers in literature. 7. Economics in literature.
8. Ethics in literature. 9. Women in literature. 10. Rape in literature.
PR448.M57M36   1999   99-17695
820.9'353—dc21

The aesthetic is going to come back:
The question is, on what terms?
—Cora Kaplan

Contents

Figures

Acknowledgments

This work was inspired by an observation: in eighteenth-century texts in general and Jonathan Swift's texts in particular, Laura Brown has noticed "the necessary intimacy of structures of oppression and liberation." Each of the texts discussed in this work mingle together sexism and feminism in very disturbing ways, so that I was drawn to understand their "intimacy" and how it might be fostered or curtailed by literature. Enlightenment rationality entwines progressive and oppressive discourses in ways that we are still untangling at this moment; I hope this book contributes to that end.

I would like to thank the many people who inspired and helped to shape this work, including Henry Abelove, Fredric Bogel, Laura Brown, Frances Dolan, Donna Landry, Mary Jacobus, Lori Merish, Lisa Moore, and Charlotte Sussman. The manuscript was written thanks to various forms of support. I would like to than the Woodrow Wilson foundation for a Mellon Fellowship, Cornell University for a Sage Fellowship, and Miami University for various research grants. Thanks also to Gilbert Mandell for driving a piece of the manuscript over the mountains during a snowstorm to Federal Express, located conveniently in the valley; and to Gregory Gundzik who spent New Year's day with me at Kinkos.

I dedicate the book to my husband, mother, and father, and especially to Josef—in the words of Anna Barbauld, "a little invisible being who is expected soon to become visible": may he witness less and understand more about misogyny than I.

Chapter 1 was previously published as "Bawds and Merchants: Engendering Capitalist Desires," *ELH* 59.1 (spring 1992): 107–23. © 1992. The Johns Hopkins University Press. Chapter 4 was reprinted from "Demystifying (with) the Repugnant Female Body: Mary Leapor and Feminist Literary History," *Criticism* 38.4 (fall 1996): 551–82 by permission of the Wayne State University Press.

Introduction

The nymph, though in this mangled plight,
Must every morn her limbs unite.
But how shall I describe her arts
To recollect the scattered parts?
Or show the anguish, toil, and pain,
Of gathering up herself again?
The bashful muse will never bear
In such a scene to interfere.
Corinna in the morning dizened,
Who sees, will spew; who smells, be poisoned.

—Jonathan Swift, "A Beautiful Young Nymph Going to Bed.
Written for the Honour of the Fair Sex"

Although Jonathan Swift's "A Beautiful Young Nymph" has painfully detailed every disgusting, disease-ridden part of Corinna's body before coming to this conclusion, the poem's last couplet tells us that it is the "dizened" or *dressed* Corinna who will make us nauseous. What disgusts Swift is not the female body but its cultural baggage: clothes.[1] Moreover, Corinna's body is, the poem tells us, constituted by a heap of prosthetic devices: "a crystal eye," a set of teeth, "rags" to prop up her breasts, "bolsters" for hips.[2] The poem sees as nauseating the things that Corinna uses to plug up holes and prop up organs as a way of masking bodily decay. Mary Douglas has shown that cultural practices surrounding bodily orifices function symbolically as a way of representing a society to itself.[3] And, in the wake of her work, critics have shown that misogyny in representations is not about women but rather about society: representations that inspire passionate hatred of women and disgust with the female body provide a place for people to work out passionate feelings about changes in economic and social structure.[4]

Douglas's work and recent criticism make it impossible to see Swift's

1

scatology any longer as a personal psychic problem.[5] Swift does not hate Corinna; rather, Corinna gives him the opportunity to master anxieties about social changes, felt by Swift to augur the decay of a paternalist social order: enclosure,[6] the blurring of demarcations that separate aristocrats (the peerage) from the merchant, trading, and professional classes,[7] the alienability of property[8]—profound and troublesome changes accompanying the shift from agrarian and mercantile capitalism at the beginning of the eighteenth century to industrial or "full" capitalism at the beginning of the nineteenth century.[9] Since dress, as sumptuary laws indicate,[10] had long marked a person's status, it is no wonder that it would become an affectively charged (nauseating) object to members of a society changing in structure from a hierarchy based on status to a class society regulated by ideology. And certainly members of a society engaged in transforming communal into private property via "a parliamentary *coup d'état*"[11] might be obsessed, symbolically, with using stones (crystal eyes and fake teeth) to plug up entrances to a body—i.e., with closing off public access to a particular parcel of land now imagined as having the borders, unity, and integrity of a human body.

Although the title of this book indicates that it is about eighteenth-century economies, the book does not provide a historical account of the emergence of capitalism. Rather, it is about the development of affective structures around the emergence of capitalism: the economies discussed here are emotional. The following analysis of how misogyny works in both canonical and noncanonical literature tracks two changes in the structure of desire that occur during the eighteenth century, changes necessary to usher in fully capitalist modes of production. In order to *desire* engagement in capitalist activities, the image of the businessman must be rendered attractive enough for people to wish to identify with it. And, though it seems counterintuitive, the commodity form had to be *rendered* desirable—it was not automatically so. During the course of the eighteenth century, literature was reconceived as a commodifiable, canonical object and thereby lent its prestige to the commodity form. In both cases, new affective economies supported the emergence of industrial capitalism. Literature is one place in which feelings and thoughts can be circulated in new ways.

In discussing "the business of literature," then, this book is concerned with two things: first, literature's relation to business, the work it does of both promoting capitalism and critiquing it; and second, literary business, the business of making texts into highly marketable canonical objects. Albert O. Hirschman and J.G.A. Pocock offer accounts of people protesting against rather than blithely acceding to the motive of untrammeled self-interest.[12] The desire to produce profits and the desire to own commodities is not simply "natural." Capitalist desires had to be made palatable. Literature in general and misogynous representations in particular performed some of that work. By constructing ideal images of businessmen and canonical poets, and by stimulating identification with them, these representations implanted in their readers the desire to produce capital and consume commodities, literary objects being, as McKendrick and Plumb have shown, among the first mass-marketed commodities.[13] However, since misogynous representations were used to stimulate capitalist desire, they also were available to contest it: misogyny is the terrain upon which the proponents of new kinds of business, profiteering and commodification, meet their antagonists, proponents of the old, precapitalist order. My book traces the emergence of modern conceptions of business and literature in texts by authors such as Dryden, Swift, Pope, Otway, George Lillo, Mary Leapor, William Oldys, Henry Headley, William Hazlitt, and Anna Barbauld, analyzing how misogyny is used to work through, realize, resist, and critique new capitalist forms.

Most of the time, eighteenth-century misogynous representations promote capitalist desires. They instill in readers the desire to accumulate profits and commodities. More important, misogynous representations are able to redirect feelings antagonistic to the newly emerging capitalist order and to resolve those logical contradictions that it exacerbates. Their fundamental function under capitalism is to enable the desubstantialization necessary for understanding *man*kind in the abstract. For capitalism to be possible, Marx says, people must be able to think of each "man" as being, on the highest level of abstraction, equal to every other. Aristotle could not come up with a theory of value, Marx says, because he lived in a society that owned slaves who were seen as human like their masters: only conceiving all "men" as radically equal makes possible abstracting, quantifying, and thereby commodifying human labor.[14] Of course, many political theorists from John Locke onward argued that all men are equal. But merely presenting such an idea is not enough. Equalizing and abstracting "man" is quite difficult to do psychically. Cultural artifacts must perform the psychic work necessary for forming "man" into an abstract object and sustaining the object's status as abstract. A history-of-ideas approach to changes taking place conceptually during the eighteenth century does not sufficiently account for the psychic processes that make large numbers of people accept new concepts. Thus, this book uses psychoanalytic theory to show the kind of work performed by specific structures and figures in texts.

Idealizing "man" is most often accomplished by embodying someone else in a degrading way. We well know from recent work that imperialism and colonialism abetted the idealizing process by portraying the colonial other as more material, more bestial, than the allegedly universal, British, middle-class man and then insisting that the colonial other needs to be violently subdued and constrained. This book looks not at the violence of foreign but rather of domestic, literary relations. The Renaissance bequeathed idealized portraits of women to eighteenth-century writers, who then found representations of women available for de-idealizing. Such de-idealizing made idealizing male humanity possible.

To violently expel from an image all that threatens its ideal status has been called "abjection." As the work of Stallybrass and White has shown, abjection is not just a personal psychic mechanism but a kind of communal activity in which cultural representations are deployed in order to emotionally charge new concepts that are becoming current in the culture at large.[15] In two major works, *The Powers of Horror* and *Tales of Love*, Julia Kristeva describes the abjection/idealization dialectic.[16] As a developmental process, abjection accompanies the institution of primary narcissism: the infant abjects what is both its mother's and its own body in order to adequate himself to the ideal ego, the image of himself that he sees in the mirror which appears to be in control, unified, and contained. In order for the child to see the image *as* himself, he must separate from what he feels, since he feels out of control, heterogeneous, and borderless. In order for the image to *stand for* the child, the child must establish some distance from his own body (indistinguishable, from the child's point of view, from its mother's body), thereby creating a space that the ideal image can inhabit. Abjection is rejection or expulsion of the drive's body, later (after Oedipalization) seen as separation from and rejection of the *mother*, but in these early stages, before gender difference, what is actually being expelled is body and drive as such. As a rejection of the sheerly fascist domination of the drives, abjection establishes the difference between body and psyche necessary for the "triumph" of the image in the mirror stage:[17] that is, the image's ability to dominate the child's sense of himself depends upon the child's ability to disown as "not self," as an abject (m)other, whatever felt experience of his body does not correspond to the image.

Primary narcissism is therefore instituted by primary repression that takes place via the mechanism of abjecting. In "Repression," Freud describes the process of idealization as accompanying the repression of a desire that arouses disgust: "[T]he objects to which men give most preference, their ideals, proceed from the same perceptions and experiences as the objects which they most abhor, and that were originally distinguished from each other through slight modifications."[18] Ideals erected in the process of repression, he argues, are minimally different from objects for which desire has been repressed, and it is precisely disgust and abhorrence that renders those objects markedly different from ideal objects. Kristeva gives us an account of the constitution of the first ideal object, which happens to be the child's own ideal ego, through the constitution of an abject. The disgust that the child feels is the affective sign of repression. The child represses the love he feels for his mother's body, indistinguishable from his own. Via disgust, he represses his love for the materiality that is to be abjected and transports that love to the ideal image that now "refers" not to the body as experienced, but to an absence created by disavowal.

Although the creation of a human psyche necessarily requires abjection of the body, abjection does not require expelling or hating women: one abjects embodiedness as such. It is only a misogynous culture that codes the body "female," thereby rendering the process of abjection a sexist act. Furthermore, abjection is a rhetorical process as well as a psychic one.[19] It is a process of figuration: the use of recognizable and repeatable literary devices to arouse and channel passions of disgust and abhorrence. Texts that engage in the process of abjection manipulate the figure of gender to allow for identification and disidentification. In a text successfully establishing distinctions, the process of abjection requires readers first to identify with women and then to disidentify: the text first *undermines* gender differences at certain points, so that saying "woman" means "all of us," and then *augments* those differences, usually through suddenly representing women as completely disgusting and utterly different. Thus, while the repression of one's felt sense of materiality via abjection is necessary to the establishment of any psyche—universally, throughout history—the use of gender to undermine and promote abjection is historically specific, depending on how any given culture represents woman's relation to the body as such.

This dialectic of abjection and idealization was visible to early modern writers such as Jonathan Swift. In *A Tale of a Tub*, Swift gives us a passage similar to Freud's description of repression: "[Man's] first flight of fancy commonly transports him to ideas of what is most perfect, finished, and exalted; till having soared out of his own reach and sight, not well perceiving *how near* the frontiers of height and depth border upon each other; with *the same* course and wing, he falls down plumb into the lowest bottom of things."[20] Like Freud, Swift describes the usually insensible proximity of the ideal and the abject, but, instead of describing it as Freud does in the process of repression, Swift uncovers their proximity in a scenario of the breakdown of repression.

According to the story this book wishes to tell about the change in forms of abjection over the course of the eighteenth century, Swift sees the modern ego's incomplete formation, Freud and Kristeva its breakdown. Freud and Kristeva are witnessing the breakdown of the primary repression that establishes the ego in particular individuals—"borderline cases"—during a moment in history when social, cultural, and economic forms promote the ego's establishment.[21] In contrast, those forms are not yet securely in place when Swift is writing, so that he can readily see the ego's inability to establish itself, the failure of primary repression. What Freud and Kristeva can see because of their analyses of pathology, Swift can see because of his moment in history.

During Swift's historical moment, insufficiently established differences are breaking down. Chapter 2, on Thomas Otway's *Orphan*, provides an analysis of that moment in history. From the time of the Exclusion Crisis to the South Sea Bubble, an incompletely formed market system, emerging into an increasingly secular society, stimulates what René Girard has called a "sacrificial crisis."[22] The concept of abjection is deepened by connecting it to Girard's notion of mimetic violence. If, as Freud and Swift argue above, people are disgusted with things whose "frontiers . . . border upon each other," with things that "were originally distinguished from each other [only] through slight modifications," then the violent expulsion of these barely distinct things is an intrapsychic version of the public scapegoating ritual described by Girard.

In this ritual, someone who is similar to all the others must be sacrificed in order to stop the series of violent acts that equal "men" are committing against each other (the sacrificial crisis). Whereas each man's violent acts mimetically reproduce the other's, thereby rendering them identical, sacrifice of this one who is the same makes him utterly different. Disgust with another taken to its extreme—to the point of actually murdering the other, as disgust becomes utter hatred—makes that other who was at first the same different by virtue of being inanimate matter because no longer alive. To "abject" woman is to feel intensely disgusted with the female body. But abjection does not spring from an originary hatred of *women*. Rather, one abjects to be rid of things that one hates about *oneself*: women are originally hated not because different but because too much the same. Disgust with another who is visibly the same is, of course, self-hatred projected outward. If acted upon with violence, this self-hatred can thus transform this same-other into something different and separate; the self thereby disowns whatever it hates about itself. Abjection, scapegoating, sacrificing someone who is the same to one's own hatred—this is the process of erecting differences, of making other the one who was the same. It is not essence but rather the violence perpetrated against her that renders woman different from man.

Abjection involves two contradictory steps: first projecting one's bad qualities onto woman by recognizing one's similarity to her, and second, hating woman in order to establish oneself as distinct from her. Abjection is thus not simply a process of exclusion but actually an internalized scapegoating ritual, as Girard defines it, in that it requires first recognizing and then violently disavowing one's identity with the scapegoated figure. What one hates about oneself and violently disavows in religious ritual is one's own mortality. To represent men as transcendent, with immortal souls, requires some kind of scapegoating ritual, a ritual of transubstantiation, be it holy communion, in which Christ takes on the body and dies with it, or what came in eighteenth-century literature to serve the function of such a ritual: the abjection of women. Misogyny recurs in representations throughout the eighteenth century because it acquires those ritualistic immortalizing and idealizing functions that an increasingly rationalized Christianity can no longer support. In misogynous representations, a female body dies so that a male body can live forever. Because of the power misogynous texts have to evoke fears of mortality through representations of decaying flesh, and then their peculiar capacity to make mortality other, to make it female, they produce an ideal purged of all that one hates, especially the body's mortality. Misogyny is thus one element in the process of abjection that instills in people love of a masculinized, immortal ideal.

Liberal political and economic idealism perpetrates violence against those people—women, colonial others, slaves—in order to render them different (unequal, inhuman); their bodies can thus serve as a scapegoat for materiality and mortality. Abjection is the mechanism underlying the processes of desubstantialization pervasive in eighteenth-century thought: in philosophical discourses; in discourses constituting political economy; in concepts of fiction necessary both to notions sustaining the new finance (paper money and credit) and to notions of authorship; and in the construction of the novel as a genre.[23] The imperative to desubstantialize the conceptual entities "humanity" and "authorship," to abstract those notions from particularities that threatened to make generalizing about them impossible, was met during this period through idealizing "Man" by abjecting woman.

Furthermore, misogynous representations promote newly emerging capitalist practices by creating new ideal objects available for identification. Two of these ideals, this book shows, are the businessman (chapters 2 and 3) and the poet (chapter 5). One wants to be like the businessman and the poet because such identifications promise immortality; identifying with them means incorporating their desires to profiteer and commodify. Eighteenth-century misogynous representations induce abjection in order to make profiteering, consuming, and canonizing into desirable ideals. However, while this book shows that eighteenth-century misogynous representations turn the businessman and poet into ideal, immortalized images, it also shows that such representations also sometimes subvert the idealizing process, either inadvertently or intentionally. Usually idealization of men is success-fully accomplished through de-idealizing women: in George Lillo's *London Merchant* (1731) and Bernard Mandeville's "Modest Defence of Public Stews" (1724), discussed in chapter 3, the capitalist is idealized by virtue of scapegoating female courtesans and prostitutes as immoral kinds of busi-nesswomen in contrast to the virtuous male profiteer. These two texts there-fore participate in the cultural work necessary for the advent of capitalism, as Hirschman's *Passions and the Interests* has shown: they transform Chris-tian vice into capitalist virtue.[24]

However, misogynous representations that formulate the ideals neces-sary for promoting bourgeois ideology do not always succeed. Thus, in Thomas Otway's *Orphan* (1680), discussed in chapter 2, misogynous rep-resentations fail to secure entrepreneurship as an ideal: the figure of the woman in this she-tragedy is too sympathetic to allow the audience to com-pletely sever its interests from hers. If the subversion of emergent ideals is inadvertent in Otway, the use of misogynous representations to contest capi-talist ideals is sometimes quite conscious. In the poetry of Jonathan Swift and Mary Leapor (chapter 4), the female body is portrayed as disgusting in order to criticize idealizations of women: for Swift, such an exposure en-ables him to critique new scientific and mercantilist modes of objectifica-tion that make use of those idealizations; most paradoxically, Leapor uses her misogynous portraits to critique antifeminism itself. Their antiblasons thus partake of the "counter-movement" against pastoral idealizations that were marshaled throughout the eighteenth century to promote a new capi-talist ethic.[25]

The analysis of the workings of misogyny as serving to promote and critique capitalism extends to representations of the poet as a commodifiable object. In order to become canonical objects, poems must be conceived as the eternal property of an immortal poet. Conceiving of the poet and his works as canonical is possible only through the abjection of women. To say that women are abjected from the canon is not to say, simply, that they are excluded; abjection involves more than simple rejection. For readers, abjecting women in order to establish the canon requires first identifying with them so that what pertains to all poets—their materiality or imma-nence and historicity—can be projected onto women poets, and, only after this identification has taken place, excluding them in an act of disavowal. Thus, when disciplinary anthologies come into existence as purveyors of the canon, at precisely that moment, there is also a proliferation of miscel-laneous collections of verse containing women poets that do not claim to offer The Great British Poets.[26] Women are cordoned off in their own mis-cellanies, cultural productions designed to assert that women have what transcendent male poets do not: body (the poets collected in *Poems by Eminent Ladies*,[27] by definition, are embodied, because the title establishes them as a collectivity on the basis of having female bodies) and historicity (women poets are collected in antiquarian miscellanies, showing how people wrote during a certain historical moment). When critics say that women write poetry that is valuable only because of its specific location in time, they in fact transport to it a historical materiality that is thereby transported away from "great" (male) poets, "great" works seen as transcending time. Women's poetry is scapegoated for being materially bound, so that canonical works can live forever.

As Terry Eagleton points out, the ability to abstract "a universal subject" out of the individual, concrete, and particular is a tremendous feat, and the emerging middle class turned to aesthetics for help with the process.[28] Projecting historicity and physicality onto women's poems, collected in miscellanies, and then excluding them from disciplinary anthologies, is what creates the canon as we know it: it is what makes possible seeing works of literature and poetic identities as eternally and universally valuable objects. John Guillory rightly argues that canonical works cannot be seen as simply "endors[ing] the hegemonic or ideological values of dominant social groups" and, conversely, that noncanonical works cannot simply "be seen to express values which are transgressive, subversive, antihegemonic."[29] Thus, some of the noncanonical literary works discussed in this book are shown to promote hegemonic points of view. These works were excluded from the canon because they are propagandistic rather than literary, because they come down too heavily on the side of one, emerging ideology rather than reflecting, as does genuinely good literature, the play of competing ideologies and interests. Put another way: since language itself is never sheerly an instrument of ideology, what makes any work of literature "bad" is the formalistic extremes it has to go to in order to refuse to interrogate the ideology it purveys.[30] But although it is true, then, that some literary works were not included in the canon because they too stridently promote a certain political point of view and are consequently more like propaganda than like literature, it is nonetheless by now obvious that works *have* been excluded from the canon based on sexism. That is, Guillory is certainly right that canonical works do not need to express sexism in order to get into the canon, and noncanonical works written by women are not necessarily feminist.[31] Nonetheless, sexual difference has been harnessed to structure the aesthetic field itself. The process of constituting "the field of restricted production" or high culture[32] has required abjection of a materiality coded in Western culture as feminine.

Despite the fact that this book systematically exposes the ideologies that shape the list of canonical works, sexism most prominent among them, it does discuss "good" and "bad" (propagandistic) literature. The book proposes criteria for determining literary value. In contrast to critiques or re-valuations of the canon that see "literariness" as a mystified concept, literariness is here defined as a value. To claim that certain works have literary value is not to ignore but on the contrary to expose the "social determinants of literary value."[33] There are some works that can be demonstrated to have literary value and were excluded from the canon despite having that value. These works should not have been included in the canon simply because they were written by Mary Leapor and Anna Barbauld, two women poets, but because they were written by these poets and are great. One can only say that anthologies contain some "great" poetry, poetry determined to be valuable based on social rather than aesthetic criteria, because some *great* poetry has been systematically left out. This book itself exposes the notion of aesthetic value that developed during the eighteenth century as faulty insofar as, out of structural necessity, it blinds us to a specific kind of literary value. But exposing what was at stake in calling certain literary works "great" is not the same as rejecting any attempt to value certain cultural products over others. We should adopt other criteria of value rather than to abandon the project of valuation altogether. If, as Cora Kaplan maintains in the epigraph to this book, the aesthetic will return,[34] some feminist work ought to be dedicated to consciously negotiating the terms of that return. We need to formulate various feminist aesthetics.

Is the enterprise of valuing literariness retrograde? Only if one were to say that whether a cultural product has literary value determines whether it has *any* value, whether it is worth writing or thinking about at all—an idea I certainly reject, since two chapters of this book are devoted to works that, according to the specific criteria for literary value developed here, are bad art. As it turns out, texts described here as "bad art" are works that have also not been canonized, suggesting some overlap between canonical valuations of the literary and the definition of literariness, given below, used in this study. Aesthetic determinations have been ideological, but they have not been only that: the aesthetic exceeds ideology.[35] What has been canonized, for the most part, does have the quality of literariness valued here. But many works written by women and excluded from the canon also have that quality. As I show in chapters 4 and 6, these authors have managed to write feminist, profoundly literary poems by relying on traditional aesthetic values, in the case of Mary Leapor, and by fabricating their own aesthetics, as does Anna Barbauld. Leapor's work is parasitic on literary conventions, but if read properly it can be seen to resist misogyny inhering in them. Barbauld avoids the debilitating equation of female matter with historically situated, expungeable material, by formulating her own aesthetic, incompatible with the dominant aesthetic that ultimately devalued most of her poetry and reduced her "canonical" work to a few lines from one poem, "Life."[36] It is progressive to show that works by women authors excluded from the canon do in fact meet traditional standards of aesthetic value as well as promote their own.

This analysis is progressive in another way as well. Distinguishing qualitatively among cultural artifacts can in fact disrupt a misogyny latent in critical approaches to cultural artifacts that do not distinguish good from bad literature. To value literariness is important at this moment in literary history.[37] Now that it has finally become possible to talk about works by women writers, we do not want to invalidate aesthetic criteria that attest to their importance. Proposing new reasons to value the literary need not resuscitate the distinction between "high" and "low" culture as it was constituted during the Enlightenment, which, as this book demonstrates, is grounded in sexism. I argue that women cannot be *canonical* authors because the task of canonizing is grounded in a sexism that designates women's writings as historically interesting rather than aesthetically pleasing. It is not because men hate women that Anna Barbauld's works are excluded from the canon. Excluding Barbauld's works from the canon and *including* them in myriad miscellaneous collections of contemporary (rather than eternally interesting) poetry serves the fundamental function of distinguishing the historicity of her writing from the transcendence of (male) canonical poets. But such structural sexism is not in fact abrogated merely by taking a cultural studies approach to literary texts. The sexism designating Barbauld a noncanonical writer is in fact carried over into an analysis that calls her work interesting *only* as a cultural artifact—*only* as material. Deconstructing the opposition between "high" and "low" cultural artifacts can in fact repeat the sexist gesture that structures the canon itself. In the absence of any reason for studying Barbauld's works, a feminist/cultural studies approach presumes it is interesting because written by a woman poet—a poet with a body—and/or fails to distinguish between Barbauld's works and Thomas Bowdler's "translations" of Shakespeare (for instance)—both are interesting material artifacts. If such approaches render her work interesting *only* because embodied, they are as sexist as was canonizing itself. Paying attention to women poets is therefore an incomplete feminist gesture: to be complete, one must recognize works by women as poetically valuable.[38] The literary must be distinguished from the popular without demoting the popular to the uninteresting; one can thereby refuse to oppose high to low art as a means for establishing disciplinary boundaries. But, to avoid repeating the sexism analyzed here, this book defines "the literary" and determines two women's abilities to construct it. Poems by Leapor and Barbauld are aesthetically valuable according to very specific criteria that can be shown to apply to much canonical literature as well.

What determines aesthetic value is a work's literariness. "Literariness" differs from literature—the latter being the disciplinary object that is commodified and canonized. Any commodified object of literature may or may not be literary, depending on its structure, but also partly depending upon what kinds of ideological pressures have been put on readers, visible in their ways of handling texts.

My definition of literariness comes not from the field of aesthetics, although it has something in common with definitions proposed by literary critics.[39] Rather, it comes from the field of psychoanalysis, in particular from D.W. Winnicott's notion of "potential space."[40] Play occurs in "a potential space between the baby and the mother" (41), and this "playground" (47) later becomes a space of "shared playing," of "cultural experiences" (51), and of psychotherapy itself (46): "The place where cultural experience is located is in the *potential space* between the individual and the environment" (100). Potential space is the place where what the child identifies as "me" because of his or her sense of fusion with the mother, and indeed everything in the world, gets sorted out via introjective and projective identifications into the "me" and the "not me" (88, 130). The "good-enough mother" and the good-enough work of art are able to present objects to the child or the reader that gratify his or her sense of omnipotence (I created the object with which I am playing) while simultaneously calling that omnipotence into question (I found the object already created by another) based on intersubjective intimacy (47, 71, 100–101): it's my mother's/the author's object, although she thinks just the way I do.

Because the mother or the artwork both grants and contests the child's or the reader's omnipotence, the potential space that mother and artwork create connects subjective fantasy to objects in the world (a person or a text). At first, play is, like fantasy, purely subjective or internal. In play, as in fantasy, a child fabricates a scene and identifies with multiple positions in it. As Judith Butler puts it, "Fantasy . . . is not to be understood as an activity of an already formed subject, but of the staging and dispersion of the subject into a variety of identificatory positions." Butler is explaining Laplanche and Pontalis's notion of the "original fantasy," in which "the subject . . . is himself represented as participating in [a] scene, although in the earliest forms of fantasy, he cannot be assigned any fixed place in [that scene]."[41] But ultimately the child connects fantasy to external reality—or, put another way, creates external reality out of fantasy—by the process of fixing identifications. In potential space (play or art), there is a dynamic of identification and disidentification, introjection of a (loved) object and projection or expulsion of the (hated) abject. Finally the play of identifications ceases: the fixing of identification marks the child's move out of the potential space that contains a combination of hallucinated self-objects and real objects (52) and into a shared reality or intersubjectively constructed world.[42] The cessation of play is temporary, of course; child and reader can eventually begin playing again.

What can be said of play and fantasy can be said of reading literature. "Literariness" is a valuable quality in texts that allows reading to be a "playground" for adults in which, like children playing cowboys, one is invited to engage in multiple identifications, to switch from one to another (white to black hat) and back again at various moments. Such play reveals the nature of identification itself: "[I]dentification is the phantasmatic staging of [a desired] event. In this sense, identifications belong to the imaginary; they are phantasmatic efforts of alignment, loyalty, ambiguous and cross-corporeal cohabitation; . . . Identifications are never fully and finally made; they are incessantly reconstituted and, as such, are subject to the volatile logic of iterability. They are that which is constantly marshaled, consolidated, retrenched, contested, and, on occasion, compelled to give way."[43] Identifications are unstable and discursive, dependent upon "iterability," as good literature reveals. A text is literary (i.e., it counts as *good* literature) insofar as it constitutes potential space, a playground: features of that text allow a reader to identify with multiple positions rather than getting stuck in any one position.[44] By identificatory positions in a text, I do not necessarily mean "characters." Reading is a matter of identifying with positions generated by a sentence: one considers oneself as able to utter such a sentence, or the one who listens to it, or the one whom it addresses. Multiple points of identification constitute multiple possibilities of interpretation. As Diana Fuss puts it, there is a "play of identification in every act of interpretation."[45]

Literariness is a structure in text allowing people to explore and play with identities, try them all on. The pleasure of reading comes from the mobility of identifications, from moving from one to another, back, moving onto a third position, and so forth. What Butler says of people actually applies much more to texts: "Identifications are multiple and contestatory, and it may be that we desire most strongly those individuals [those texts!] who reflect in a dense and saturated way the possibilities of multiple and simultaneous substitutions."[46] Mobility of identifications is generated by structures in a text promoting such substitutions, but multiple identifications must be actuated by an economy of reading—by the way a reader invests her interest, allowing or prohibiting the play of substitutions.[47] This book discusses two economies of reading, two ways that readers move through texts, which are related to the ways that affect moves when someone fantasizes.

The first reading economy resembles what a person does when having a sadomasochistic fantasy. In "A Child Is Being Beaten," Freud describes sadomasochistic fantasies that all human beings have at a certain stage of development. If we forget the element of pain operating in sadomasochism and think about it instead as the name for an economic system, then "sadomasochism" names an economic structure that differs from getting and spending, from credit and debit; it names an economy of unmitigated expenditure. This economic organization describes a reader's investment in texts in which literariness operates: the reader invests in one identification, then another, then another, without getting any investment back; the reader continually spends by expending interest. People get pleasure from literariness in the same way as does the person who fantasizes a sadomasochistic scene, described by Freud: from continuously shifting "perspective"—or to put it in formal terms, from continuously imagining oneself as the one who is writing and/or addressed by specific sentences in a text, and then other specific sentences that contest the former, and then others, and so on. To say "get pleasure from" is, however, to misconstrue the sadomasochistic economy: pleasure is not a return on the investment; it comes from the activity of spending or investing psychic energy, from expending interest.

Literariness is indeed a structure like that described by Freud as the structure of sadomasochistic fantasies. It can be found in texts that offer multiple positions for a reader to identify with and that encourage the reader to move from one to another. But literariness cannot be seen as "contained" by a text; it has to do with the capacity of the reader as much as it does with opportunities provided by a text. A text can proffer an identification and nudge a reader toward it through discernible formal means, but it is up to the reader to take the offer and move into a new position.

Whether a reader is willing to take an invitation to move from one identification to another is not a personal matter. It is instead a matter of ideological pressures. Literariness, or the playful mobility of identifications, begins to be shut down when "literature" comes into existence as an object. It is well known that the word "literature" meant book learning even up to the 1790s when *The Life of Samuel Johnson* was first published: Boswell could still say "he had literature" and not mean "he had books on his shelves" but rather "he was learned."[48] The eighteenth century transforms literature from a process, the activity of learning, into a thing that one can buy. When faced with the question of what prevents readers from enjoying literariness, we can say that it is, in fact, because a text has become "literature," both commodity and disciplinary object. This reduction is easiest to see when discussing a literary work with someone who wants to use it as cultural capital, to be able to "ace" the test or impress people over cocktails: he wants to know what the text is saying, not to discuss a myriad of possibilities about what it might be saying. One has access to a text's literariness when all of its contradictory meanings remain open and possible. But to know a work of literature (to own it as cultural capital) means having mastery of a (more or less) univocal meaning. For example, the answer on a test to the question "Does Swift want to eat babies" is "No, 'A Modest Proposal' satirizes English oppression of the Irish." But the "answer" that would stand in for a process of reading "A Modest Proposal" would be "Yes, at moments Swift and I (the reader) want to eat babies; at moments I identify with that position and enjoy its sadism; but also no, I do not want to eat babies—I at moments identify with the author who is satirizing such a point of view by exposing its sadism." The literariness of "A Modest Proposal" consists in its capacity first to make it possible for a reader to identify with certain things that the proposer says by *undermining* one's sense of difference from him, and second to make it possible for the reader to identify with certain things said against him by *augmenting* difference. But the text's capacity to shift the point of identification is nothing without the reader's capacity to momentarily take up a position proffered by the text and then move onto others, a capacity diminished by the desire to master the text. Literature as a static object, a commodity or cultural capital, is distinct from literariness itself. The transformation of texts into literature forecloses on literariness, on the play of identities made possible formally within those texts, and thus reduces their capacity to create potential space.

In addition to meeting the economic need for commodities and the disciplinary need for cultural capital, there were distinctively social pressures for reducing literary play. Under a feudal socioeconomic structure and (more or less) absolute monarchy, secure structural positions do not depend upon the individuals who inhabit them. In contrast, under liberal, bourgeois, democratic capitalism, the individual defines through personal attributes the structural position that he or she can inhabit.[49] Class climbing is possible through self-improvement, as any reader of *Pamela* well knows. But such self-improvement was defined by the culture of bourgeois conduct manuals as discovering and revealing one's own "inner worth" or true identity.[50] When the social structure is itself not rigid and therefore not secure, people acquire a position in it by demonstrating their "inner worth" conceived of as their essence: one achieves a new status by revealing what is alleged to be one's own "real" identity. The new dispensation put pressure upon literature, upon its readers as well as its writers, to reduce the mobility of identifications in a text because such play is too threatening to the secure establishment of identity: according to Fuss, "at the very same time that identification sets into motion the complicated dynamic of recognition and misrecognition that brings a sense of identity into being, it also immediately calls that identity into question."[51] When status is secured by occupying a position, the play of identities is welcome. When status depends upon an allegedly fixed identity, such play is intolerable. Class mobility, a defining attribute of bourgeois society, is hostile to the mobility of identifications in literature. Bourgeois persons operate under the imperative that play be real: all the signs of identity they perform in order to claim a certain status must be signs of a real, underlying fact.

The desire to pin down the play of identities, a capitalist desire, did in fact stimulate bad writing such as George Lillo's *London Merchant*: the play so much insists upon readers identifying with one position in the text, that of the thoroughly good merchant "Thorowgood," that it is in fact more like propaganda than literature. But the pressure to limit play did not always or even necessarily affect writers—I am not arguing that, in 1757, authors began to mumble to themselves while at their writing desks, "OK, there has to be only one good guy in the text." Although literariness is a structural attribute, it is one that can be activated only by readers. We could almost go so far as to say that literariness is not "in" the text; if it is "in" anything, it is in various readings of texts. According to this view, *The London Merchant* is propaganda only insofar as we reduce its ambiguities when reading it. Readers gain full access to the literariness of a text when participating in a reading economy that is sadomasochistic in structure: it involves the complete expenditure of reading effort without being given any return, any paraphrase as to what the text "says" that is itself salable or that can be converted into that admiration for one's acquirements essential to class climbing and identity for the bourgeoisie, as well as to the profession of literature.[52] The pleasure generated by this sadomasochistic economy comes not from a return on an investment but from the activity of spending itself.

Raymond Williams sees "the aesthetic," one of the "great modern ideological systems," as housing two ways of thinking about the work of art, first as "process" and second as "instance." "The making of art," he says, "is always a formative process," and indeed some aesthetic discourse about great art sees it as such, as "experience, immediate feeling . . . newly generalized and assembled."[53] In the terms developed here, seeing the aesthetic object as process requires a reading practice that is sadomasochistic in its economic structure. Much canonical literature has the capacity to sustain a sadomasochistic reading economy, but canonical literature has very often not been read that way; often it has been read, to put it in Williams's terms, as "instance," as a finished product. Reading literature as literature rather than to activate its literariness—reading it as a commodifiable and exhaustively knowable object—such reading participates in another kind of economy and produces another kind of pleasure, one that is sadistic in structure. The second, sadistic reading economy is of the same sort of structure as that which produces economic capital. It is a pleasure that comes from getting back more than you spend, the pleasure of dispossessing another of a good that one wants.

Early in the eighteenth century, misogyny is a representational structure that is used to activate a text's literariness, to make it OK and even good for a reader to engage in multiple identifications. Why misogyny? At the moment historically when it is becoming necessary to fix woman conceptually as utterly, disgustingly other, she is not yet quite seen as absolutely different. People can still see the figure of any one gender as not absolutely excluding the other.[54] That is, a figure in a text can be female and still encourage a male reader to identify with her, but "secretly," as it were. People consciously see men as different from women even at this moment, when in cultural fantasy gender distinctions are not so firm. Misogyny superficially hides while structurally keeping open the play of identifications offered by a text. Misogyny therefore usefully protects literariness at a moment when it is threatened by ideological pressures.

However, as the century progresses, gender difference becomes more and more fixed.[55] Essentializing, transforming gender from a figure into a word with a literal referent (female anatomy), renders misogyny a representational strategy that is no longer capable of preserving the literariness of texts. Gender no longer secretly conveys a reader to another identity but rather blocks a reader's identification. That is, once woman is seen as essentially different from man, the reader of a text representing the figure of woman can now completely deny any similarity between a male (or male-identified) reader and a female figure or passive position in a text. This new sadistic economy is not a feature of the text—that is, texts are still literary in structure. But misogynous representations begin to be read in a way that reduces the figure of gender to a literal referent, prohibits the reader's desire for cross-gender identification ("cross-corporeal cohabitation," as Butler puts it),[56] and thereby fixes the meaning of a text as univocal.

To summarize, then: early in the century, misogynous representations serve to keep open the play of identifications or the literariness of a text; later in the century, misogynous representations work in a sadistic economy. Although some propagandistic texts do not in fact allow readers to identify with multiple positions in the text, this shift from one reading economy to another is more a matter of reading practices than it is a matter of a change in the structure of misogynous texts themselves. If this shift in reading practices has indeed occurred, then that means that we read early-eighteenth-century misogyny in a way that it was not read during the time it was written. As demonstrated fully in chapter 1, Swift, Dryden, and Pope did not read their own and each other's satires in the same way that we read them now. Seeing their satires as *literature*, as commodities and disciplinary objects, has involved suppressing the literariness of those texts, and we can see that suppression in the history of literary criticism about misogynous satire. However, we *can* read as did Pope and Swift. We can as readers activate literariness and participate in a sadomasochistic economy that resists rather than promotes the oppressiveness latent in Enlightenment thought. We can read like Pope and Swift only by employing a feminist method. Am I here calling contemporary feminist readings of eighteenth-century literature sadomasochistic? No. But feminist readings can restore to texts the indeterminate structure of identifications characteristic of sadomasochistic fantasies.[57]

The treatment of misogyny in this book is distinctive from all other works on eighteenth-century misogyny insofar as it presumes that misogyny is not at all natural, that it is not even a natural response to historical moments during which women demand equality or in other ways try to usurp patriarchal power.[58] It is necessary for feminists to maintain that misogyny is pleasurable to men because of what it is used to do rather than because men naturally hate women: only if overcoming the *desire* to oppress women is possible can we imagine a society in which antifeminism would be eradicated. The necessity of maintaining such a stance is not so much moral or political as it is methodological. That is, what Georg Lukács says about "realism" applies to criticism that attempts to realistically portray history. According to Lukács, "the possibility of realism . . . is bound up with that minimal hope of change for the better offered by bourgeois society."[59] Only hope for the better will inspire historians to take subaltern points of view as well as dominant ones into their account of reality. I personally believe that misogyny can be abolished, that it is unnatural, and that it persists only for the ideological purposes that it serves. But even if those things are not true, assuming that misogyny can be eradicated is a good method: adopting that assumption produces a more "realistic" history, as defined by Lukács, of eighteenth-century literature.

To say that misogyny preserves literariness in the face of emergent ideologies designed to destroy it (chapter 1) and that misogynous representations can serve even feminist purposes (chapter 4) is not to see misogyny as good. As chapter 1 argues in greater detail, we circumscribe the rhetorical power of misogynous representations by misreading them as about real women rather than as literary structures; we read sadistically if we do not see that the figure of woman is a transfer point in a text, a place for affect to come to and depart from. Thus misogynous representations serve many functions, both good and bad. But no matter what function such representations perform, they do indeed have invidious effects on the world. They promote misogynous culture. It is only within the context of a misogynous culture that misogynous representations can be used to serve good as well as bad causes: if sexism were abolished, the rhetorical effects described here would have to be achieved another way.

Whether misogynous representations are used in the service of good or bad politics, they have very real and deleterious effects in culture at large, effects that are themselves unaltered by an analysis such as this one in which misogyny is shown to be not about women but about something else. But this kind of analysis can affect reading practices in the field of eighteenth-century studies that tend to monumentalize (if not valorize) misogyny by presuming it to be "natural." Whether we read misogyny as only an attempt to demean women or as also an attempt to come to terms viscerally with socioeconomic changes depends upon us. Only a feminist analysis of misogyny reveals to us that such aggression has been aggravated and harnessed to perform cultural work necessary for an emerging dominant order; such an analysis thereby allows us to redirect eighteenth-century writers' anger to its proper target.

This book shows how virulently misogynous representations evoke the affect of disgust and induce abjection in order to establish crucial ideological differences: between entrepreneurship and competitive jousting (chapter 2), between the profiteering man of business and immoral greediness (chapter 3), between canonical literature and works of passing historical interest (chapter 5). Ideological success usually involves artistic failure: chapters 2 and 3 show misogyny operating in its most virulent, sadistic form; here misogyny shuts down play through the kind of abjection that establishes gender distinctions. However, as chapter 1 shows, abjection can also structure texts that are, ideologically speaking, failures because literary in structure. Often theorists of "phantasmatic identification" envision the abject only as that which one disidentifies from.[60] But as Kristeva specifies, abjection is a process that occurs when distinctions are being established *and* when they are breaking down.[61] If certain eighteenth-century texts are read, as they should be, using a sadomasochistic reading economy, they can be seen to deploy misogyny in order to keep open the play of figural substitutions: here abjection dissolves gender distinctions, thereby facilitating a greater mobility of identifications.[62] In this case, the reader first refuses to identify with a filthy female figure but then is brought to a "narcissistic crisis" as sexual difference that distinguishes him from the filthy figure breaks down.

Abjection, the affect of disgust aroused at the dissolution of difference and the failure to sustain an ideal, is especially visible in Swift's scatological satire, when Cassinus has gone too insane to clean himself after defecating, and so with "embrowned" legs himself, madly raves in horror at the fact that "Celia shits."[63]

Abjection is a kind of disgust or hatred one feels during a process of projection and exclusion that erects distinctions. It is also what one feels and undergoes at the moment when these distinctions are disintegrating. As Mary Jacobus puts it in a review of *Powers*, "the casting out or 'abjecting' of the mother [involves] in Kristeva's terms the radical exclusion of what threatens to collapse all distinctions between the self and other."[64] Such radical exclusion is necessary only when "the collapse of all distinctions" is imminent. Disgust with someone is a last-ditch effort to proclaim that person different from oneself, a use of affect to construct a perceptual and cognizable difference. Differences often come undone in those moments when they are first being put in place because they are not strong or conventional or commonsensical enough to withstand scrutiny.

Swift's and Pope's satires contain the rhetorical process of abjection because they undo differences and deflate ideals. I suggest in the following chapter that we have reduced the threat to our ideological constructs by the way we read Augustan satire: in Swift's and Pope's writings, abjection marks the undoing of distinctions; in the way that these texts have been made readable as canonical literature—viz., in the way they have been rendered morally respectable—we turn that abjection around and make it successfully work to erect difference. The modern reader doggedly shores up those distinctions not quite upheld in these early modern satires.

1

---·---

Misogyny and Literariness
Dryden, Pope, and Swift

Literary pleasure comes from texts that are structured sadomasochistically. While such an idea is rather easy to believe about early antifeminist satires, this sadomasochistic structure can be found in *all* types of eighteenth-century texts representing women. Both idealizing and satiric eighteenth-century poems encourage the reader to identify with many positions in the text, passive and active, sadistic and masochistic. Often professional readers of early-eighteenth-century satire have tried to convince themselves that the satiric is nothing like the passive satiric object. And yet there are moments when satirist and object become identical. If the satirist at moments resembles the person or character trait that he satirizes, then we as readers would be encouraged by that resemblance to shift from identifying with him to identifying with the object satirized. Whereas later canonizing readers disavow similarities between satirist and object in order to reduce the play of identifications stimulated by these texts, a satiric persona is portrayed in early-eighteenth-century texts as "bawdy" thereby is made to resemble the satiric object. In Dryden's translation of Juvenal's Sixth Satire, for instance, woman is attacked for her lasciviousness by a plainly lascivious narrative voice. Early-eighteenth-century satires structurally push readers toward making multiple identifications, so that the desire among twentieth-century literary critics to see the satirist as "the good guy," to fixate upon one point of identification in the text, betrays a change from sadomasochistic to sadistic reading practices. These practices have stimulated a kind of tunnel vision: it is easy for us to see the masochism in blason love poetry (a male speaker dies for the love of an ideal woman), and easy to see the sadistic treatment of women in satiric deflations of love poetry,

21

but it has not been so easy for us to see the sadism in idealizing poetry and the masochism in the satiric. Our reading practices, in other words, have rendered invisible one half of the sadomasochistic structure of both kinds.

Misogyny in the Ideal

Feminist analyses of lyric poetry have shown that ideal portraits of women in the lyric are themselves misogynous. Ellen Pollak, Mary Poovey, and Margaret Doody have all argued, for different reasons, that idealizing women constrains and denigrates them.[1] As feminists are beginning to discover, the pleasure imparted by ideal representations resembles satiric pleasure in startling ways. Barbara Johnson has analyzed the *male* masochism inherent in ideal portraits of women in the Petrarchan tradition.[2] Nancy Vickers has analyzed the sadism inherent in descriptions of ideal beauty.[3] In fact, idealistic portrayals of women provide sadomasochistic pleasure. The blason, the love poem idealizing parts of a woman's body, offers the same kind of pleasure, though through slightly different mechanisms, as do early-eighteenth-century satiric denigrations of women.

It is usually assumed that male satirists represent "the female monster" or the grotesque female body to express fear of female sexual appetites and needs,[4] and conversely, that idealized portraits of women represent "selfless, sexless" women for the sake of constraining female desire.[5] The lustful woman was satirized, the asexual woman idealized. As Marlene LeGates puts it, "[t]he misogyny which had characterized traditional satire and philosophical thought from the ancient Greeks through the seventeenth century was replaced by the eighteenth-century version of the Cult of True Womanhood."[6] With the rise of "domestic virtue,"[7] satire became less popular.

However, although many critics are able to explain the function of the ideal of virtuous, sexless woman, they do not explain why this ideal was attractive either to women or to men. What is enjoyable about ideal representations? Why do people desire to be virtuous women, or to have them as wives? We cannot assume that an ideal becomes desirable simply by being represented. As Charlotte Sussman says in her discussion of Armstrong's work, "[Armstrong's] crucial insight into the mechanics of novel-carried ideology would benefit from a more rigorous account of how 'virtually anyone' was interpellated into the subject position of the 'domestic woman.' How, for instance, were novel heroines, and their readers, made to desire this particular 'gratification'?"[8] That the representation of ideal femininity serves a social or economic or political function, that the middle class defines itself around it,[9] or that it helps separate private and public economic realms,[10] does not explain why readers enjoy it nor why it has ideological force.

We assume that ideal representations just are desirable and enforceable and so assume that satire is appealing because it deflates or parodies the ideals society forces us to care about: Swift's dressing-room poems are enjoyable, it seems, because they present "a parody of the idealization of the sex"[11] and "the deflation of romantic stereotypes and sentimental literary conventions";[12] they give us temporary relief from the values society forces on us.[13] In fact, the opposite is true: ideal representations are appealing *only* because they bear an obvious relation to parodies of them.

To begin with, parody does not provide relief from literary or social conventions; on the contrary, such conventions are not even recognizable until they have been parodied. Critics insist that the coupling of ideal and parodic portraits is "accidental," but that is not true: every *Romance of the Rose must* have its Jean de Meung: the blason was not defined as a genre until after the appearance of Jean de Tournes's ironic contre-blasons.[14] As Paul Salzman puts it, "one cannot see anti-romance as an attempt to destroy or refute romance"; "it is quite wrong to see romance and anti-romance as in some way mutually exclusive."[15]

But parody sustains ideal representations in an even more essential way than simply providing an ironic ground for the ideal figure. In a purely morphological way, ideal representations of woman are inherently violent in the same way that satires of woman are violent. Both chop up women's bodies, as is suggested by the fact that the name "anatomy" has been applied to both. The first collection of blasons, written by Clément Marot, Maurice Scève, Saint Gelais, and others, was published under the title *Blasons anatomiques du corps féminin* (written 1536, collected 1543) precisely because each poem described one body part, a foot, or a tooth, and in Marot's famous poem the breast. Satires on women were also called "anatomies,"[16] but in this case dissection reveals their hypocrisy rather than the "deliciousness" of their parts. Thus, idealizations and parodies perform the same procedure, but with what are apparently different results.

I say "apparently" because in fact the results are not different. The rose is very often used in carpe diem poetry to threaten women with the loss of their beauty: they should comply with men's wishes now while they are young "buds" because they will soon become "blown" blossoms.[17] Yet the rose metaphor cloaks threats beyond the mere onset of old age. This can be seen in George Etherege's "To a Very Young Lady":

Sweetest bud of Beauty, may
No untimely frost decay
Th'early glories, which we trace,
Blooming in thy matchless face;

But kindly opening, like a Rose,
Fresh beauties every day disclose,
Such as by Nature are not shewn
In all the blossoms she has blown:
And then, what conquest shall you make,
Who hearts already dayly take?
Scorcht in the Morning with thy beams,
How shall we bear those sad extreams
Which must attend thy threatening eyes
When thou shalt to thy Noon arise?[18]

The speaker's masochism is most evident in these lines: he has been "scorcht" and taken. Not so evident, however, is their sadism. If one pictures what is being done to the rose as being done to the lady, this poem threatens violence: "Nature" stands by ready to pull off all her petals (to undress her, or to disfigure her?) if the young lady unkindly refuses to "open" up her "beauties" to this man.

In "Beauties Periphrasis" (written in 1674, published in 1683), Thomas Shipman parodies the conventional metaphors used to describe woman in sonnets and blasons, and thereby brings out some of the violence and humiliation latent in these metaphors. As Shipman's parody shows, the metaphor of nature opening the rose can be used by the poet to defend taking off his lady's clothes:

Her Garments I will first disclose;
Then naked lay my blushing Queen,
The same procedure has the Rose;
First Leaves, and then the Bud is seen.[19]

In the second line of this stanza, the poet has elided "I will": *he* will "naked lay [his] blushing Queen" after stripping her. This line thus elides the agency that is itself being elided through use of the rose metaphor. The metaphor conceals the agent of violence, naturalizing it and making it seem blameless: the "rose" is not "opened" by a rapist, but rather "naturally" opens of its own accord.[20] If one pictures what happens to the rose happening to a woman, one can see the violence inherent in the metaphor. Idealized portraits of women impart the very pleasure proffered by misogynous satires insofar as they both depict violence perpetrated upon women's bodies. Furthermore, just as Etherege's love poem contains both sadism and masochism, satires generate pleasure—not through sadism alone—but through a slippage in which the aggressor becomes identified with the object of attack.

Misogyny in Satire

In an early article, Felicity Nussbaum presumes that satiric representations of women provide a check on lust, that they work as a kind of *remedia amoris*, "an antidote to the madness of love."[21] Yet these satires gave all readers, male and female alike, a great deal of pleasure.[22] Rather than discouraging male desire, misogynous attacks present sadomasochistic fantasies just like the fantasy "a child is being beaten" described by Freud, in which gender differences serve only to distinguish the onlooker from the group of children being beaten. In "the third phase" of the fantasy of a child being beaten, as Freud describes it, there are many indeterminacies that match the indeterminacies of scatological satires on women: the person doing the beating (satirizing) is unknown, and the onlooker (reader) does not definitely identify with any one position in the fantasy, beater (satirist) or beaten (satiric object). Identifications are more mobile than that. In "the third phase,"

> [t]he person beating is never the father, but is either left undetermined . . . , or turns in a characteristic way into a representative of the father, such as a teacher. The figure of the child who is producing the beating-phantasy no longer itself appears in it. In reply to pressing inquiries the patients only declare: "I am probably looking on." Instead of the one child that is being beaten, there are now a number of children present as a rule. Most frequently it is boys who are being beaten (in girl's phantasies), but none of them is personally known to the subject. The situation of being beaten, which was originally simple and monotonous, may go through the most complicated alterations and elaborations; and punishments and humiliations of another kind may be substituted for beating itself. But the essential characteristic [of this phase] . . . is this: the phantasy now has a strong and unambiguous sexual excitement attached to it.[23]

The pleasure of this fantasy comes from mobility of identifications: the fantasist identifies with no one position, or with all of them; the source of the violence is unknown, as the passive construction "being beaten" suggests.[24] The gender switch—a male audience watches the humiliation of women (satire), or a female audience the humiliation of men (Freud's fantasy)—simply serves to keep identifications mobile.

As some recent work on satire suggests, satire characteristically encourages the reader to suspect that the satirist or beater has a great deal in common with his satiric object and is thus in his very diatribes being beaten rather than beating. The satirist or attacker often appears as a character in the poem (thus more properly referred to as a satiric persona) and is identified by the poem with the satiric object.[25] Thus in Swift's "Cassinus and

Peter: A Tragical Elegy," Cassy—Celia's satiric attacker who cries out in despair,"Oh! Celia, Celia, Celia shits"—appears in the poem and is identified with the very Celia who disgusts him. Peter finds Cassy straddling "His jordan," his legs "well embrowned with dirt and hair."[26] Therefore, Cassy is horrified at Celia for being "embrowned" like he is. Even the reader is implicated: insofar as the reader is horrified by the excrement described by the poem, the reader is like Cassy, who is like Celia.[27] The reader's identification with Cassinus and also, because Cassinus is made similar to Celia, with Celia herself renders completely ambiguous who is being beaten.

The same kind of ambiguity occurs in the blasons and sonnets idealizing women, discussed above. Nancy Vickers sees ideal descriptions of women as containing within them the threat of dismemberment because of castration anxiety. Cathy Yandell analyzes Béranger de La Tour's "Blason du miroir" as an "only partially successful" attempt to "reassemble, through a complete image of the lady in the mirror, the dismembered body of the *blasons anatomiques*."[28] The blasons by Marot and Scève anatomize or dismember the female body, and La Tour tries but fails to unite them in a mirror image. In discussing the sixteenth-century Italian vernacular *ekphrastic* tradition, the "detailed presentation of the individual perfections of women," Elizabeth Cropper marvels that "the conventional description of the beautiful woman became so closely identified with a lyric poet who never painted her complete portrait."[29] The blason gives us only female body parts; the woman is more "beautiful" in pieces than she is whole.

However, the threats to male integrity come *not* from a male father figure, but rather, Barbara Johnson argues, from the very aggressive female "object" being described: "The image of being the prey rather than the hunter, the penetrated rather than the penetrator, would seem to pervade the Petrarchan figuration *not* of femaleness but of maleness."[30] It is for that reason that Johnson calls male masochism "the secret that it is lyric poetry's job to keep" (176). Analyzing the violence inherent in ideal descriptions in courtly-love poems as male-to-male violence, as the threat of castration, helps keep masochism a secret by transforming it into the aggression of the father. In fact, the threat of dismemberment is something "earlier" than castration, the aggressivity of part-objects described by Kristeva as abjection: the poet is threatened by parts of the mother-woman's body that threaten to devour him, the body that he himself has dismembered for the sheer pleasure of oral gratification;[31] such pleasure was called "primary masochism" by Laplanche in an early work, designating a kind of sadomasochistic pleasure that precedes object-relations.[32]

But if the positions with which a reader can identify are ambiguously sadistic and masochistic in satire and in ideal portraits of women, it is difficult to imagine that all Augustan misogynous satires collapse the distinction between satirist (or satiric persona, the "satirist" who appears as a character in the poem) and satiric object and thereby represent a sadomasochistic scene in which readers can participate. Since, in the case of satire, the moral outrage that we share with the satirist is what invites us to identify with him, it is difficult to imagine that satiric poems, especially scatological satire, impart pleasure through enabling a fantasmatic identification with the satiric object. Yet one can argue that moral outrage is only ever pleasurable insofar as the outraged person "secretly" identifies with the object of his rage.

Satiric Pleasure

John Guillory has called literature a quintessentially bourgeois object.[33] And, as Stallybrass and White amply show, in becoming a "high" rather than a merely popular form, English literature had to become more respectable.[34] For example, many miscellanies produced during the long eighteenth century are entitled *The Ladies Miscellany*: during the Restoration and early in the century, this title designates collections designed to seduce women;[35] toward the end of the century, it designates those designed to instruct women in virtue.[36] With the bourgeoisification of literature, poetry is desexualized.

In the 1690s, before the bourgeois movement of the reformation of manners begins, Dryden published his "Discourse concerning the Original and Progress of Satire,"[37] a work that is almost impossible to read because it points to the fact that satire is sexually titillating and simultaneously tries to desexualize it, to represent it as motivated by purely moral, asexual concerns. After distinguishing between the virtuous satirist and the immoral libeler, Dryden spends no fewer than twenty tedious pages arguing that satire did not originate in Greece: one immediately wonders, What could possibly be at stake? Why does Dryden try so hard to dissociate satire from the Satyr (the half-man, half-goat god), the Greeks, and drama itself (Greek comedy)? The Satyr was lascivious, as British satirists who associated themselves with it well knew;[38] Greeks were associated with voluptuous heterosexual sexuality,[39] and theater was, of course, associated in the 1690s with libertinism. In dissociating satire from the Greek origins imputed to it, Dryden tries to separate the pristine rustic whose moral outrage is justified from the lascivious goat who attacks for pleasure; he wants to distinguish the legitimate "Reprehension of Vices" from the questionable "License" of Greek feasts.[40] But Dryden's repudiation of the sexiness of satire is not confined to the *Progress*. He also suppressed from his translation of Juvenal's Sixth some clearly pornographic verses, including passages in which urination either figures ejaculation or is taken to be a sexually stimulating act in itself.[41]

Dryden's "Progress" is nonetheless ambivalent. It sets up Juvenal as honest and serious, unlike Horace, who was himself not virtuous enough to lash great vices[42] and unlike Persius, who though chaste and modest himself, too often enjoyed the "Crime" of being "broad and fulsom" in his attacks (4:52). The "business" of satire, Dryden says, is "to Reform great Vices," and Juvenal takes the palm in this task since he himself is virtuous enough to attack them and since he "lashes" them with the greatest vehemence (4:62, 65, 68). Juvenal causes the most pain, involved as he is in "the slovenly Butchering of a Man," and on that account Dryden contrasts him with Horace, who can "make a Malefactor die sweetly" (4:71). One would imagine, then, that Horace gives more pleasure; but a few pages later, Juvenal finally wins the contest as best satirist because he gives the most intense pleasure (4:73): Juvenal gives the most pain, and thus the most intense pleasure. Dryden describes the pleasure imparted by satire as sexual pleasure in a passage where he shows his preference for Juvenal: "[T]he Delight which *Horace* gives me, is but languishing. . . . He may Ravish other Men, but I am too stupid and insensible to be tickl'd. . . . [H]is Wit is faint; and his Salt, if I may dare to say so, almost insipid. *Juvenal* is of a more vigorous and Masculine Wit, he gives me as much Pleasure as I can bear: he fully satisfies my Expectation" (4:63). If one were to replace in this passage "Masculine Wit" with "sexual prowess"—a substitution encouraged by the word "Salt," which connotes sexual energy—one would have a description of who is better at giving the reader sexual pleasure.

The same kind of substitution can be performed in Pope's description of satire in *Epilogue to the Satires*, where, if one substitutes "penis" for "Weapon," satirizing becomes a (mono)sexual act:

> O sacred Weapon! left for Truth's defence,
> Sole Dread of Folly, Vice, and Insolence!
> To all but Heav'n-directed hands deny'd,
> The Muse may give thee, but the Gods must guide.
> Rev'rent I touch thee! but with honest zeal;
> To rowze the Watchmen of the Publick Weal,
> To Virtue's Work provoke the tardy Hall,
> And goad the Prelate slumb'ring in his Stall.[43]

I believe most readers will feel that it is irreverent for me to insinuate that this passage is an allegory of masturbation. But if this passage inspires reverence, that "awe" has been manufactured, I would like to suggest, precisely by institutionalized, disciplinary literary histories within which Popean and Swiftean satire have always made an uneasy fit.

One could summarize a dominant trend in the criticism of Pope and Swift, from their own time through the New Criticism, this way: Pope is proud, Swift clinically insane. Those who voice this criticism, however, are not simply those who read their poems. The "adversaries" (as they are called in descriptions of classical satire) are the interlocutors in satires by Pope and Swift and say the same things about the main, satiric personae of these poems as we say about Pope and Swift. The "Friend" who ends Pope's *Dialogue II* with "Alas! Alas! pray end what you began, / And write next winter more *Essays on Man*" (254–55) might have been an editor of the Norton anthology that contains the *Essay on Man* but not the *Epilogue to the Satires*. The friend admonishes P. by rendering P.'s probity suspect, to say the least: "You're strangely proud," says the Adversary to "P." (205). P.'s pride is "strange" because the friend does not know why P. considers it his duty to vituperate bad, sycophantic verse, nor why such vituperation has to be formulated in scatological images: "Hold Sir! for God's-sake, where's th'Affront to you? / . . . / This filthy Simile, this beastly line, / Quite turns my stomach" (157, 181–82). Why doesn't it turn yours? the Friend insinuates. Does P. wish to *attack* using scatological imagery, or does he merely wish to *use* that imagery, reveling in it as do the bad writers described in the *Dunciad*?

In Swift's "Cassinus and Peter: A Tragical Elegy," Peter introduces Cassinus's horrific revelation (that "Celia shits") with, "Dear Cassy, thou must purge and bleed; / I fear thou wilt be mad indeed."[44] Peter is thus the first in a long line of eminent critics, from Lord Orrery to Middleton Murray, who are horrified at "[t]he mad Irishman's wandering dirty thoughts."[45] But the antagonistic position taken by readers of *Dialogue II* and "Cassinus and Peter" is formulated in these poems by more than simply the adversarius.

Pope and Swift deliberately exaggerate their satiric personae in order to make stick the Friend's and Peter's implicit charges against them; it is almost as if Pope and Swift were asking the Curlls, the Gildons, the Lord Orrerys, the Fidelias, and other correspondents to the *Gentleman's Magazine*—the critics of their time—to call Pope proud and Swift insane. One of the first New Critics to point out that the satiric persona is constructed by and thus not reducible to the satirist, Alvin Kernan, analyzes this exaggeration.[46] Given that Stallybrass and White are correct in seeing Augustan satire as the place where individual psyches, and thus individuals per se, were first constructed, Kernan most aptly calls the excess or obsessiveness of the satiric persona its "private personality": "[t]here is always . . . a darker side to his nature, . . . which [makes] suspect his pose of a simple lover of plain truth" (264). The satirist goes "beyond mere prurience"; "[t]he more effectively he builds up catalogues of human vice, the more it will appear that he is merely purveying salacious material to satisfy the meaner appetites of his audience" (25). Or, one might add, his own.

In answering the Friend's question as to why he satirizes bad writers, P. of *Dialogue II* displays an egotism that strains belief:

> Ask you what Provocation I have had?
> The strong Antipathy of Good to Bad.
> . . . .
> Yes, I am proud; I must be proud to see
> Men not afraid of God, afraid of me.
> (lines 197–98, 208–9)

The reader begins to realize that, although P. may not write verse to flatter George II (as, he says, Henry Fox does [line 166]) nor to flatter Walpole (as does Bubb Dodington [line 161]), he certainly writes to flatter himself. P. is caught in an adolescent narcissism, imagining himself in an almost onanistic fantasy to be the chosen scourge of God.

In contrast, the Cassinus of "Cassinus and Peter" epitomizes the madman obsessed with excrement, inveighing against it with the most intense fervor (Cassy wants to die because "Celia shits") and, at the same time, adoring it, wallowing in it:

> Scorched were [Cassy's] shins, his legs were bare,
> But, well embrowned with dirt and hair.
> . . . .
> His jordan stood in manner fitting
> Between his legs, to spew or spit in.[47]

Pope's pride and Swift's anal fixation are not only artificial constructs, problems and diseases that the poets gave to personae in their poems; these constructs are also incredibly heavy-handed. Kernan insists that we recognize the satiric voice as a persona, that we not make it part of an author's biography. And Maynard Mack tells us not to "overlook the distinction between the historical Alexander Pope and the dramatic Alexander Pope who speaks" his poems.[48] It is therefore unwise to read the "O Sacred Weapon" passage as Pope's own serious proclamation of his satire's effect.

Thus, if substituting "penis" for "sacred Weapon" has no other effect than restoring the playfulness to this satiric form (which, if not playfully but seriously meant is not awe-inspiring or sublime but ridiculous), if it has only the effect achieved by adding "in bed" to the end of each message written for a fortune cookie, it restores to satire its original indetermination: the indistinguishability of satiric persona from satiric object; the satirist, and any reader who identifies with him, is being satirized in these poems as much as is the object of attack.

Canonizing readers such as Maynard Mack do indeed at moments misunderstand satire by seriously envisioning it as a "sacred Weapon" "To all but Heav'n-directed hands deny'd."[49] The dangers of taking these satirists too seriously—that is, in pinning their identities down to those of their personae—is dramatically visible in Claude Rawson's analysis of *Gulliver's Travels*. "One of [the] bleakest implications [of the *Travels* is] . . . that the most thorough-going positive in the entire fiction [Houyhnhnm society] is tartly established as outside human possibility."[50] Rawson then speaks of "the yawning failure of men to live like angels or even Houyhnhnms" (48)—which, if one remembers that Houyhnhnms are horses, translates into "the yawning failure of men to live like angels, or even horses." The playfulness and indeterminacy subtracted from canonized satire can be partly restored by recalling the context of Pope's allusion to quadrupeds—in the "sacred Weapon" passage, he calls the prelate's room an ox's stall. To imagine that the satirist speaking in the poem is Pope, or that Pope means the passage seriously, is like believing that Swift condones rationalism in *Gulliver's Travels* when he portrays rationalists as horses: everywhere in writing of the period, horses (and oxen) are symbols of concupiscence.[51]

The satirists were not only "gloomy"; they were also bawdy. The portrayal of the satiric persona, the satirist or attacker, within a satire as morally righteous but suspect, as himself someone who resembles the object of attack serves, precisely, to give sadomasochistic pleasure: by portraying the satirist as a scourge who himself secretly identifies with the object he attacks, the satire permits the reader to secretly identify with the object of the satirist's attack. In early-eighteenth-century satire, indifferentiation between satirist and satiric object therefore promotes sadism and masochism, the possibility of identifying with any of the positions (attacker or attacked) in a scenario of humiliation. Misogyny, engendering the attacked body as female, serves the same purpose as depicting a suspect satiric persona: it gives male readers the opportunity for disidentification and simultaneous identification with the object of attack. The moment of disidentification with the assaulted satiric object is the moment of moral outrage; identification is the moment when one recognizes an inescapable similarity between the satiric object and the outraged satirist with whom one has identified. The moment of disidentification in misogynous representations involves abjection: the assaulted object is a filthy materiality that is "not me" but "female."

"Me" in the preceding sentence is a male reader. But abjection can occur for female readers as well—because nothing forces a reader to read like a woman, least of all biology. That women can enjoy misogynous, scatological satire suggests *not* that the gender switch is nonessential in the construction of fantasies, but that misogyny is a peculiarly *literary* sadomasochistic pleasure for which we have acquired a taste. In other words, misandry is also pleasurable—according to Freud, quoted above, misandrous sadomasochistic fantasies are most pleasurable for women. But if more men are read than women, and men more often express sadomasochistic desire in misogynous literary representations than women writers do in misandrous literary representations, misogyny can thereby become a distinctively literary pleasure.

Swift's dressing-room poems are *not* "poems that nauseated their readers . . . to release men from passion and its attendant madness";[52] rather, male and female readers enjoyed misogynous scatology, and still do. In fact, rhetorical flourishes that point to enjoyment of the very misogyny being denounced can be found throughout Sandra Gilbert's and Susan Gubar's *Madwoman in the Attic*: there are moments when their text revels in its own descriptions of "filthy femaleness."[53] In other words, there are moments in *The Madwoman in the Attic* when it is not clear whether Gilbert and Gubar are exposing a misogyny "hidden" in the text or whether they are actually manufacturing misogyny for literary pleasure.[54] At times in feminist works, the exposure of misogyny and enjoyment of it are indistinguishable. Misogynous desires have been sanctioned and perhaps even instilled by the high literary culture that has formed Gilbert's and Gubar's taste and has taught them to write "interesting" and "appealing" prose.[55]

Literary pleasure comes from a sadomasochistic economy at work in both lyric love poetry and satire. One feature of satire that makes it possible for the reader to identify with multiple positions is the satirist's undermining of the satiric persona: the satirist deliberately calls into question his "probity" as scourge. If the satirist is deliberately portrayed as lascivious, then he is no better than his object: he resembles what he attacks. Criticism denies such a resemblance for the sake of reducing the text's play and thereby attempting to fix who the reader identifies with. Structurally, Swift's satire pushes readers toward multiple, contradictory identifications. Practically, we have foreclosed on such identifications by seeing the satiric persona's self-righteousness as justified rather than deluded.

There are three kinds of denial required for canonizing satire that I have just discussed: (1) a denial that satire's misogynous representations are pleasurable; (2) the denial that Augustan satire attempts to be bawdy; and (3) most important, the denial that the bawdy satirist resembles his lascivious satiric object. To admit the latter would require admitting that the pleasure of satire comes from the extent to which our identifications with positions in it can be mobile. Jean I. Marsden opens her essay "Ideology, Sex, and Satire: The Case of Thomas Shadwell" with an excerpt from the prologue to Shadwell's *The Lancashire Witches*:

But [satiric] Poets and Young Girls by no mishaps
Are warn'd, . . .
Their former Itch will spite of all perswade,
And both will fall again to their old trade.

As Marsden points out, Shadwell here explicitly "link[s] the satiric urge to female sexual desire."[56] Despite passages in writings of the Restoration period and the early eighteenth century that equate satire with the salt and itch of sexual desire, literary criticism of canonical Augustan texts has, as Rose Zimbardo claims, "cut the . . . morally uplifting model for satire in stone": "we have always had difficulty in trying to fit Swiftian satire to the binary, moral-emendation model [of satire and] have usually solved the problem by assuming that Swift was far in advance of his time."[57] The "morally uplifting model" of satire has made satiric poetry by Pope much more canonical than that by Swift because Pope's satiric personae have been, despite Alvin Kernan's best efforts, seen as less contaminated, as sharing fewer of the attributes of the satiric object, than have Swift's.

Swift's satiric persona, or the point of view we are supposed to sympathize with as readers, is typically contaminated. We are sometimes forced to move out of it into another perspective. Edward Said credits Swift with "the discovery of the intellect's madness" and sees in "Swift's mind" the "essential resistance to any fixed boundaries"; for Said this anarchy is fundamentally at war with a Tory literary tradition and form.[58] And one can see this madness operating as identificatory instability in "An Argument against Abolishing Christianity."[59] The projector of "An Argument against Abolishing Christianity" argues "for the retention of 'nominal' Christianity"[60] so that the pamphlet itself argues the opposite (Swift's) view, which is that society should retain "real" as opposed to "nominal" Christianity. However, when this projector argues against retaining "real" Christianity, he argues too well:

To offer at the Restoring of ["of *real* Christianity"], would indeed be a wild Project; it would be to dig up Foundations; to destroy at one Blow *all* the Wit, and *half* the Learning of the Kingdom; . . . to ruin Trade, extinguish Arts and Sciences with the Professors of them; in short, to turn our Courts, Exchanges and Shops into Desarts: And would be full as absurd as the Proposal of *Horace*, where he advises the *Romans*, all in a Body, to leave their City, and seek a new Seat in some remote Part of the World, by Way of Cure for the Corruption of their Manners.[61]

The projector says, in effect, that "only a satirist would advocate a plan as crazy as following real Christianity"; he attributes this idea to the writer of the satire who has constructed him. One cannot tell here whether Swift is satirizing the projector or the projector is satirizing Swift. The projector, who was supposed to be the satiric object, is winning in an argument against the satiric persona: in order to know this, we have to be identifying with the projector's point of view and therefore with the position of the satiric object. The identification is temporary; in a moment, we will slip back into the satirist's point of view.

I have shown that the mechanism by which readers procure literary pleasure from misogynous satire and idealizing lyrics is best explained by Freud's "A Child Is Being Beaten." In my view, Freud's descriptions of how fantasy works are not really about the operations of a timeless psyche but rather about how reading practices established in the early modern period operate. We deny that misogyny is pleasurable because we are currently participating in a new, sadistic affective economy that requires reducing identifications to one. Whether we choose to identify with assaulting satirists or attacked women, such fixity is accompanied by moral outrage. The pleasures of literariness, of the promiscuous mingling of identities in a scene of indifferentiation, cede to the pleasure of sadism.

Abjection and Literature

The literariness of satire, I have argued, consists in the mobility of identifications for the reader. But the mobility of identifications resides not only in the representation: the possibility for identifying with multiple positions can be foreclosed by the reader. Insofar as we take seriously the gloomy moral outrage proffered by the satiric persona in Pope's *Dialogue II*; and further, insofar as we read misogynous satires as really about men's "natural" hatred of women—in both cases, we build a bulwark against identifying with the satiric object. It is precisely those kinds of reading that canonizing Augustan scatological satire has involved. In other words, turning Augustan misogyny into a literary object has reduced its literariness.

For Pope and Swift, who did not see their satirists, their weapon-holders, as sublime, moral outrage—the most violent way to proclaim oneself as different from the outrageous object—does not work: in their satires, differences between moral satirist and immoral object of attack are done and undone in a continual vacillating process. They wrote their satires, and probably expected us to read them, relying upon a sadomasochistic economy. Those of us who have seen the satiric personae in their texts as "Pope" and "Swift" themselves, and who have then read their satires as expressions of disappointment with the world of politics or a secret hatred of women, are reading according to a sadistic economy. For us, abjection works: we see them as successfully outraged, successfully abjecting. Insofar as we do so, we reduce to nothing the literariness of their satires by putting a halt to the play of indeterminate and incomplete identifications they proffer.

But the pleasure of indeterminacy is not forgone for nothing. The sadistic pleasure that we get in exchange works this way: the reader sees that the morally virtuous satirist is in fact identified with the morally impure object; in a sadistic moment, the reader pulls away from that identification via self-righteous differentiation. "The satirist and I are not ourselves promiscuous as is a promiscuous woman; she is a disgusting slut, just like a piece of 'blown' meat hung up by the Butcher to attract flies."[62] The amount of hatred or disgust, the affect generated by misogyny, is what puts the distinction in place. That amount of affect is not "in" the text, but "in" the reader, or, more truthfully, in the circumstances surrounding the reader that make adamant differentiation so necessary.

The next two chapters analyze precisely those pressures put upon writers and readers of texts to make a distinction, pressures I see as coming from capitalism. I am going to analyze texts that are not canonical: Otway's *Orphan*, George Lillo's *London Merchant*, and Bernard Mandeville's *Modest Defence of Publick Stews*. Successful abjection makes texts canonical, and two of these texts do indeed successfully project onto women morally repugnant qualities of the capitalist businessman that are then disowned through disgust. All three texts were immensely popular during the eighteenth century, and Otway was considered until the beginning of the nineteenth century to be a playwright of national stature. But these works are nonetheless rarely considered to be canonical texts. There are two reasons why texts that perform the work of successfully idealizing the businessman by abjecting women are not canonical. First, canonical literature is not capitalist propaganda. If it purveys capitalist ideology, as this book argues, it does so only at the expense of a risk: canonical literature also provides a place for dismantling the ideologies it contains. To the extent that Swift's and Pope's satires are canonical, they are so because they have a sadomasochistic structure capable of demystifying forms of conceptualization required by capitalism but are susceptible of being read sadistically, that is, in accordance with capitalism's conceptual needs. Canonical texts offer the possibility of identifying secretly with a satiric object while waging self-righteous attack; noncanonical, propagandistic texts do not offer the possibility of secret identification along with overt disidentification through moral outrage. The two texts analyzed here that are structured sadistically, Mandeville's *Defence* and Lillo's *London Merchant*, are not canonical because there is no sadomasochistic affective economy underlying the sadistic. They contain, simply, the good (male businessman) and the bad (woman).

Second, successful abjection depends upon a moment of identification with the female figure that is then, in a subsequent moment of virulent abjection, violently disavowed. As shown in the next chapter, using the figure of woman successfully as a scapegoat requires "animating" her to the perfect degree: that is, the character must be animated or human enough to attract some sympathy, but not so animate that one cannot violently abject her, that is, disidentify with her via disgust and hatred that reduce her to the monstrous or inhuman, a sheer thing. In she-tragedies, identification with the heroine is easy; it is disidentification that has become problematic. The amount of sympathy that readers will have for female figures is overdetermined by structures in the text and the reader's capacity for identification, depending upon socioeconomic pressures. Before the establishment of a possessive market society is secure, abjection fails to promote sadistic capitalist pleasures over the sadomasochistic pleasures enjoyed by the knightly courtier. Otway's *Orphan* and she-tragedies in general evoke what is for us too much passion for their heroines because the distinction between entrepreneur and courtier that abjecting such heroines would serve to put in place could not be established. But also, what makes an eighteenth-century reader just barely identify with a female figure could make us identify with her whole hog: Millwood's feminism and Mandeville's feminist statements, which were lures for identification to their readers and auditors, are to us reasons for never relinquishing our identification with the female figure.

2

Capitalism and Rape
Thomas Otway's *The Orphan*

Thomas Otway's *The Orphan* eroticizes rape by using it to figure specular relations of power. The play renders rape appealing, represents it as procuring sexual pleasure, while simultaneously using rape to figure competitive business relations among entrepreneurs. The heroine of the she-tragedy plays the part of an abjected materiality that threatens to undermine the idealization of business relations: the raped, inert female body left over at the end of she-tragedies such as Otway's *The Orphan* and Nicholas Rowe's *Jane Shore* is the price and remainder of the idealization process. The world-annihilating scenes of chaos portrayed so often at the end of she-tragedies, and decidedly at the end of Otway's *The Orphan*, show us that the idealization process is not yet complete, that competitive relations do not look ideal by the end of this play as they should. Too much sympathy in writer and audience animates the abject remainder of the distinction being made, the figure of the woman, and her refusal to be thingified threatens to undo her role as mere object in an idealized, pleasurable scene of exchange between men.[1]

Feminists have for a long time seen rape as not fundamentally erotic—as an act of violence rather than a sexual act. However, ten years ago Catherine MacKinnon argued that heterosexual relations under capitalism are a version of rape and consequently that rape is indeed a sexual act, is in fact a more overt manifestation of the violence in all heterosexual relations.[2] It has been the premise of this book that no form of the oppression of women is "natural," thus that no representation of violence committed upon women's bodies is in itself sexually exciting, meeting the needs of a biological instinct or natural sexual drive. Given that premise, Mackinnon's argument does not apply to rape throughout time but only to rape under capitalism. In fact, rape should not be seen as a self-identical set of actions existing in every historical period but as itself structured by the ideological work performed in representations of rape. As Hazel Carby puts it, "Rape itself should not be regarded as a transhistorical mechanism of women's oppression [but] as one that acquires specific political or economic meanings at different moments in history."[3]

If MacKinnon's argument is historicizable, if, that is, we can see rape as a sex crime rather than a crime of violence under the capitalist system that came into existence *during the early modern period*, then we need to know how capitalism sexualizes the violent misogyny present in representations of rape. The "she-tragedies"[4] of the late seventeenth and early eighteenth centuries help to answer that question. They show us that rape is represented as sexually pleasurable to the rapist insofar as the relations of power figured by rape are themselves erotic. Those power relations become eroticized as part of the cultural work of promoting relations among capitalist entrepreneurs. If sympathy for the heroine is not too great, the disfigured, abject, and ultimately inanimate body of the raped woman serves a function in securing these sadistic, capitalist relations.

Audiences watching she-tragedies derive a great deal of pleasure from the spectacle of victimized women. Judging from the lyricism of violent scenes in Otway's *The Orphan* of 1680 and Nicholas Rowe's *Jane Shore* of 1714, and from the protracted scenes in which the women chastise themselves for the crime that has been perpetrated against them, the authors obviously *enjoy* depicting virtuous women who have been raped. Jane Shore has been raped by King Edward IV, the "royal spoiler," to whose progeny she nonetheless professes allegiance, and the play ends with her wandering the streets barefoot, bleeding, unable to eat some conserves her loving husband tries to feed her, and finally dying of starvation. Audiences of the late eighteenth century began to enjoy the spectacle of a virtuous woman suffering for having been raped offstage. Why? What ideological function does portraying those completely abject women, social outcasts, who die after having been raped, serve? This chapter shows that the fantasmatic representation of rape in *The Orphan* allows the play to reconceive business relations in a way conducive to an emerging market society. But it is important first to sketch out the difference between business relations in a feudal society and those in a capitalist society.

From Courtier to Competitor: Regulating Expenditure

In the feudal society of manorial lords, wealth and rank were inextricably aligned: wealth was an inevitable result of nobility, coming "naturally," as it were, from the tribute of vassals and baronial conflict. Necessary for the consumer revolution and the birth of a market society was the redefinition of status as determined by "purchasing power" rather than hereditary right.[5] Of course, in the old hereditary system, there had been greater social mobility than strict inheritance of property and titles would seem to allow: the number of titled families increased from 55 during the sixteenth century to 160 by the end of the seventeenth.[6] Lisa Jardine describes how status was acquired in Tudor England. Land was granted to families by royal charter, "in return for direct services to the Crown."[7] The crown consolidated its power by "maximis[ing] the wealth and landholdings of a small, select group of nobles" (80) who then opposed any transfer of property except by inheritance: "it was these new peers," Jardine says, "who set their faces most firmly against any further social mobility" (142); "Landlords (and the Crown) were opposed entirely to alienation of land" (79), to allowing land to be sold rather than inherited or reapportioned through royal charter. It is precisely the alienability of land, C.B. Macpherson has shown, that was required for a possessive market society to come into being.[8] Ideologically, property had to be seen no longer as an inherited "right" to income from rents, a right earned through service to the king, but rather as a salable thing. Doing business had to be reconceived, from courting favor to exchanging goods for a profit.

According to Neil McKendrick, the consumer revolution began in earnest in the 1690s with "the unleashing of the acquisitive instincts of all classes."[9] It is undoubtedly true that the detachment of wealth from rank made emulative spending possible for more classes of people. But the notion that the consumer revolution "*unleashed* acquisitive desires" should not blind us to the intensity of such desires, even among poorer people, preexisting the birth of a consumer society. Sumptuary laws in Tudor England tried to prevent wealthy commoners from buying clothing inappropriate to their rank.[10] Yet the 1563 Statute of Apparel prohibits people from buying such clothing *only* if they do not have the "ready money" to do so, and it warns the garment-maker not to take any "assurance . . . by bond, surety, promise, or pain of the party or any other" as credit instead.[11] Thus, as Frances Baldwin says, the statute tries, among other things, "to prevent the poorer classes from buying clothes beyond their means" (209 n. 48). In his treatise of 1583, *The Anatomie of Abuses*, Phillip Stubbes complains that people with incomes of forty shillings a year buy silk stockings costing twenty shillings, and they have several pair.[12] The Act of Apparel of 1563 thus seeks to prevent people from spending all or more than all that they have. In thinking about the change from a feudal to a market economy, we need to entertain the counterintuitive possibility that the desire to spend did not have to be stimulated but rather limited; that a self-destructive and sadomasochistic desire to expend all of one's means to the point of total ruin had to be curtailed.

Two Kinds of Business in The Orphan

According to the *OED,* it is between 1670 and 1727 that the meaning of the word "business," arguably the word uttered most often on the Restoration stage, began to have its modern sense, to shift from designating primarily public life or affairs at court to specifying trade, commerce, and mercantile transactions.[13] Otway's *The Orphan* opposes the change. The play can be seen as a sort of cautionary tale, warning us of what will happen if merchants try to achieve status in their own way and thereby proclaim that the courtier's rank is not indisputable but up for grabs. The play figures as rape the attempt to acquire status that one has not been born into nor received as a gift from the king, rape being, to the courtier, an apt figure for the predations of monied men.

Yet, for all its royalism, the play is not able to admonish against the new mode of business and portrays the pleasures of the new man just a little too well. The moral of the tragedy is that upstart younger brothers should not try to usurp the fortunes of their elder brothers, whose right to their inheritance is inalienable; however, that the play has a moral marks it as one of the new domestic tragedies, bourgeois in form.[14] Thus, even though the play depicts the disastrous consequences of acquiring wealth independently of royal sanction, it does its part in the ideological task of convincing people to transfer affect from the old mode of business to the new. In fact, the play ultimately contradicts the argument it wants to make by showing us that the pleasures of the business of service are not lost in the transformations of a market economy but, on the contrary, subsumed and intensified by the business of competition. By examining the pleasures proper to both kinds of business, and the transfer of affect from one to the other in this play, we can see how the sadomasochistic desire to utterly expend one's means is redirected and curtailed, transforming it into a sadism that makes rational exchange possible.

The representation of the new businessman in *The Orphan* is, from the point of view of the emergence of capitalism, successful: capitalist entrepreneurship undertaken for profit is shown to be as pleasurable in a sadomasochistic way as is feudal courtiership, despite the play's explicitly articulated moral promoting inherited wealth and status over earned wealth and status. However, the ideological success of this representation in promoting capitalist business relations is purchased at a cost: the change from the relations between men obtaining in a gift economy succeed to specular relations at the cost of the unleashing of mimetic violence that, as René Girard would say, can only be stopped by scapegoating.[15] At the end of *The Orphan*, it is not just the raped woman who is murdered; rather, the world is represented as being completely annihilated, a fact which suggests that this scapegoating ritual has not worked to stem the violence intrinsic to capitalist relations.

Scapegoating rituals can fail if the female scapegoat is not seen as fully human, on the one hand, or on the other, if an audience refuses to relinquish its identification with her—it can fail, that is, if she is represented as having too little or too much psychological depth. A woman who is a flat character will not serve as an effective scapegoat. In she-tragedies, being raped endows the female figure with a sense of personhood because a raped woman is someone who had an invisible intention made visible in its violation, who has an inner volition differing from outer actions, and therefore who is a person with psychological depth.[16] Insofar as she is a person, the figure of woman can be identified with. But because she is, during the rape, rendered a passive object, disidentification should follow. In the identificatory moment, aggression can be projected onto her; in the moment of disidentification, one's own projected violence will be seen as coming from the other. If like Lucretia, she is murdered by herself. Self-murder makes visible that she did not consent to rape, and thus that her mental intention differed from her (forced) sexual, physical action, but it is also an act of violence that imitates the original rape. In murdering herself, she embodies violence rendered impotent, which is thereby temporarily stopped. However, if the text and/or audience refuse to relinquish their identification with the murdered heroine—if she is too well-rounded—her self-murder doesn't provoke the deanimation of and consequent distancing from her that is necessary for the scapegoating ritual to work. In that case, both she and the world are annihilated. The play of identifications that promote or undercut the scapegoating process will be illustrated fully below in discussing Otway's play, the South Sea Bubble, and G.B. Tiepolo's painting "Tarquin and Lucretia." One further point will be made in the conclusion to this book about the figure of the raped woman. From being a subject capable of multiple relations, she is reduced to the status of an object through violence that deanimates her. Insofar as her virtue is represented as wealth, and this is appropriated from her, the figure of the raped woman is a protocommodity, and the incessantly repeated story of Lucretia is an allegory of the commodification of human labor. As will be seen here, the figure of the raped woman is a commodity exchanged in a relation of specular violence, the relation between two entrepreneurs.

The Business of Love

At the very end of Otway's *The Orphan*, after Castalio, Polydore, and Monimia have all killed themselves and the patriarch Acasto is ready to die at any moment, one of the marginal characters, Acasto's daughter Serina, tells us that she will go to London, take "some city lodgings," and pretend to be a rich heiress: these actions "may produce a story worth the telling, / Of the next sparks that go a fortune-stealing."[17] The question immediately arises, has *The Orphan* been about two "sparks that go a fortune-stealing"? Monimia, though of noble birth, is a penniless orphan, Acasto's ward and beneficiary of his charity. Out of respect for her noble birth, Acasto has promised to give her a portion of ten thousand crowns or twenty-five hundred pounds. But that is hardly a fortune: the *average* portion for a peer's daughter at the time was almost four times that amount.[18] In fact, the play continually emphasizes her poverty and thus her defenseless state. But as it does so, the play figuratively equates sexual pleasure with a valuable commodity. When planning their secret tryst in which they will consummate their marriage, Castalio says to Monimia: "When shall I come? For to my joys I'll steal / As if I ne'er had paid my freedom for them" (3.300–301). According to Castalio, marriage is a business in which the freedom a husband gives up pays for the sex he can have with his wife. Sex itself is figured as money. When Castalio goes to Monimia's room, he expects

> To take possession of Monimia's arms.
> . . . .
> At midnight thus the us'rer steals untracked
> To make a visit to his hoarded gold
> And feast his eyes upon the shining mammon.
> (3.506–10)

Later, when Polydore is revealing to her that he has substituted himself for Castalio—her husband and his brother—at the tryst and has slept with her in Castalio's stead, Polydore explicitly equates with wealth the sexual pleasure Monimia has given him. He claims to be a "man that's rich / [because now] in possession of thy sweetness" (4.416–17). The "fortune" these sparks have tried to "steal," as Serina puts it, is not a portion—Monimia has no money—but rather sexual pleasure from intercourse with her.

In order to make its explicit argument about how business affairs should be conducted, the play sets business at court and courtship at home in a mirror relation to each other. *The Orphan* opens by telling us that Acasto has prohibited his twin sons Castalio and Polydore from seeking either favor at the Bohemian court or fame in the emperor's army. The ambitious boys feel that they are literally rotting at home (1.100–101). Thus, lacking the opportunity to distinguish themselves in the emperor's service, Castalio and Polydore redirect their ambitions toward winning Monimia. Monimia is often called a "tyrant" (1.142, 5.225) or a "sovereign" (2.337); she is figured as a lord (2.385–89) and is said to possess an empire (3.554). The main characters try each in their own way to increase their value in the monarch Monimia's eyes.

Castalio tries to win Monimia through serving her in courtly fashion. Monimia, angry that Castalio has allowed Polydore to "affront [her] with his brutal passion" (2.349), threatens to break off relations with him. "But, oh, Monimia," he protests, "when th'hast banished me, / No creeping slave, ... / Shall ever dote [on thee] as I have done" (2.386–89). Monimia is, he proclaims, "the sovereign of my joys" (2.337); "I am a doting honest slave, designed / for bondage, marriage bonds—which I've sworn / To wear" (2.312–14). Castalio is a knight in her service, literally enthralled—in thrall or serfdom to a lord. Later in the play, when neither of them know that Monimia has slept with Polydore, she thinking it was Castalio and he angry because he was not admitted into her room, Castalio shouts at her: "I know my charter better" (4.120). In the paternalistic system portrayed by this play, the business of court is the business of love: in return for service, the monarch grants the courtier a charter to pure pleasure.

The Business of Rape

Polydore at first tries to win Monimia by doting, just as Castalio has done. But he is not a true courtier like his elder brother; rather, Polydore is one of the false courtiers who practice "the trade of courtship, / And . . . deal love out with art" (3.109–10). That is, instead of doting, he flatters. Flattery is associated with the new kind of business: not with the total self-expenditure of the enthralled courtier, but with exchange of currency, which flattering words figure. Polydore's father Acasto denounces the court where he has recently been disappointed, where "[a] huffing, shining, flatt'ring, cringing coward" (1.23) was raised in honor above him. Flattery, Acasto says,

> is a little sneaking art, which knaves
> Use to cajole and soften fools withal.
> If thou has flatt'ry in thy nature, out with't,
> Or send it to a court, for there 'twill thrive.
> . . . 'Tis next to money current there.
> (2.16–20)

Polydore first tries to purchase Monimia with flattery,[19] but when that fails, he plans her rape:

Who'd be that sordid foolish thing called man,
To cringe thus, fawn, and flatter for a pleasure,
Which beasts enjoy so very much above him?
The lusty bull ranges through all the field,
And from the herd singling his female out,
Enjoys her, and abandons her at will.
It shall be so. I'll yet possess my love.
(1.361–67)

For Polydore, performing the courtier's service does not give pleasure in itself; rather, flattery purchases sexual pleasure. He doesn't want to spend the coin of flattery and so vows instead to steal pleasure through rape.

Insofar as Otway explicitly advocates aristocratic values, the winner in the contest for Monimia's love has been predetermined. The first son out of the womb, Castalio, claims her as his hereditary right: "I loved her first," he says to Polydore, "and cannot quit the claim, / But will preserve the birthright of my passion" (1.135–36). When Monimia, "polluted" as she says by incest, tells Castalio that she must leave him, he replies: "Thou art my heart's inheritance; I served / A long and painful, faithful slavery for thee, / And who shall rob me of the dear-bought blessing?" (5.280–82). Polydore, of course, has already robbed him of his inheritance. But the play tells us that Castalio is to blame for the tragic events (5.445–54) because he encourages Polydore to compete with him over an inherited right that should be indisputable. Castalio's fault, Otway contends, is that he should not have agreed to a contest in which Polydore can try to make good his illegitimate claim. By allowing Polydore the opportunity to compete, Castalio turns Monimia into a whore before Polydore has even raped her: "Am I then grown so cheap," she asks, upon being told about their pact, "just to be made / a common stake, a prize for love in jest?" (1.260–61). As the engine of the tragic dénoument, competition itself changes love into rape.

The Pleasures of Hatred

Just like a fairy tale, the play has given us a good brother and an evil one, good business and bad, love and rape; they are as different as night and day. However, if one closely examines, inside the play and out, the kind of pleasure that accrues from service, paternalism, "love," on the one hand, and competition, capitalism, "rape," on the other, the distinction collapses. As we have seen, the play distinguishes paternalistic doting from the flattery of the new economic man. Doting, it contends, is service performed out of true love; flattery is performed simply for the sake of outdoing another server: Polydore wants to win Monimia only to overcome "the start [Castalio] got of [him] in birth" (3.374), only to overturn an inherited right. His pleasure in raping her will come not from the sexual pleasure she gives him but rather from hearing Castalio's cries at being refused entrance into her room, that is, from knowing that he has deprived his brother of pleasure. Polydore tells us this in a soliloquy in which he figures out how "[t]o cheat this brother" by standing in for him at their meeting:

> Oh, for the art of Proteus but to change
> The happy Polydore to blest Castalio!
> She's not so well acquainted with him yet,
> But I may fit her arms as well as he.
> Then, when I'm happily possessed of more
> Than sense can think, all loosened into joy,
> To hear my disappointed brother come
> And give the unregarded signal [for entrance into her room]. Oh!
> What a malicious pleasure will that be!
> (3.411–19)

The Orphan shows us here how pleasurable it is to watch someone suffer in dispossession. The play represents a new desire, a desire absolutely necessary, according to Marx, for turning large sums of money into capital proper. While villainizing the new desire thematically (i.e., in making Polydore its proponent), the play also represents as pleasurable the very actions that it condemns on moral grounds. For money and means of production to be transformed into capital, the owners of these things have to be "eager to valorize the sum of values they have appropriated by buying the labor-power" of the peasants they have expropriated from the soil;[20] they have to want to enjoy, I would say, watching those who were peasant farmers and are now dispossessed laborers suffer from the loss of the goods that the capitalists themselves now possess. The distinctively capitalist pleasures represented by Polydore are not only sadistic but also, insofar as the capitalistic predator identifies with the man he has dispossessed, sadomasochistic.

In its explicit argument, *The Orphan* would like to pretend that such pleasures are absent from a paternalistic society. However, Raymond Williams has called into question the so-called benevolence of paternalism. Whereas *The Orphan* wants to pretend that the sadistic Polydore corrupts a benevolent system, Williams says that "the 'intruders,' the new men, were entering and intensifying a system . . . already established [and already,] by its internal pressures, developing new forms of predation."[21] As to the consolidation of lands through dispossessing the peasantry, Williams says, "It needed no merchant to teach it to landowners."[22] Where, then, *is* the sadomasochism in paternalistic relations?

Castalio describes his doting service as absolute, complete expenditure. When begging Monimia for her favor, he says:

> Which way shall I court thee?
> What shall I do to be enough thy slave,
> And satisfy the lovely pride that's in thee?
> I'll kneel to thee, and weep a flood before thee;
> Yet prithee, tyrant, break not quite my heart.
> (5.221–25)

Monimia's brother Chamont repeats this masochistic fantasy of total self-expenditure; for him, loving is just like expending oneself in the emperor's wars:

> Onsets in love seem best like those in war,
> Fierce, resolute, and done with all the force.
> So I would open my whole heart at once,
> And pour out the abundance of my soul.
> (3.111–14)

And again, Acasto proclaims himself to be one of those men who "[h]ave spent their blood in their dear country's service, / Yet now pine under want" (2.61–62). In service, one expends all one's bodily liquids, tears and blood, or like Chamont, "*pour[s]* out the abundance of [one's] soul." But total expenditure is not a free gift.

Every sort of masochism involves some kind of contempt for the tyrant who inflicts the suffering. Theodore Reik puts it this way: "The masochist exhibits the punishment but also its failure. He shows his submission certainly, but he also shows his invincible rebellion. . . . He has an inexhaustible capacity for taking a beating and yet knows unconsciously he is not licked."[23] Castalio, Chamont, and Acasto claim the ability to expend themselves totally in service to their tyrants; the claim to have "an inexhaustible capacity for taking a beating," for being able to spend oneself down to the last drop of blood and tears, is, as Gilles Deleuze insists, a "provocation": "[There is an] element of contempt in the submission of the masochist . . .: his apparent obedience conceals a criticism and a provocation. He simply attacks the law on another flank. . . . [H]e overthrows the law as radically as the sadist, though in a different way."[24] That the masochist's assault on the tyrant who makes him suffer is as violent as the sadist's rebellion can be seen if one understands what total expenditure means in a precapitalist gift economy.

In *The Gift*, Marcel Mauss has made visible the violence of giving. Insofar as any giving, in any economy, makes the receiver indebted to the giver, it renders the recipient vulnerable. But in a gift economy, the failure to return a gift equal to or better than what one has received means loss of status. In *that* case, a giver's total self-expenditure ("potlatch") is a violent attempt to humiliate the receiver who may not be *able* to repay.[25] Thus, Chamont fears greatly for his sister Monimia because the defenseless orphan has been subjected to Acasto's benevolence. Acasto's gift to her, Chamont fears, may force her to pay it back by giving her virginity to his sons:[26]

> Great spirits bear misfortunes hardly;
> Good offices claim gratitude, and pride,
> Where pow'r is wanting, will usurp a little;
> May make us (rather than be thought behindhand)
> Pay over-price. . . .
> . . . I fear her weakness
> May make her pay a debt at any rate.
> (2.176–82)

Pride makes potlatch progressively more violent, each participant returning the gift with interest as a way of doing violence to the other.[27]

In the business of service, sadomasochistic pleasure comes from potlatch, from sheer expenditure, in which nothing is retained. As discussed above in connection with the 1563 Act of Apparel, when people began to believe that they had the right to aristocratic pleasures, they at first tried to spend everything, even their future income; like those aristocrats who continued to practice the sheer expenditure of luxury, these people would have made very bad capitalists, bankrupt ones, to be exact.

The pleasures of a gift economy are in this play represented as transferrable, however, to a capitalist system in which competitors are in a specular relation competing for a prize (Monimia) that (or, in this case, whom) is not an end in itself but a medium of exchange, the "thing" competed for. Monimia is merely currency in the primary affair between Castalio and Polydore. Often, specular relationships such as Castalio and Polydore's are figured as homoeroticism.[28] Here specular rivals are represented as twins, and Polydore's rape of Monimia as incest: "Sure we're such friends," Castalio says to Polydore, "So much one man, that our affections [for a woman] too / Must be united as we are" (1.151–53). Competition for the object covers over but also enacts a desire to merge into a unity with the other, to become him. The workings of capitalist desire are often obscured by homophobia;[29] here, we are prevented from seeing the sadistic desire coupled with masochistic identification inherent in destructive specular rivalry by the violent figure of rape.

Insofar as we imagine that the rapist's gratification comes from the fact that rape resembles certain kinds of sexual intercourse, we are prevented from seeing that rape is not essentially erotic but rather eroticized by the power relations it enacts, that the rapist's pleasure comes from the sadism of dispossessing a competitor. Polydore does not only rape Monimia; he also ravishes his specular rival of their common stake. In the case of the second kind of business, that of competition and exchange, the sadomasochistic pleasure is preserved, but no longer gained from sheer expenditure; now the pleasure comes from sadism, from taking rather than receiving the gift, and from secretly, masochistically identifying with one's beaten rival. *The Orphan* shows its audience that the sadomasochistic pleasures available in the total expenditure of courtly service are still available in sadistic commercial competition.

That one of the relations of power under capitalism is specular, often (although not necessarily) on that account figured as homoerotic, and that women figure into the specular, imaginary battle as chattel, we could have known from reading with Eve Sedgwick *The Country Husband*, a Restoration comedy dating, as does *The Orphan*, from the time of the Exclusion Crisis. But *The Country Husband* represents seductions, not what gets called rape, and the women in the play do not die: *The Country Husband* is a comedy, *The Orphan* a tragedy. As a tragedy about woman, as a she-tragedy, it is performing very specific ideological work. *The Orphan* represents capitalist competition as pleasurable. It tells auditors that they will not have to forgo the sadomasochistic pleasures of courtly service, but rather that those pleasures can accrue from competition that allows for both sadistic and masochistic pleasures. But what the play itself performs differs entirely from what it represents. One would expect a work that heralds the new capitalist order (despite Otway's conscious intention) not only to represent sadistic pleasure but also itself provide it: one would expect the play to perform a sadistic act for the sake of securing as ideal the businessmen it represents. But it does not do that. In fact, *The Orphan* is not able to successfully differentiate aristocrats from capitalist businessmen, nor to idealize the latter. This play performs the failure of abjection, the collapse of sadism into sadomasochism.

René Girard's account of tragedy and Mary Douglas's account of pollution rituals together provide a way of understanding what ideological work the she-tragedy performs as itself a ritual reenactment of crisis. Girard and Douglas describe scapegoating rituals—what causes them, how they operate—in a way that deepens Kristeva's notion of abjection.[30] The abject is a scapegoat in a ritual that takes place in a text or a psyche. Thus it is structurally identical to what the ritual commemorates—to scapegoating rituals that take place in the world.

The Sacrificial Crisis

In *Violence and the Sacred*, Girard plots the life of any given social structure on a continuum that ultimately proves to be a circle.[31] At one end, a scapegoating event brings a community into existence: the members of a group project all the violence they wish to perpetrate upon each other onto the violent interchange of two antagonists; at some moment during the violent interchange between these rivals, the distinction between them and thus among all of the members of the community whom they represent disappears. It is necessary for the members of the community to identify with both of the rivals in order for scapegoating one of them to work to stem violence within the community: only if all members can identify with the scapegoat can the scapegoat be an effective locus of their projections; only if they can see the scapegoat as a version of their violent selves can they kill off that violence by killing the scapegoat.

The community unanimously decides to victimize one of the rivals, thereby establishing an originary and arbitrary social definition (a definition that is necessarily arbitrary, since both antagonists, and indeed all members of the community, are at the moment of the sacrificial crisis "the same"). The scapegoating event establishes social distinctions, laws, the society's controlling fictions. They are fictions because they are arbitrary, because the community has unanimously "decided" to regard them as facts. The arbitrariness must not be too visible, however, for these fictions to function well.

Next, ritual recollections of the original event, ritual sacrifice, reinforces and sustains those fictions. At a later stage, the community withdraws belief in its fictions and ritual loses its effect: ritual reenactments of the violent event cede to actual violence; violence is no longer contained within the ritual frame. During this deritualization, mimetic desire or mimetic rivalry, the desire to be the same or rivalry for the same place within society's structure, devolves into mimetic violence, a violence that is not only wrought upon a rival but also necessarily undermines the ritually sustained social structure itself. As they rival for the same place, rival in effect to be the same, as they commit the same acts of violence upon each other, antagonists necessarily do violence to the structure that distinguishes them.

Finally, when mimetic violence reaches its peak, the structure disintegrates; it no longer distinguishes between rivals. Everyone in the community, until now polarized because all its members identified themselves with either one rival or the other, becomes indistinguishable from and identified with each other. Like the original sacrificial crisis that established the community and was commemorated in ritual, this sacrificial crisis ends when one rival—now identical to and indistinguishable from the other rival—is scapegoated: this arbitrary and unanimous act of violence consists in massive disidentification. Members of the community arbitrarily and unanimously distinguish themselves from an outsider who is both evil (containing as he does the community's disowned aggressions) and divine (in retrospect, since the death of this hero gave birth to unanimity and a new social structure). The scapegoated victim becomes a mythic hero, the focus of subsequent ritual reenactments of the event, whose distinctive tragic flaw both requires disidentification and abandonment by the spectator and exalts the hero to divine status.

In *Purity and Danger*, Mary Douglas analyzes the "dirt" of a society, "that which must not be included if pattern [social structure] is to be maintained."[32] Society's dirt, its "inarticulate forms" (37, 95–100), are a source of power and danger. It is at first glance hard to see how Mary Douglas's analysis of pollution rituals designed to ward off the danger of nonstructure (123) might be plotted so that it parallels Girard's scheme in which a community comes into being by violently excluding its own violence. Douglas rigorously distinguishes between two kinds of religious fears that sustain and undermine secular power structures (secular systems of differentiation): pollution danger, fear of transgressing structural boundaries because of a power inhering in the structure itself, and sorcery danger, fear of power believed to be wielded by agents who either consciously ("sorcerers") or unconsciously ("witches") threaten social structure. In pollution rituals, the community faces the threat to its definitions posed by anomaly and ambiguity. Another way to clarify social definitions is to accuse someone of being a sorcerer who perverts the power accorded to them by the social structure. The accusation allows "guilt to be pinned on [a] source of confusion and ambiguity" (107) other than the structure itself. Even though Douglas does not explicitly say that pollution rituals devolve into accusations of sorcery as social distinctions lose their efficacy, one can link Douglas's pollution rituals to the earlier stage in Girard's scheme in which ritual effectively reinforces social distinctions, and link the fears of sorcery Douglas analyzes to Girard's mimetic violence.

Douglas's "dirt" is inanimate matter that has been excluded by social definitions because it contradicts them. It is "matter out of place."[33] One could think of dirt as a corpse: it is neither entirely a thing nor entirely a being; it is partially animated by the power it has to disturb these two categories. The more dirt threatens to undo the system sustained by its exclusion, the more animated it becomes: marginal matter becomes a marginal or interstitial *person*, a witch. This is to say that, instead of rejecting and thereby deanimating the exclusions that threaten their laws, members of the community begin to identify with them, to endow them with subjectivity or personhood. In a witch, dirt is half-animated; she or he is seen as operating unconsciously, mechanically, without intent. As the social system further disintegrates, members of the community attribute its disarticulation to sorcerers who abuse the system: what threatens the structure is now fully endowed with personhood and conscious intent; dirt is now fully animated. A witch embodies, as a sorcerer thinks the structure's contradictions.

In describing the African tribe she studied, the Lele, Douglas talks about their pangolin ritual in which anomalies considered to be polluting (they threaten the structure, which is defined only by virtue of their exclusion) are confronted and affirmed: "The Lele pangolin cult is only one example of which many more could be cited, of cults which invite their initiates to turn round and confront the categories on which their whole surrounding culture has been built up and to recognise them for the fictive, man-made, arbitrary creations that they are."[34] But the Lele are not always a "dirt-affirming" society (170): "The elaborate system of anomalies rejected and affirmed which their cults present is regularly superseded by the latest anti-sorcery cult which is nothing less than an attempt to introduce the millenium at once" (171). When their social structure is most threatened, the Lele see sorcerers as consciously using the power of inarticulate forms to undermine structure.

Consciousness of dirt always threatens the social structure: the threat of a structure's disintegration can instill belief in its necessity, but it can also truly threaten to undo not only that particular system but all systems for differentiating. In the latter case, the community's reaction is twofold and, although the reaction seems to make sense, from the point of view of structure, it is absolutely disastrous: first, the community tries to eliminate the threat to the structure by eliminating all dirt; second, the community looks forward to "the millenium"—the elimination of all structure, of all the injustices due to differentiation: "[a]ll evil is caused by sorcery. [The Lele] can clearly visualise what reality would be like without sorcery and they continually strive to achieve it by eliminating sorcerers."[35] The community rejects the arbitrariness of social distinctions and animates excluded dirt: it is a sorcerer. The desire to purify social structure of its fictionality or arbitrariness paradoxically leads to its destruction. If members of the community would only ritually affirm whatever threatens their social structure, instead of trying to eliminate it, the structure would be strengthened. Intolerance of dirt leads to arbitrarily ascribing evil intent to a sorcerer and then scapegoating that sorcerer, an event that will stem violence only if it does not incite vengeance and provoke a chain of scapegoating events.[36]

For Girard, if violence is to end, the scapegoated sorcerer must be a "surrogate victim," differing enough from the original antagonist so that her family will not take revenge, but similar enough to both antagonists, who are now, in the throes of antagonism, themselves virtually identical. Girard talks about a community averting a sacrificial crisis by identifying with a tragic hero, a victim of the system, and then abandoning that identification. To put it in terms of conscious intent, members of the community recognize the necessity of the system even when confronted with the injustice they must commit for the sake of establishing and maintaining social distinctions. To put it in other terms, members of the community identify with social structure by distancing themselves from the hero, deflating their personification of inarticulate forms, deanimating, that is, the exclusions that the tragic hero represents.[37] By withdrawing identification, members of the community say, in effect, that its insight into the tragic hero is, finally, a fiction, and that the social structure alone (unjust or not) is real.

For tragedy to work at all in clarifying the social structure, members of the community must be able to identify with the tragic hero at the outset. The sacrificial crisis is precipitated by tragedy when the community refuses to abandon identification with the scapegoated tragic hero. In Girard's account, tragedy fails to allow ritually recognizing the arbitrariness of the system (and thereby strengthening it) when writers and audiences no longer see the scapegoated victim's death as necessary. In that case, audiences retain their identification with the tragic hero even after his death, envisioning him as an antihero victimized by a worn-out system.[38] Social fictions are seen as unjust and fictitious (and indeed, if unsanctioned, they are no longer "real"). The possibility of eradicating dirt, arbitrariness, fictionality, and, in short, systematicity per se is seen as real: people believe that overturning the system will bring about the millenium. Once the sustaining arbitrariness of the system is eradicated, the system topples.

According to Girard, asserting difference or claiming status will "swell the flood" of violence unleashed by indifferentiation when status is not predetermined but achieved and lost in "perpetual confrontation"[39] among the members of a community, when, that is, assertions of difference lead to indifferentiation.[40] Because we erroneously blame structuration itself for those crises in which claims to status proliferate, as opposed to blaming the loss of structure to which such a proliferation attests, we cannot see that differentiation itself, and with it inequality, actually stem violence:

> Order, peace, and fecundity depend on cultural distinctions; it is not these distinctions but the loss of them that gives birth to fierce rivalries. . . . Modern society aspires to equality among men and tends instinctively to regard all differences . . . as obstacles in the path of human happiness. . . . [A]n "antidifferential" prejudice often falsifies the ethnological outlook . . . on the

origins of discord and conflict. . . . Although usually implicit, its principles are explicitly set forth in Victor Turner's *Ritual Process*: "Structural differentiation, both vertical and horizontal, is the foundation of strife and factionalism, and of struggles in dyadic relations between incumbents of positions or rivals for positions." When differences come unhinged they are generally identified as the cause of those rivalries for which they also furnish the stakes. This [is] not always their role. . . . [W]hen they no longer serve as a dam against violence, they serve to swell the flood.[41]

According to Girard, Victor Turner is correct in connecting assertions of difference with the outbreak of violence, but not "structural differentiation" itself with such outbreaks. Violent differentiation only breaks out when the system for differentiating is breaking down.

The Exclusion Crisis and subsequently the Glorious Revolution mark exactly such a moment in British history: they mark the birth of British liberal theory, insofar as John Locke's *Second Treatise of Government* is a product of the Exclusion Crisis[42] and insofar as the Declaration of Rights punctuates the end of absolute monarchy.[43] This sense of the fundamental equality of human beings is also essential, Marx maintains, to the birth of exchange value as human labor in the abstract.[44] If the emergence of exchange value does not in and of itself make a system "capitalist," it is the crucial component that makes labor alienable and appropriable for the generation of surplus value—which is to say, of capital. If Girard's notion that indifferentiation produces violence is right, then there would be one perpetual sacrificial crisis in a liberal, capitalist system. Such a system attempts to eradicate differences among people for the sake of furthering humanitarian concerns and, at the same time, paradoxically, for the sake of rendering human beings exploitable. And in fact the distinguishing feature of bourgeois hegemony, class mobility, might be seen as a perpetual assault upon those in particular places in a hierarchy, and in fact as a perpetual assault on structural differentiation itself.

The South Sea Bubble: The Crisis "Legally" Resolved

In his *Memoirs of Extraordinary Popular Delusions and the Madness of Crowds*, Charles Mackay describes the South-Sea Bubble crisis from the point of view of a member of the class whose status was threatened by the crisis and clarified by its outcome;[45] thus, the "facts" he describes and the way he describes them illustrate the salient features of an outbreak of sorcery fears and the sacrificial crisis as described by Douglas and Girard. During 1720, rumors that the Spanish government would open the ports of its colonies to the South Sea Company enabled the company to sell stock on Exchange Alley at incredibly high prices, allowed them to cash in on future trading opportunities. Since "the inordinate thirst of gain that had afflicted all ranks of society was not to be slaked even in the South Sea"(52), entrepreneurs began other joint-stock companies ("Bubbles"). Once buyers were assured that any Bubble's petition for a royal patent would be granted, the price of its stock rose. When the price of stock was at its peak, the original projectors, the directors of the Bubble company, sold out, "the scheme was at an end," and the stock purchasers were ruined (54–62):

> Each poor subscriber to the Sea,
> Sinks down at once, and there he lies;
> Directors fall as well as they,
> Their fall is but a trick to rise.[46]

What horrifies Mackay about the activity on Exchange Alley is the intermingling of classes and sexes. "Everybody came to purchase stock":[47] "[a] speculating frenzy had seized [peers] as well as the plebeians" (51); a "frantic eagerness [seized] people of every class to speculate" (54); "[p]ersons of distinction, of both sexes, were deeply engaged in all these bubbles" (56). He quotes "A South-Sea Ballad":

> The greatest ladies thither came,
> And plied in chariots daily,
> Or pawned their jewels for a sum
> To venture in the Alley.[48]

Worse, success in these ventures allowed drastic changes in status. As J.H. Plumb shows, movement from one class to another was relatively easy during the early part of the century, even out of the Alley:

> Towards the end of their careers, ["the merchant princes"] often bought up great estates to endow themselves with the social prestige which went with land ownership and which would enable their sons and daughters to marry into the aristocracy or to acquire a title in their own right. These were the men who controlled the Bank of England and the great chartered companies .... With property came standing in society and a future for one's children, for in the early part of the century it was relatively easy to pass from one social class to another—a fact which amazed Voltaire and others.[49]

Mackay portrays the sudden changes in status that occurred during 1720 this way: "The overbearing insolence of ignorant men, who had arisen to sudden wealth by successful gambling, made men of true gentility of mind and manners blush that gold should have power to raise the unworthy in the scale of society." For Mackay, these changes in status bring with them "a corresponding laxity of morals": corrupted manners, "scenes of infamy disgraceful . . . to the morals of the offenders," and (here Mackay quotes Smollett) a "'picture of tasteless vice and mean degeneracy.'"[50]

Activity on Exchange Alley constituted a crisis of indifferentiation: it presented in exaggerated form disintegrating definitions of class occurring throughout the early part of the century. For Mackay and Smollett, the new-monied men are "dirty," which is to say "degenerate" and immoral. Significantly, Mackay and "A South-Sea Ballad" figure class indifferentiation as the corruption of fine ladies.

The crisis of indifferentiation on Exchange Alley came to a head in the larger crisis, the bursting of the Bubble, the first stock-market crash. Both crises arose because once a title can be purchased by "hard cash,"[51] the ficitionality or arbitrariness of class distinctions has become too visible. But these crises did more than expose the definition of "aristocrat" to be a fiction once sanctioned by a now visibly shaken feudal social structure: the contradiction also exposed the fiction that "cash" is in any way "hard."

Some of the proposals for establishing companies by raising capital through selling stock seem like "normal" economic ventures to us. Thus, among those ventures listed in Mackay's summary of the companies that were, after the crash, outlawed by the order of the Lord Justices, 12 July 1720, there are projects for making money through manufacturing products; "purchasing and improving leasable lands" or "lands to build on"; "buying and selling estates"; insuring against wage loss, fire, robberies, and theft; lending money; importing; and, like the South Sea Company itself, "carrying on trade." However, most of the Bubble companies were purely "monetary corporations," corporations that, like the South Sea Company, intended to make money less by actually undertaking their projects than by inflating the price of their stock: as mentioned above, the more unabashedly monetary, the more absurd and "scientific" (in the Royal Society sense of the word) were their projects. The project "for a wheel for perpetual motion [which required] capital [of] one million [pounds]" and the company "for carrying on an undertaking of great advantage, but nobody knows what it is" were both declared illegal, along with insurers and importers, by the order of the Lord Justices.[52]

As absurd as these and other projects were, it is important to note their affinity with what we consider "normal" economic ventures: what we consider "legitimate" capitalist enterprises and out-and-out scams are here equated; "normal" and "absurd" economic ventures occur on the same list of illegal joint-stock companies. Thus, in answering the question as to why, even in the hands of "aggressive, inventive" industrialists and merchants, "progress [in the early eighteenth century] was so slow,"[53] J.H. Plumb concludes that the greatest "hindrance to rapid commercial and industrial expansion was the lack of capital," a lack directly attributable to "[t]he financial panic of the South Sea Bubble" and the subsequent "Bubble Act of 1721, which forbade the formation of joint-stock companies without a royal charter—an instrument which was costly and difficult to get; and, therefore, the easiest method of raising the capital necessary for large-scale industrial organization was not available" (26). The South Sea Bubble was a crisis of indifferentiation arising from the market economy's attempt and failure to supersede feudal class definitions.

The panic and run on the banks of September 1720 occurred because the idea that a projector wants to raise capital in order to undertake an enterprise that would make products, jobs, money, and commodities suddenly became too obviously a fiction: that a projector wanted to raise capital merely to enrich himself was so obvious that most projectors skipped the intermediary steps of investing the capital they received from stock jobbing in any actual enterprise. It is not that a capitalist sorcerer today would not, like the "unknown adventurer" who proposed "[a] company for carrying on an undertaking of great advantage, but nobody knows what it is," "be contented with his venture [in selling stock], and set off the same evening for the Continent";[54] rather, laws limit the degree to which an undertaking can be fictional.

Mackay, like William Maitland, whom he quotes, is amazed at public credulity, amazed that people believed any of the more absurd projects would ever be undertaken.[55] He cites numerous examples of satire that exposed the projects as scams, among them the "Bubble Cards" (62–64): "every card of the pack exposed some knavish scheme, and ridiculed the persons who were its dupes" (64). But Mackay errs in telling the story "of a plundered people" (70), of "a whole people shaking suddenly off the trammels of reason, and running wild after a golden vision, refusing obstinately to believe that it is not real" (71). Contemporary accounts of the crisis, such as that which appeared in the *Political State*, reveal a people fully conscious of the delusiveness of their own hopes: "[Projects were] set on foot and promoted by crafty knaves, then pursued by multitudes of covetous fools, and at last appeared to be, in effect, what their vulgar appellation denoted them to be—bubbles and mere cheats."[56] In Mackay's words, "The populace are often most happy in the nicknames they employ. None could be more apt than that of Bubbles."[57] If a whole group of people call a bubble a bubble, a cheat a cheat, a fiction a fiction, they cannot be poor fools imposed upon by knaves. It is *because* of the fictionality, and *not in spite of it*, that people bought stock. The rash of satires that exposed projects as fictions did nothing to dissuade buying stock because no one cared about the reality of the projects themselves. Everyone was a director investing in a purely monetary corporation and hoping to sell at just the right moment.

What is most interesting about Mackay's account is that, while he attempts to arouse pathos for the poor imposed-upon victims of projectors, and while he relishes describing the punishment of the directors, punishment that takes the form of mob violence, Mackay also recognizes the arbitrariness of this scapegoating process, recognizes that in fact the crisis was not caused by criminals who cheated victims but rather by a whole slew of would-be criminals.[58] To put this in terms of Girard's account, one would say that Mackay attests to the efficacy of Parliament's punishment of directors in stemming violence and arresting the crisis *not* despite but precisely *because* he recognizes its injustice. Mackay quotes Gibbon's defense of his grandfather (a director of the South Sea Company), in which Gibbon laments the punitive actions of "a lawless majority" who exacted "arbitrary fines and forfeitures"; Gibbon points out that "[o]ne man was ruined because he had dropped a foolish speech, that his horses should feed upon gold."[59]

Mackay repeatedly points out the arbitrariness of scapegoating directors for the actions of a whole nation.[60] If we take Girard seriously, we can say that seeing the punishment of directors as arbitrary paradoxically allows feeling that their punishment *was* necessary. One needs to see the acts of violence that brought the crisis to a close as arbitrary in order for them to work. For indeed, it is after pointing out the arbitrariness of punishing the directors that Mackay attacks them with excessive rhetoric:

> The overbearing insolence of ignorant men, who had arisen to sudden wealth by successful gambling, made men of true gentility of mind and manners blush that gold should have power to raise the unworthy in the scale of society. The haughtiness of some of these "ciphering cits," as they were termed by Sir Richard Steele, was remembered against them in the day of their adversity. In the parliamentary inquiry, many of the directors suffered more for their insolence than for their peculation. One of them, who, in the full-blown pride of an ignorant rich man, had said that he would feed his horse upon gold, was reduced almost to bread and water for himself; every haughty look, every over-bearing speech, was set down, and repaid them a hundredfold in poverty and humiliation. (71–72)

The rhetorical force of this passage, the sense of the justice of the class distinctions it upholds, is not undermined but enhanced by the excessive and arbitrary punishment wreaked by this rhetoric on the man whose horse would eat gold. Girard would say that scapegoating various directors resolved the crisis because everyone in "the mob" became identified with the directors during the progress of the crisis, and this identification allows the violence perpetrated against them to be, like Mackay's rhetoric, *visibly* arbitrary and excessive. But the selection of scapegoats must also not be so visibly arbitrary that they don't seem culpable at all, in which case killing them would serve no scapegoating function. These directors seem to be at once equally guilty *and* more guilty than everyone else.

Fictional Scapegoats: Tragedy

During the sacrificial crisis, mimetic rivalry or the attempt to displace another within a system becomes mimetic violence, the attempt to seize *"kudos"* (divine and inviolable status) "once and for all": seizing *kudos* consists in trying to fix a hierarchical definition upon one person, to reify it, rather than to allow social distinctions to define an empty place in a structure that can then be filled by any number of people;[61] if the structure and what threatens it are fixed in, embodied, and animated by two individuals who attack each other, the structure will disintegrate because it can no longer recognize what threatens it by incorporating and thereby enlisting that threat in the process of structural definition.

For members of the society in a crisis, one "sorcerer" presents pure fact, the other pure fiction; one is good, one is evil. Members of the community believe that they need only choose one and eliminate the other in order to establish the millenium. From within the crisis, they think they are trying to establish a permanent social structure and definitions that, since not arbitrary, will not be at all fictional or unjustly exclusive; in fact, eliminating indifferentiation also eliminates the differences that it sustains. Reciprocal violence between contenders for a position within a system, between "sorcerers," breaks down the system itself: "Although the targets are individuals, it is the institutions that receive the blows. Legitimate authority trembles on its pedestal and the combatants finally assist in the downfall of the very order they strove to maintain."[62]

During sacrificial crises, tragedy devolves into invective and a battle among "sorcerers" such as Oedipus and Tiresias, who embody the social institutions that have granted them the status they are fighting to maintain. The scapegoating event that ends the sacrificial crisis only succeeds after the two antagonists engaged in seizing *kudos* have, by using the same weapons to attack each other and by the rapidity of attack and counterattack, become identified with and indistinguishable from each other and all other members of the community: once identified with each other, the necessary inextricability of fact from fiction and vice versa is recognized; the violent murder and expulsion of one of them (re)establishes the social order because, since the scapegoat is recognizably "the same" as his opponent (and everyone else), the violent exclusion of him, his violent reduction to the dirt of the system, is recognizably an arbitrary act; system is (re)established when it can again incorporate fictionality or arbitrariness, when the community can recognize that the system is real *only* by virtue of their unanimous "decision" to act as if it were real.

Difference is established only when asserted and undermined at the same time,[63] only when it is possible to recognize the arbitrariness of definition in the very act of distinguishing. One might talk about the strength of a social order in terms of an "optimum distance" between the consciousness and unconsciousness of that system's arbitrariness or fictionality.[64] Effective differentiation requires some recognition of arbitrariness, of the community's complicity in granting the system factual status, of the community's guilt in and responsibility for establishing it. Any demand to purge a system of its fictions, to literalize dirt by locating it in an enemy who can then be expelled, comes from being too aware that the system is a fiction.

Scapegoating to Uphold the New System

At the time when *The Orphan* was first produced, entrepreneurship looked fictional because it was still new, because it was not yet in fact a reality that ambition should follow business rather than curry favor at court. The tragedy itself attempts to expel fictionality from the new system of capitalist relations by staging a sacrificial crisis. The crisis begins with indifferentiation. In the relationship between Castalio and Monimia, Castalio is in her service or thrall and continually designates himself as her slave (2.306). Yet, with all the instability of a truly specular relationship, their roles keep switching, he becoming her "lord" and "tyrant" (1.279, 2.337, 4.110–33) and then she becoming his (1.142, 2.306, 5.191–225) in rapid alternate succession. Their "love" consists in a competition for superiority, in bouts of love and hate in which master and slave switch their roles. Castalio and Monimia are contestants in a joust for superiority, just as Castalio and Polydore are contestants in a "joust" for Monimia's love.

The woman's superiority in the she-tragedies of *The Orphan* and *Jane Shore* consists in her capacity to retain and capitalize upon the chastity that constitutes her own value on the marriage market. She is an entrepreneur like Polydore, with this difference: she is a she.[65] Mominia is thus on one level identical with Castalio and Polydore—all three being competing entrepreneurs—but, insofar as her gender is represented as a salient and essential difference, she is also susceptible of being scapegoated, differentiated from, and deanimated. And in fact, the play kills her by her own hand. Her self-murder puts an end to the sacrificial crisis insofar as it cannot be avenged, and no one is left alive by the end of the play for the cycle of vengeance to continue.

A Difference That Works?

There is a problem if gender difference does not distinguish Monimia enough from Polydore and Castalio. Also, her self-murder identifies her with them even more. Similarly in Rowe's *Jane Shore*, Jane and her oppressor Gloster become identified when he scourges her with curses:

Glos. Ha! do'st thou brave me, minion!
        Do'st thou know
        . . . .
        That I can let loose fear, distress and famine
        To hunt thy heels like hell-hounds thro' the world;
        That I can place thee in such an abject state
        As help shall never find thee; where repining,
        Thou shalt sit down, and gnaw the earth for anguish,
        Groan to the pitiless winds without return,
        Howl like the midnight wolf amidst the desart,
        And curse thy life in bitterness of misery.[66]

Jane returns this curse that renders her abject with an almost identical cursing of herself:

J. Sh. Let me be branded for the publick scorn,
        Turn'd forth, and driven to wander like a vagabond,
        Be friendless and forsaken, seek my bread
        Upon the barren, wild, and desolate waste,
        Feed on my sighs, and drink my falling tears,
        E'er I consent to teach my lips injustice.
        (4.1.170–75)

The "e'er" of the last line quoted here shifts her self-cursing away from mere repetition of Gloster's, but not by much.

Just as Monimia is identified with both Castalio and Polydore in their attempts to be tyrants or usurpers, the raped Lucretia identifies, by murdering herself, with her rapist, stabbing herself in just the same way that he would have done in the act of rape had she resisted. Critics have noticed in the iconography of paintings of Lucretia that she physically "quotes" her assailant in stabbing herself.[67] In "Tarquin and Lucretia," by G.B. Tiepolo

Figure 1. Giambattista B. Tiepolo, *Tarquin and Lucretia* (1750). Courtesy of Staatsgalerie am Shaezler-Palais, Städtische Kunstsammlungen, Augsburg, Germany.

(see fig. 1), the two characters are almost identified because the elbow of Tarquin's knife-wielding arm intersects with Lucretia's elbow, making the painting a bit ambiguous as to whether Tarquin is threatening to stab her or Lucretia is stabbing herself.

Self-murder expresses an intention that differs from what the woman's body expressed in the physical activity of being raped. To have an intention that differs from action is to have a psyche capable of consent—a modern psyche.[68] Although representing the self-murder of the raped victim gives her a psyche, it does so in the process of depriving that psyche of a living body to inhabit. As someone identifiably the same as all of us whose feelings differ from the activities that express them, but different because polluted, material, and dead, the raped woman is the perfect scapegoat for the capitalist market's violent crimes. But insofar as the playgoer's sympathy animates her too much, she does not quite remain the inanimate scapegoat that she is meant to be.

In fact, at the end of the play, there is an exchange of curses among characters, "plagues" that go from Polydore to Castalio (5.421, 95), a curse in Monimia's last wish for Castalio (5.486, 98), and plagues from Chamont to Castalio (5.489, 98) and back again (5.514, 99), culminating in a scene of chaos:

> Confusion and disorder seize the world,
> To spoil all trust and converse amongst men;
> 'Twixt families engender endless feuds;
> In countries, needless fears; in cities, factions;
> In states, rebellion; and in churches, schism:
> Till form's dissolved, the chain of causes broken,
> And the Originals of Being lost.
> (5.516–22, 99)

This looks less like the end of a sacrificial crisis through scapegoating and the consequent establishment of an arbitrary difference, and more like a continuation of the sacrificial crisis. Insofar as Monimia is a genuine tragic heroine, our chaos is come again, a chaos of indifferentiation.

The Orphan successfully represents the sadomasochistic pleasures of the gift economy and how one might change from giving gifts to getting goods without forgoing those pleasures. But it unsuccessfully performs a sadistic, differentiating act. For our tastes, the play is too pathetic, the world-annihilating emotion over Monimia's death far too overdone. Whereas we can transform at least some of Swift's and Pope's satires into works that effectively distinguish good moralist from bad sexually promiscuous woman, this play leaves us with no "good" and "bad" objects. We cannot effectively distinguish between good and bad capitalists via the effective scapegoating of a woman, as we are able to in reading George Lillo's *London Merchant* and Bernard Mandeville's *Modest Defence of Publick STEWS*, discussed in the next chapter. *The Orphan* performs a sadomasochistic economy, but it requires huge amounts of pathos in order to keep the audience sympathizing with its heroine. For us, exaggerated pathos will have exactly the opposite effect—it will turn off our sympathy. But the exaggeration suggests that Otway and Rowe, and writers of she-tragedy generally, had to go to great lengths to make the passive woman in this humiliating scene someone with whom one can identify. Writers of she-tragedies wrote with a sense that it might be difficult to get their auditors to identify with female victims. We can here see misogyny failing to keep up the play of identifications necessary for literariness: the woman is not hated enough to be disidentified with at the end of the play, and so no distinctions are made fixed or fluid. (There is no indeterminacy without determinate positions to be undecided about!). *The Orphan* does not fix identity in one determinate position, but it also does not give us numerous positions with which to identify, continually offering readers a way out of every determinate position. Instead of the indeterminacy central to literariness, it gives us indifferentiation. The texts by Lillo and Mandeville discussed in chapter 3 do not collapse into indetermination, nor do they restore indeterminacy. Instead, for the sake of fixing the reader's desire to identify on one character, the ideal businessman, they shut down literary play, perhaps because the danger of setting off a sacrificial crisis is, after the South Sea Bubble, seen as too great.

3

Engendering Capitalist Desire

Filthy Bawds and Thoroughly Good Merchants in Mandeville and Lillo

Bernard Mandeville's *Fable of the Bees* and *Modest Defence of Publick STEWS* and Lillo's *London Merchant* engender capitalist desires. By first gendering them female, these texts can scapegoat the figure of woman for morally repugnant aspects of capitalist pursuits. Such scapegoating engenders the desire to maximize profits not only by cleansing profiteering of its morally reprehensible features, but also by eroticizing the quest to capitalize on one's investment.[1] My larger reason for examining this scapegoating process is to try to understand how at certain moments feminist sentiment surfaces in what are otherwise antifeminist works of the period. I am not interested in whether Mandeville and Lillo were feminists,[2] but rather in the contradictory conjunction of feminist arguments and misogynous portrayals in their texts. Unlike Otway's *Orphan*, Mandeville's *Defence* and Lillo's *London Merchant* successfully erect distinctions between (bad) women and (good) businessmen. *The Orphan* is caught in a sadomasochistic affective economy, she-tragedies in general generating too much pathos for their heroines so that audiences cannot easily relinquish their identification with them. Such an identification must be relinquished in order for a text to successfully scapegoat women for unsavory aspects of capitalist enterprise; a sadistic moment is needed for disidentification to take place. Mandeville's treatise on prostitutes—a shadowy counterpart to his defense of mercantile capitalism in *The Fable of the Bees*—and Lillo's bourgeois tragedy sadistically deanimate their heroines (prostitutes; businesswomen who trade in bodies) in order to animate and beautify capitalists (capitalists; businessmen who truck only in abstract labor, labor allegedly disengaged from particular bodies). Mandeville's and Lillo's texts successfully idealize the capitalist, as I

64

will show, by abjecting women, and it is through abjection that these texts attempt to engender the desire to produce profits.

Prologue: The Desire to Consume

Raymond Williams talks about representations of the desire to consume luxuries in early-seventeenth-century literature. He finds portrayed in country-house poems like Ben Jonson's "To Penshurst" a certain "willing and happy ethic of consuming [which is unaware of] the possible grossness of [such consumption]." There is a sense of "prolonged delight," he says, in "that easy, insatiable exploitation of the land and its creatures."[3] Later in the century, Williams maintains, people become much more self-conscious about the exorbitance of capitalist desires. As Laura Brown has demonstrated in her recent article "Reading Race and Gender: Jonathan Swift," early-eighteenth-century texts associate female desire with the desire to consume foreign products.[4] Not only in those mercantile tracts that deplored importing goods, but also in the "Whig panegyrics" that celebrated trade, the desire to consume imports was rewritten as the female desire for fashion, for sexual attractiveness, hence as woman's inordinate sexual appetites.[5] Bernard Mandeville's *Fable of the Bees*, reprinted throughout the 1720s, partakes of this trend.[6] A great trading nation, Mandeville contends, consists in "[m]illions endeavoring to supply / Each other's Lust and Vanity" (1:18). *The Fable* represents unbridled consumerism as vicious but defends it as a necessary evil: ". . . they, that would revive / A Golden Age, must be as free / For Acorns, as for Honesty" (1:37); those who preach against acquiring luxuries had better be ready for discomfort, he says.

Economists writing later in the century did not follow Mandeville's lead of portraying consumerism as a necessary evil, but rather, as Albert O. Hirschman has shown, tried to reconcile the desire for luxury with traditional notions of virtue.[7] Thus, Adam Smith's *Theory of Moral Sentiments* (1759) portrays some forms of consumerism as bad and others as good: "It is the great fallacy of Dr. Mandeville's book [*The Fable of the Bees*] to represent every passion as wholly vicious which is so in any degree and in any direction."[8] It appears as though a change has taken place between the writing of the *Fable* and of Smith's *Theory*, a change that allows capitalist desires to be seen not merely as an evil, albeit a necessary one, but also as an ideal; in fact, however, it is precisely Mandeville's representation of the desire to consume that enables Smith to make these distinctions of degree and direction, that enables him to call some forms of consumerism virtuous and others reprehensible. Mandeville's tract scapegoats women for consumerism and depicts male merchants as trading merely for the sake of satisfying their wives' vicious desires.

Since consumerism is portrayed as unequivocally evil in Mandeville's *Fable*, one might expect it to be an antimercantile tract.[9] It is not such a tract precisely because the evil consumer it portrays is Woman. The *Fable*, subtitled *"Private Vices, Publick Benefits,"* argues that the public benefits from the vicious habits of private citizens; trade is stimulated by the desire for luxury. However, Mandeville formulates the argument so that a *male* public benefits from the private world of evil *women*. The essays or "Remarks" appended in 1714 to Mandeville's original poem explicitly attack women: if the wives who now demand goods from their husbands, it says, were to change suddenly and "behave themselves as a sober wise Man could wish them," "nothing could make amends to the Detriment Trade would sustain" (1:225). The reader must realize, Mandeville asserts, "that a considerable Portion of what the Prosperity of *London* and Trade in general, and consequently the Honour, Strength, Safety, and all the worldly Interest of the Nation consist in, depends entirely on the Deceit and vile Stratagems of Women. . . . [The virtues women should have] could not possibly be a thousandth Part so serviceable, to make an opulent, powerful, and what we call a flourishing Kingdom, than their most hateful Qualities" (1:228). In this passage, Mandeville attacks women and condemns consumerism: the desire for things leads women to use "Deceit and vile Strategems." However, it is by way of that condemnation of women that Mandeville is able to quarantine the vicious part of capitalism and then idealize the capitalist enterprise of trading: an honorable, strong, safe, opulent, powerful, flourishing kingdom is a trading kingdom, and the activity of trading itself in no way involves the deceit or vile strategems of consuming women. By confining the vicious part of capitalism to the female consumer, the text purifies the merchant's desire to get goods.

Mandeville's *Fable* can distinguish between the abject[10] desire to indulge in luxury and the ideal desire to trade because of its use of the figure of woman: vicious consumerism is female, virtuous mercantilism is male. As René Girard has shown in his work on the scapegoat, the scapegoat must be recognizably the same as its ideal counterpart in order for that ideal to be established. Scapegoating must be recognizably arbitrary: that which is to be idealized and its abject counterpart must visibly share those attributes for which the abject will be scapegoated; in order to assume any given society's ideals as their own, members must be able to identify both with the ideal *and* with the scapegoated victim who takes the punishment for the ideal's repulsive qualities.[11] To put this in terms of Mandeville's *Fable*, English merchants can only feel wholly good about searching the world for treasures if they can punish women with whom they identify, the consuming women who force their husbands to "rob the State" and "ransack" the Indies in order to get what they want (1:33): it is only through identifying with these vicious women whom they castigate or symbolically murder that merchants can purify and elevate their own motives.

At times, Mandeville's *Fable* reveals the arbitrariness of pinning on the figure of woman the vicious desire to consume. It is either out of love or "out of Vanity," Mandeville says, that some men are "lavish to their Wives, and . . . croud New Clothes and other Finery upon them faster than they can ask it" (1:227). Here, the *Fable* almost recognizes that the female consumer is not always female. Intuitively one might read this moment in the *Fable* as profeminist: women are not really to blame for consumerism, Mandeville seems to say; men are. But Girard's account offers a counterintuitive reading of this passage: identifying with the abject female consumer allows the proper businessman to successfully disown his own excessive desires by punishing these female figures for them. The female consumer must be identical to the male writers and readers who are victimizing her in order to effectively take the blame for their faults. Thus, what appears to be a feminist moment is in effect an invitation to identify with the scapegoat for the sake of making that scapegoating process effective.

As the case of consumerism demonstrates, then, works of the Restoration and the early eighteenth century engaged in the project of rendering capitalist desires morally respectable are able to degrade and elevate the same passion by splitting it in two, splitting it into its ideal male and abject female forms. I will now examine this dynamic in the case of the desire for profit. It makes sense that in its abject female form, such a desire would be pinned on prostitutes—they are profiteers easily degraded. I turn therefore to Mandeville's treatise on legalizing prostitution.

Mandeville's *Modest Defence of Publick STEWS* (1724) sets up an abject and decidedly female version of the desire to intensify profits; it creates the version of it that, in a certain degree and direction, is "wholly vicious," so that in another degree and direction it can be ideal. For this reason, moments in this treatise that appear to be feminist are actually moments when the text invites identification with women in order to better scapegoat them. These feminist ideas and figures are sympathetic precisely to the degree that the ideal capitalist appears to readers and writers to be contaminated by abject desires; victimized females are the more sympathetic the more the capitalist needs to be cleaned off. Anxieties about the excesses of profit-hungry merchants get displaced onto the fear that prostitutes are reaping too much profit, excessive pleasure as well as too much money. In Mandeville's *Modest Defense of Publick STEWS*, the rule goes, when anxious because businessmen can control the fate of Spain, then regulate the business of bawds.

Profiteering: Filthy versus Clean

A Modest Defence is a satire on reformers, the same group Mandeville attacked in his "Essay on Charity and Charity-Schools" of 1723. Mandeville writes his treatise on streetwalkers in the character of the "Reformer" "Phil-Porney,"[12] a lover of prostitutes.[13] Phil Porney's "Dedication" is addressed to the "Gentleman" of the Reforming Societies whose method of "converting" prostitutes does not seem to be working: "[I]t would not be amiss, if You chang'd somewhat your present Method of Conversion, especially in the Article of Whipping. It is very possible, indeed, that leaving a Poor Girl Penny-less, may put her in a Way of living Honestly, tho' the want of Money was the only Reason of her living otherwise; and the Stripping of her Naked, may, for aught I know, contribute to Her Modesty, and put Her in a State of Innocence; but surely, *Gentlemen*, You must all know, that Flogging has a quite contrary Effect" (x-xi).

A Modest Defence of Publick STEWS thus satirizes "the Defence of Modesty and Virtue" (i) undertaken by reform societies; however, as I will now show, it is not so much about reform as it is about business.

Richard Cook maintains that Mandeville seriously proposes state-run prostitution.[14] Cook contends that Mandeville exaggerates the mercantilist position not to parody it but rather for the sake of baiting his opponents. The grand jury had condemned the author of *The Fable* a year earlier, saying that Mandeville had endeavored to apologize for and praise "the very *Stews* themselves. . . . with Design, we conceive, to debauch the Nation."[15] However, as Cook recognizes, Mandeville could be satirizing the mercantilist stance: Phil Porney's discussion of the importation of foreign women and the retail price of various kinds of prostitutes might be designed to outrage readers over the alienating effects of mercantile practices. It is always possible, therefore, to argue that Mandeville exploits what Cook calls the "comic potentialities" of mercantilism in order to satirize it. Like *The Fable of the Bees,* which could be read as a rigorist rejection of capitalist values, *A Modest Defence* could be read as an antimercantilist tract.[16]

We can avoid the whole issue of Mandeville's seriousness by reading the text *not* for his opinions about prostitution and mercantilism, but rather for the ideological work it does, whether serious or not.[17] There is no simple relation between the growth of prostitution and the proliferation of texts on prostitution, nor between mercantile expansion and the use of it as a figure. The Reform Movement and (anti)prostitution tracts should not be seen as simply a reaction to a preexisting social problem, any more than Whig panegyric depicts a preexisting economic reality. By defining "Vice" and campaigning against it, reformers work toward channeling desire in new ways.

Henry Abelove has suggested that "sexual intercourse so-called," that is, those sexual activities that promote reproduction, "became importantly more popular" during the eighteenth century, and that this popularity accompanied and may not be distinct from the privileging of productivity in profit-intensive economic pursuits.[18] The plan for state-regulated "public stews," Phil Porney asserts, will restore the "Inclination to Matrimony" (29). He insists that state-run prostitution will increase "the Number of [the state's] Inhabitants" on whom its "Prosperity" depends (5) by restoring to marriage its true "Ends and Purposes" (30): people will not marry for Love, which they can get more easily at the government stew, but rather will marry to propagate (26–34; cf. 4–5). If the reformers and other prostitution tracts attempt—seriously in their case—not only to inspire young men "to quit the Gaiety of a Single Life" (30), but also to persuade them that the function of marriage is propagation, then they may be seen as part of the movement toward privileging reproductive sexual behavior that accompanied privileging production. Abelove does not intend to imply that a rise in reproduction caused a rise in production, or vice versa: "Neither of these causal arguments would seem to me to be sound, and both would of course depend on a too-easy and conventional distinction between the sexual and material realms."[19]

At the level of argument, Mandeville's treatise works toward establishing what is now for us this "too-easy and conventional" distinction between sexual pleasure and business. However, A Modest Defence also simultaneously seems to dissolve this distinction: it represents profit-making as sexually pleasurable, ideal in its male form, abject in its female form. Representing the distinction between the two as arbitrary does less to dissolve the distinction than it does to establish it.

A Modest Defence sets up two kinds of capitalists: Mandeville directly addresses the people to whom he is speaking about regulating prostitution in their capacity as reasonable businessmen, and indirectly he figures the women about whom he speaks as abhorrent capitalists. Occasionally obscene, the treatise spends pages describing woman's irrational and overly "eager Pursuit of Pleasure" (45–46) in contrast to man's necessary and rational business pursuits. According to the Defence, all women essentially want to lose their chastity (44, 51), but they manage their "modesty" as men manage property, capital, and credit. Mandeville's Modest Defence renders virtuous the capitalist's exorbitant desire for profit by contrasting it with the prostitute's business activity. This contrast forms an arbitrary distinction between good and bad versions of the desire to exploit others for the sake of one's own pleasure. The arbitrariness of it is especially visible when sexual behavior is figured as economic activity and vice versa.

Phil Porney begins his treatise by saying that "mischievous Consequences" do not come from "Whoring, consider'd in itself, but only proceed from the Abuse and ill Management of it; our Business is certainly to regulate this Affair in such sort as may best prevent [many] Mischiefs" (6). In this projector's mercantilist dream, turning "Private Whoring" ("rape, seduction, and adultery without the exchange of money")[20] into "Publick Whoring" or prostitution (8) by erecting public stews will eliminate "the ill Consequences of this Vice" (2). But the projector gets lost in his own mercantile zeal. In a way that certainly scandalized most of Mandeville's readers,[21] Phil Porney discusses female prostitutes as commodities, dividing them "into four Classes, who for their Beauty, or other Qualifications, may justly challenge different Prices" and elaborately detailing why one woman should cost "Half a Crown" while another should rate "a Guinea" (13). As is visible even in the projector's excess, the ostensible argument is that changing stews from whatever they are into business will promote the public good, that therefore private whoring is at this moment *not* a business. However, as shown below, the effect of the treatise is to demonstrate that women are already good managers of their most valuable commodity, their feigned or real chastity.[22] Sex is indeed a business, and women are not mismanaging it, but managing it too well.

Mandeville's projector wants to argue that women cannot manage their chastity because in women passion predominates over businesslike rationality: "In short, there requires no more to convince us of the Violence of Female Desire when raised to a proper height, but only to consider, what a terrible Risque a Woman runs to gratify it. Shame and Poverty are look'd upon as Trifles, when they come in Competition with this predominating Passion" (41). To further support the treatise's premise that passion opposes financial interest and therefore must be publicly managed, one would think that Phil Porney would go on, from his discourse on the violence of female desire, to describe how women forget their financial interests in the heat of sexual desire, and the treatise does do that to a degree—it is designed to be titillating. However, in Phil Porney's taxonomy of types of women and how they manage their chastity, Mandeville's treatise actually demonstrates that women manage their honor so as to both gratify their passion and serve their financial interest. In fact, at moments during this account of women's maneuvers, financial gain and sexual pleasure become indistinguishable. The most successful businesswoman is (or will become) the most passionate, and Mandeville describes their strategies in economic terms.

Passion, honor, and interest are the three terms used in Mandeville's treatise to perform a surprisingly structuralist analysis of types of women: each of the four types of women is defined by the presence or absence of passion, of a strong desire for honor, and of a strong sense of financial interest. The first type is naturally chaste; this kind of woman desires honor and has little or no passion (42). The second type, the woman who values her reputation as much as the first but is naturally amorous—Mandeville calls her "a Wanton Woman of Honour" (45)—tries to maintain her reputation by concealing her amorous escapades. Phil Porney describes these efforts at concealment as trying to buy sexual pleasure on credit: by hiding their sexual encounters, these women try "to purchase Pleasure without the Expence of Reputation" (45).

In the passage in which he describes the third type, middling women who want to marry well, Mandeville equates financial interest with sexual desire. These women have neither honor nor inclination; that is, since they do not *yet* have honor (and with it, money), they completely repress their inordinate sexual appetites: "[F]or when a Woman has her Interest and Fortune depending upon her Reputation, as all the middle Rank of Womankind have, she is a Woman of Honour of course. Interest, indeed, is inseparable from Female Honour. . . . The bare Puncto of Honour, when abstracted from Interest, would prove but a small Rub to Women in their eager Pursuit of Pleasure: Thus we see the Conduct of a Maiden Lady, how much more Circumspect is it whilst her Fortune in Marriage is depending, than afterwards, when that Point of Interest is secured by a Husband" (45–46). This passage deviates from the argument Phil Porney wants to make. He wants to say that female desire is so strong, the only way to contain it is by preventing men from laying siege to it. Here, in contradiction to that contention, a woman's desire is perfectly in tune with her financial interests: she is naturally a woman of honor ("a Woman of Honour of course"), naturally "circumspect" until her "Interest" has been "secured by a Husband." Once comfortably married, however, "let their natural Chastity be ever so great, the smallest Spark of Desire is capable of being blown up and rais'd to a considerable Pitch" (46). In other words, for those who have secured their interest through marriage, financial well-being incites desire.

According to *A Modest Defence*, then, all women manage their own desire just as a businessman manages his "Accounts," with a view to procuring the greatest amount of financial gain and pleasure. As the treatise describes their endeavors, pleasure is equated with financial gain by being figured as success in capitalist enterprise. Lower-class women who have no chance of gaining a fortune through marriage "can't promote their Interest by preserving their Chastity, yet, if they have the least Spark of Beauty, they will find their Account sufficiently in parting with it" (47). A woman who wants a man to marry her will "bribe his After-Love, by the great Value she seems to put upon her Chastity before she makes him a Present of it" (48). A woman who tries to raise the value of her chastity by actually remaining chaste instead of merely resisting temporarily must have "a good Stock of Virtue, [or] an unaccountable Series of good Fortune if she escapes" from passion (52).

The most striking and disturbing figure represents men as essentially better capitalists than women because men have penises. A woman's vagina, Mandeville says, is "like a Debtor's House upon the Verge of two Countries, [and so] is liable to be attack'd both Ways; à parte ante, & à parte post" (49). Collecting a debt is here equated with laying siege to a vagina, with rape. In "Commerce with Women" (30), a vagina owes and a penis makes it pay. The tropological argument of the text equates profit with sexual pleasure.

The logical argument of the Defence, however, pretends that only bawds are merchants driven by passion. It contrasts bawds with the business managers to whom Phil Porney speaks, the men who should take over and run houses of prostitution and who habitually practice "that cool Exercise of [their] Reason" (8) unless they are distracted by (sexual) desire (4, 8). At the level of argument, A Modest Defence thus explicitly disconnects sexual pleasure from the pleasure of making money. Erecting public whorehouses, the argument runs, will keep businessmen from falling in love and therefore will help business; it will save businessmen from "the Expence [love] occasions, and the Neglect of Worldly Business" (22). The sexual desire that rules women and that men can rationally regulate in order to keep themselves fit for business "is quite inconsistent with Industry, the main Support of any, especially a trading, Nation" (4). As part of this attempt to separate business from sexual pleasure, women become associated with the realm of leisure in two ways: they are said to be too passionate to take care of their own financial interest, as seen above, and are relegated to the status of objects in the realm of leisure and pleasure. It is through these representations of the figure of woman, therefore, that A Modest Defence is able to establish a series of oppositions: "Men of Business" versus "Men of Pleasure" (24); industry versus "Indolence" (22, 4); business versus leisure (26).

Tropologically, as we have seen, the text equates business and sexual activity. It does so for the sake of inviting businessmen to identify with the bawds who will be scapegoated for the desire to exploit others to increase their own pleasure. The whores appearing on Mandeville's pages are filthy embodiments of and containers for the kind of pleasure that has been excluded from, that one denies that one gets through, profit-intensive business management: indolence and pleasure in excess are here figured as sexual pleasure, and sexual pleasure is quarantined, as it were, from the clean concerns of business. At the very moment when the distinction between the drive to obtain sexual pleasure and the desire for financial gain most threatens to collapse, the prostitutes in *A Modest Defence* are "abjected," in Kristeva's sense of the term. They are figured as "dirt": a stew is "a Boghouse"—an outhouse; a whore is a piece of "blown" or spoiled meat that "a Modern Butcher. . . . hang[s] up for a Cure," that he uses to attract the flies away from his fresh meat (xi). They are insidiously evil: a prostitute has the power to contaminate the businessman, to "drain his Pocket, and make him unfit for any Business" (25), to make him contract "a Seminal Weakness" (32); furthermore, Mandeville carefully argues, it is really women who spread venereal disease to men, and not vice versa (20–22). Here Mandeville's treatise renders the figure of the businesswoman revolting and marshals horror at her for the sake of making a distinction where one did not exist before, or of shoring up a distinction that threatens to collapse: in these passages, prostitutes are represented as filthy for the sake of distinguishing business from sexual pleasure.

Feminism, Capitalism, Aesthetics

A Modest Defence of Publick STEWS animates in the figure of the prostitute the evils to be excluded from the ideal of prudent business management: women get (sexual) pleasure out of capitalizing, men do not; women capitalize in the service of indolence, men do not.[23] *A Modest Defence* allows the businessman to prosecute a victim recognizably as innocent (or as guilty) as he is and yet completely other; it allows him to identify with and simultaneously distance himself from, to abject, the evils of an exorbitant desire for profit. The prostitute offers businessmen the perfect opportunity for both identification and disavowal.

A Modest Defence sets businessmen and prostitutes up as identical antagonists: Mandeville speaks to "*lewd Men of Honour*" (17) about "*a wanton Woman of Honour*" (45). But there is another way of inviting identification: arousing sympathy for female victims by pointing to the arbitrariness of condemning them. In Mandeville's treatise, there is no subtle transition between passages that recognize the arbitrariness of scapegoating women and those that assert that these women are completely other (i.e., that they are deserving victims). Open acknowledgments that condemnation is arbitrary contrast starkly with passages that scapegoat. Thus, Mandeville describes

"*Whoring* as a Kind of Peccant Humour in the Body-Politick, which, in order to its Discharge, naturally seizes upon such external Members as are most liable to Infection, and at the same time most proper to carry off the Malignity. If this Discharge is promoted by a Licence of *Publick Stews*, which is a Kind of legal Evacuative, the Constitution will certainly be preserv'd" (57). Prostitution is the discharge of infected bodily fluids, a "Virulence" and a "Contagion" (58) that threatens to "[seize] upon . . . external Members . . . most liable to Infection"; it is truly revolting. But a page before comparing whorehouses to outhouses and prostitutes to maggot-infested meat, Phil Porney, in what appears to be real understanding and sympathy, admonishes overzealous reformers "that leaving a Poor Girl Penny-less, may put her in a Way of living Honestly, tho' the want of Money was the only Reason of her living otherwise" (x). *A Modest Defence of Publick STEWS* abjects women—offers identification with them, allowing them to become the locus of all projections, and then violently debases them so that identification is withdrawn—in order to idealize capitalist desires. It is because of this dynamic that real disgust with prostitutes stands in stark contrast to what appears to be real profeminist support of them. This text thus seems to contain feminist sentiment, which is in fact only a tool for implementing an ideological effect, the promotion of capitalist desires.

In Mandeville's treatise, as in Lillo's play, examined below, feminism is not proposed for its own sake, but to stimulate temporary identifications: identifying with female figures is necessary in order to turn them into effective scapegoats. Mandeville's text is hobbled aesthetically by the task of performing abjection for an audience that needs to be regaled with rational arguments about equality to make identifying with prostitutes possible. Because of the seesaw of invitations to identify with women, proffered and then violently withdrawn, the text does not look unified, and Mandeville does not look like a unified personality. We might call him "borderline" now because of the radical swings he makes between sympathizing with and hating women, though it would be wrong, as well as anachronistic, to psychologize these rhetorical structures. Moreover, for Mandeville's audience, the seesaw worked to effect a difference.

Staging Difference

As seen in chapter 2, *The Orphan* and *Jane Shore* do not successfully represent their heroines as different enough from those for whom they are scapegoated, and their deaths unleash a chaos of indifferentiation rather than effectively resolving social ambiguity. In contrast, in William Wycherley's *The Country Wife* and George Lillo's *The London Merchant*, difference is successfully established.[24] The process of abjection successfully erects an image of the ideal businessman: immoral in Wycherley's case, as one would expect in Restoration comedy, because the pleasure he takes in business is too evident; hypermoralized in *The London Merchant* as one would expect of bourgeois, "realist" drama. Lillo's play is of the genre that Denis Diderot called "la comédie larmoyant" and defined in his *Entretiens sur Le Fils naturel* (1757) as the kind of play that arouses intense emotion and then causes the spectator's "own emotion [to be] augmented by the large number of those who share it."[25] *The London Merchant* is able to establish its ideal through scapegoating a woman (abjection) and transferring the pleasures of indifferentiation to the pleasure of "discovering" a difference that is an essence.

As Katherine Eisaman Maus has argued, in order for women to appear on the English stage, there had to be a fundamental change in the conception of woman that rendered it "unrealistic" for boys to play the parts of beautiful women. When woman is conceived of as an undeveloped man, then a young boy can easily pass for Cleopatra; but when woman is conceived of as essentially different from man, then such imitation is "unrealistic."[26] Thomas Laqueur has analyzed eighteenth-century medical texts on reproduction in order to show that the conception of woman did change at this time: she had been seen as a "lesser" or underdeveloped man and was now being seen as essentially different. According to Laqueur, the change takes place in order to allow the continued subordination of women despite new theories of the equality of all human beings.[27] However, it is most analytically useful to see the oppression of women in society not as an end in itself, but rather as a structure capable of carrying an ideological load. The political import of early-eighteenth-century gender distinctions has been examined in detail by scholars who analyze cross-dressing.

Unsettling disguises, genuinely transgressive kinds of cross-dressing, contrast with those kinds that merely reinforce the norm and stabilize social structure by stimulating resistance to "the deviant." This distinction is Jonathan Dollimore's.[28] To put it in terms relevant to early-eighteenth-century practices, a truly transgressive kind of disguise is "blacking," whereas a recuperable transgression is "masking."

In his book *Whigs and Hunters*, E.P. Thompson describes the practice of blacking both in forests and in cities during the 1720s, to which the Black Act of 1723 was a brutal response.[29] Rural protesters reasserted their rights to use newly enclosed common lands by blacking their faces and hunting deer on private property. The notorious Black Act made deer hunting in disguise a capital offense. One way to explain the severity of such punishment is to say that such an act was necessary to enforce the new definition of property as "private." However, as an act passed by Parliament in 1722 clearly shows, capital punishment was invoked not so much against theft as against blacking. "Theft or poaching," Thompson says, "might be conformable with due daylight deference. It was, above all, malice to the gentry which the act was designed to punish" (256).

And not only malice, but also symbolic usurpation. For one thing, blacking was of a piece with those customary practices that, on special feast days—and then, beginning in the early 1720s, during public protest—allowed for the temporary overturning of hierarchies: customary practices and the forms of protest that evolved out of them that have been described by Bob Bushaway and by Stallybrass and White[30] often involved men dressing as women and sometimes also playing the part of royalty. For example, the turnpike rioters at Lebury in 1735 blackened their faces and dressed in women's clothes,[31] thereby pointing to the fact that disguise is meant to overturn hierarchies, in this case that of gender. But class hierarchies were also threatened: the leader of the Hampshire blacks active from 1720 to 1723 was named "King John." And authorities perceived the threat as one directed at social status. Thompson writes that, for the sake of prosecuting metropolitan imitators of the Windsor and Hampshire Blacks, Parliament passed "an almost forgotten act (9 George I c.28) . . . with a death-clause for anyone who, from a pretended place of privilege, joined in disguise or riot" (249). It was not deer-stealing but deer-stealing *in blackface* that so much threatened economic distinctions. In the early eighteenth century, disguising oneself through blacking had the same effect as did cross-dressing in the early seventeenth: these were not acts of hiding one's own person but rather of hiding one's status. Blacking was a way of defying social structure by covering its marks on one's body.

In contrast to blacking, masking as described by Terry Castle did not pose a radical threat to social structure but rather reinforced that structure by allowing a temporary release from it.[32] Masquerades were like a safety valve; they protected society by providing a place specifically for the transgression of social and sexual norms. Allocating space within social structure for its violation protects the structure from direct challenges to it.

It is not quite possible to argue that, from the Renaissance to the Restoration, blacking changed into masking: both were going on in the 1720s. And similarly, it is possible to see, during the early eighteenth century, female cross-dressing that is genuinely subversive as well as instances of it that merely flirt with ambiguity while containing it. Thus, Kristina Straub argues that, although gender ambiguity became "intolerable" when connected with male actors during the Restoration and the early eighteenth century, female cross-dressing remained genuinely subversive: "The cross-dressed actress of the early to mid–eighteenth century seems to constitute a historical possibility for pleasure in sexual gender ambiguities."[33] But Straub recognizes that this kind of pleasure gets shut down as the century progresses: "By the end of the century, discourse about the cross-dressed actress is both more condemnatory . . . and more insistent that female cross-dressing, like the male, was mere travesty, an obvious parody which left gender boundaries unquestioned" (127). It is therefore possible to impose a narrative of change on these two kinds of phenomena. Just as the genuinely threatening blacking gradually ceded to a contained kind of subversive behavior, masking,[34] there was a change on the English stage from truly transgressive to merely recuperative cross-dressing, or cross-dressing that is mere masking. When characters like Shakespeare's Rosalind disguised themselves as boys on the Renaissance stage, their gender was truly ambiguous and therefore defied social definition: "Rosalind" was a boy actor playing the role of a female disguised as a boy. Lisa Jardine has shown that what was titillating for Renaissance audiences was this genuinely transgressive ambiguity itself: "the boy player," she says, "is liable to be regarded with erotic interest which hovers somewhere between the heterosexual and the homosexual around his female attire."[35] During the Renaissance, Jean Howard has argued, cross-dressing by women off the stage was not just transgressive but too revolutionary to be borne: cross-dressed women "signal not only the breakdown of the hierarchical gender system, but of the class system as well."[36] What made female cross-dressing not only bearable, but enjoyable enough for cross-dressed women to appear on the stage?

Shortly after women began acting on the stage in 1660, they not only played roles in which female characters cross-dress, they were also cross-cast: plays such as Thomas Killigrew's *Parson's Wedding* and William Congreve's *Love for Love* were staged using actresses to play all the parts, male and female. But the attraction of these spectacles, Pat Rogers has argued, the attraction of women playing "the breeches part" on the Restoration stage, came from their *failure* to pass themselves off as men, revealing the essential womanliness that lay "beneath" any disguise.[37] The cross-dressed woman on stage who cannot be manly proves the rule that women are not like men, and it was this reinforcement of the law that gave audiences such pleasure. By emphasizing the fact that female cross-dressing gave early-eighteenth-century audiences pleasure from genuine gender ambiguity, Straub does not wish to overturn Rogers's argument, but rather to say that he is "correct up to a point": that the change he imagines "may have been only emergent at this moment in history."[38] Clearly, in the 1720s, cross-dressing stimulated two kinds of pleasure. As in the case of the boys-playing-women-dressed-as-boys of the Renaissance stage, titillation on the early-eighteenth-century stage comes not only from sexual ambiguity, as Straub maintains. However, in contrast to Renaissance cross-dressing, pleasure also comes from the resolution of ambiguity, as Rogers demonstrates.

Williams's notion of dominant, emergent, and residual ideological structures is an especially valuable analytic tool here:[39] William Wycherley's *Country Wife* and George Lillo's *London Merchant* both proffer an emergent ideology, the belief that men and women are essentially different. Wycherley's earlier play can be seen as addressing an audience who, however, still gets as much pleasure from gender ambiguity as it does from the clarification of gender distinctions. At that moment, the belief that women are underdeveloped men still dominates, but it is beginning to evanesce into a residue. By the time Lillo's play is produced in the 1730s, the dominant ideology of Wycherley's moment is even closer to becoming residual, and the emergent view that sexual difference is essential is fast becoming dominant.

If during the Renaissance one declares a definitely social identity by the clothes one wears and threatens social definitions by wearing different clothes, on the mid-eighteenth-century stage, a woman's essence is revealed by the clothes she peels off, through the rather piecemeal exposure of female body parts underneath the rind of male clothes. The new pleasure that comes from resolving ambiguity is dramatized in William Wycherley's *Country Wife*. Marjorie Pinchwife has demanded that her jealous husband take her to see a play. Pinchwife is forced to take her but determined to hide her from Horner, who wants to make him a cuckold. Pinchwife's sister Alithea recommends that she put on a mask. "A mask," he replies, "is as ridiculous a disguise as a stage-beard; her shape, stature, habit will be known." Not only that, he says, "A mask makes people but the more inquisitive. . . . Masks have made more cuckolds than the best faces that ever were known. . . . A mask! No—a woman masked, like a covered dish, gives a man curiosity and appetite, when, it may be, uncovered, 'twould turn his stomach" (3.1.93–99, 105–8). This passage eroticizes pretended depths: not knowing what lies beneath the mask makes whatever it is more valuable and attractive. That is, Pinchwife ends up being wrong about the nausea one may feel in uncovering the dish; as the libertines who seduce Marjorie demonstrate, glimpses of what is inside it increase pleasure. Pinchwife dresses Marjorie up in a suit he has bought for his brother-in-law, but covering her body succeeds no better at mitigating Horner's desire than covering her face with a mask would have done. The disguise fails because, as Pinchwife puts it, "she carries it so sillily" (3.2.381). In her behavior, she exposes the essential femaleness hiding underneath a man's clothes. And yet we cannot quite get over Pinchwife's suggestion that this essential femaleness may turn out to be something nauseating: an abject sexuality, perhaps, that is indistinguishably female or male. The pleasures of unresolved gender ambiguity are alleged to be disgusting by this play, but they have not been completely prohibited, as indeed they are by Lillo's play.

George Lillo's *London Merchant* scapegoats anyone donning blackface in representation; the play resolves indeterminate identity into an essential difference through the figural abjection of anyone whose blacking threatens the structure.[40] On a walk "at some distance from a county seat," the corrupted apprentice Barnwell decides to murder his uncle in order to get the money he needs to court a woman: "[W]ithout money, Millwood will never see me more, and life is not to be endured without her. She's got such firm possession of my heart and governs there with such despotic sway—aye, there's the cause of all my sin and sorrow. 'Tis more than love; 'tis the fever of the soul and madness of desire" (3.5.20–25, 49–50). To make sure that he can continue to have sex with this courtesan, then, Barnwell "[p]uts on the vizor, and draws a pistol" (3.5.36, 50)—he becomes guilty of blacking, of disguising himself as a highwayman. After Barnwell has killed his uncle, however, he repents, and the ambiguity caused by blacking disappears when Barnwell "throws off his mask" (3.6.16). When Barnwell is executed at the end of the play, Millwood is executed with him, but not before her gender is called into question in her interchanges with the "good" apprentice "Trueman."

The character Blunt calls Millwood "the Devil," whom he describes as "*he* that first seduces to sin and then betrays to punishment" (4.14.5, 60). Trueman then calls her "deceitful, cruel, bloody woman!" but then adds, "To call thee woman were to wrong the sex, thou devil!" Millwood responds: "That imaginary being is an emblem of thy cursed sex collected, a mirror wherein each particular man may see his own likeness and that of all mankind!" (4.18.1–7, 64). Millwood's diatribe is less a canny feminist critique than it is a rhetorical device used to call her own gender identity into question.

Gender indeterminacy renders Millwood an effective abject for erecting Thorowgood and Trueman into ideal men of business: thoroughly, truly good men. Lillo's *London Merchant* splits the capitalist in two, into an ideal and an abject capitalist, the merchant Thorowgood and the prostitute Millwood, who are indistinguishable except for gender. Millwood is the inverted, mirror image of Thorowgood. She cares for nothing but money. She ruthlessly perverts Thorowgood's apprentice Barnwell into stealing from his master. Unlike Millwood, who will attempt to get wealth in any way possible, Thorowgood teaches his apprentice Trueman that "the method of merchandise" is not "merely a means of getting wealth" but instead "a science" that must be used to "promot[e] humanity" (3.1.1–5, 40). Millwood is both the victim and the perpetrator of robbery:

> I curse your barbarous sex who robbed me of [my "uncommon perfections of mind and body"], ere I knew their worth, then left me, too late, to count their value by their loss. Another and another spoiler came, and all my gain was poverty and reproach. My soul disdained, and yet disdains, dependence and contempt. Riches, no matter by what means obtained, I saw secured the worst of men from both. I found it, therefore, necessary to be rich and to that end I summoned all my arts. You call 'em wicked; be it so! They were such as my conversation with your sex had furnished me withal. (4.18.4–20)

She presents therefore a demonic version of the ideal portrayed by Trueman:

> I have observed those countries where trade is promoted and encouraged do not make discoveries to destroy but to improve mankind—by love and friendship to tame the fierce and polish the most savage; to teach them the advantages of honest traffic by taking from them with their own consent, their useless superfluities, and giving them in return what, from their ignorance in manual arts, their situation, or some other accident, they stand in need of. (3.1.11–19, 40)

Millwood was robbed of what was essential to her without her consent, and she herself continues that process. But the merchants who trade with savages are nothing like those who originally dispossessed Millwood, and thus nothing like Millwood herself, who follows in their path. The merchants are not rapists: the "savages" with whom merchants trade, according to Trueman, have "useless superfluities," not essential parts of themselves, "tak[en] from them with their own consent," not via rape.

The play opens by representing Thorowgood as having forced Genoa to break a contract to loan Spain money for the sake of diverting "the storm that threatened our royal mistress, pure religion, liberty, and laws" (1.1.1–22). Karl Kroeber is justifiably amazed that such activities can be here called the practice of "honest merchants" and that it would inspire in Trueman the apprentice an "honest scorn" with which to reject all vice. Kroeber points out that it is hard to see how "such mercantile national self-interest differs from Millwood's mercenary egoism."[41] Millwood will be executed for persuading Barnwell to break his contracts, as an apprentice to a merchant and as a client to a manorial lord. It is precisely the similarity between Millwood and Thorowgood, their near indistinguishability, that allows the play to get away with extreme (and to our taste, ridiculous) praise of all mercantile practices as sheerly beneficial to humankind. When Millwood is scapegoated at the end of the play, she takes the blame for all the evils of mercantile capitalism.

Millwood is minimally distinguished from Thorowgood and Trueman by gender. Insofar as she is like them, she is able to stand in for whatever materiality could undermine the businessman's ego ideal. Insofar as she differs from them, she can be scapegoated for the qualities of business that are evil. But distinction by gender established in the case of Millwood is not finally secure. One would think that such indeterminacy would undo the differences that the figure of Millwood establishes, the difference between good and bad business, rape and trade, nationalist fervor and the breaking of contracts. However, in this play, instead of undermining differences, the inability to differentiate by gender is actually localized in Millwood and itself expelled. Millwood is scapegoated for being immoral in business *and* for her own gender indeterminacy. She represents the power of blacking, having learned early, she says, to protect herself by "detraction [which], like darkness and death, blackens all objects and levels all distinction" (4.18.31–32, 65). Her creed is to live according to indifferentiation: "All actions are alike natural and indifferent to man and beast who devour or are devoured as they meet with others weaker or stronger than themselves" (4.18.43–45, 65). As a representative of gender indeterminacy, Millwood thus is scapegoated for the figurative tricks that allow her to serve as a scapegoat and effectively erect mercantile practices into an ideal.

Lillo's 1731 bourgeois tragedy solves a huge problem in representation that the she-tragedies could not overcome: by using a trope customary in medieval misogyny—woman as a figure for rhetoric itself[42]—bourgeois tragedy or "crying comedy" blames the figure of woman for the very rhetorical instability necessary for making her into an effective scapegoat. That instability needs to be mustered, and then shut down for effective scapegoating, for the woman to be effectively abjected. The figure of woman needs to be seen as essentially distinct so that women can be used to establish permanent-but-male universals and ideals. To the degree that she is not essentially different, she is hateful. Since women are essentially feminine, a woman who speaks like a man simply arouses more disgust, securing the scapegoating process rather than undermining it.

Propaganda versus the Literary

It is clear from the production history of *The London Merchant*—produced between 204 and 230 times during the eighteenth century, many times "At the Particular Desire of several Persons of Distinction and eminent Merchants of the City of London,"[43]—that the play was indeed successful in idealizing the man of business. Eighteenth-century audiences did not see as unbelievable the play's unqualified praise of mercantilism: scapegoating Millwood worked. As Tejumola Olaniyan puts it, Lillo's play legitimized "the merchant self and function" in the face of "the snobbery of the landed gentry" that saw "the merchant class" as inferior to landed wealth.[44]

But although popular, *The London Merchant*, like Mandeville's *Modest Defence of Publick STEWS*, never was considered great literature. Can we conclude that idealizing capitalists and making great literature are two completely separate and opposed enterprises? As I pointed out in the introduction, literature is not capitalist propaganda. Insofar as they are distinct from propaganda, works that have been considered great and have become canonical contain literariness, a structural indeterminacy hostile to the successful establishment of ideals. In contrast to propaganda, literary texts structurally generate indeterminacy, although that indeterminacy can be foreclosed upon in the process of canonization (as shown in chapter 1) by the bourgeois consumer of high art. In noncanonical, propagandistic literature, the original structure of indeterminacy is missing. Although sadomasochistic and therefore potentially indeterminate in structure, Otway's *Orphan* is not considered to be great literature (i.e., it has not been canonized) because it generates indifferentiation rather than indeterminacy: there are not several poles with which one can identify, but ultimately only one (if everyone is the same) or none (if everyone is indistinguishable). Inculcating a sadistic affective economy that effectively differentiates women from men, Lillo's and Mandeville's texts are not "great" literature because they abjure indeterminacy for the sake of establishing capitalist ideals, refusing in the end to offer their heroines any sympathy at all. When Lillo generates too much sympathy for Millwood, or when he renders her gender indeterminate, at those moments the character engages in what look to be feminist speeches. However, in the case of all three texts, the excessive attempts to both generate and derail sympathetic identifications cause the stark juxtaposition of sexism with feminist sentiments. Excess is necessary because of the absolute difference being established between men and women, making it harder for a male audience or readership to identify with female figures and feminist statements in the first place. In Mandeville's work, as for Lillo, the requirements of effective scapegoating require them to deploy viable feminist arguments, making their female figures sympathetic enough to their audience, too sympathetic for us and perhaps for any budding feminists among their readership. If this chapter explains why such a popular play and pamphlet were not canonized, revealing some of the reasons for their propagandistic feel to modern audiences, it might also begin to explain how the uttering of feminist sentiments might seem propagandistic: it is not the starkness of feminist sentiments, nor their intrinsic "ugliness" as aesthetic objects, but the promotion of capitalism to which these feminist utterances contribute, that make them in particular part of noncanonical literature.

The Orphan, *A Modest Defense*, and *The London Merchant* are all noncanonical texts that fail to preserve indeterminacy—the former collapsing into a chaos of indifferentiation, the latter too successfully promoting capitalist ideals. I now turn to noncanonical literature that is indeed indeterminate in structure. Mary Leapor's poetry is literary despite the fact that it has never been canonized. Whereas the texts analyzed in chapters 2 and 3 do not contain the requisite structure for being great literature, whereas they are not indeterminate and literary, Leapor's work suffers from the opposite problem: her poetry has never been canonized because its indeterminacy is not reducible, because it could not be reduced to the bourgeois object, literature.

In the next chapter I examine in Leapor's poetry another coincidence of misogyny and feminism. This time, feminism is not just an epiphenomenon of the attempt to balance a system of identifications and disidentifications: Leapor uses misogyny to demystify literary conventions. In trying to understand her work, one can see that misogynous reading practices that we have inherited from the eighteenth century, practices necessary for establishing our ideals, threaten to rob Leapor's work of its feminist potential. The next chapter analyzes the effects of sadistic reading practices. Shutting down the literariness of texts is one way of co-opting feminist protest: the sexism intrinsic to certain conventions can be effectively registered only via ambiguities produced by literary form.

4

Misogyny and Feminism

Mary Leapor

Corydon: 'Tis true, her Linen may be something soil'd.
Phillario: Her Linen, Corydon!—Herself, you mean.
        Are such the Dryads of thy smiling Plain?
        Why, I could swear it, if it were no Sin,
        That yon lean Rook can shew a fairer Skin.
Corydon: What tho' some Freckles in her Face appear?
        That's only owing to the time o'th'Year.
        . . . .
        Come, come; you view her with malicious Eyes:
        Her Shape———
Phillario: —Where Mountains upon Mountains rise!
        And, as [if] they fear'd some Treachery at hand,
        Behind her Ears her list'ning Shoulders stand.
Corydon: But she has Teeth—
Phillario: ———Considering how they grow,
        'Tis no great matter if she has or no:
        They look decay'd with Posset, and with Plumbs,
        And seem prepar'd to quit her swelling Gums.

—Mary Leapor, from a poem upon herself called "Mira's Picture"

Note, This Description of her Person is a Caracture. [Note by the editors to "Mira's Picture"]

I must beg Leave to enter a *Caveat* against printing the Poem call'd *Myra's Picture*; because tho' she may be suppos'd to have made very free with herself, I think it may give the Reader a worse Idea of her Person than it deserv'd, which was very far from being shocking, tho' there was nothing extraordi-

nary in it. The Poem was occasioned by her happening to hear that a Gentleman who had seen some of her Poems, wanted to know what her person was.
—Bridget Freemantle, introduction to vol. 2 of Leapor's *Poems*

Bridget Freemantle advises against printing this antiblason written by the popular eighteenth-century, laboring-class poet Mary Leapor.[1] As her patron, Freemantle is concerned in general to present Leapor as one of the deserving poor[2] and thus is worried about this antiblason's politically subversive intent. Freemantle's caveat implies that Leapor's "Picture" poem is neither an accurate description nor a misogynous satire against women, as antiblasons are usually taken to be. Rather, it is a satire of the aristocratic gentleman Phillario, who, like the "Gentleman who had seen some of [Leapor's] Poems [and] wanted to know what her person was," has a set of expectations, gleaned from the pastoral, about rural, laboring women. Phillario addresses the "harmless Shepherd Swain" Corydon in order to find out whether "th'Arcadian Nymphs outshine / The shiv'ring Beauties of this Northern Clime" (2:294–95): he ridiculously expects rural nymphs to have white skin and teeth, despite the hardship of their physical existence. This poem de-idealizes the pastoral nymph and swain by describing skin freckled or browned from working out of doors and decayed teeth, which Phillario foolishly attributes to eating sugar plums and wine-spiced posset rather than to poverty. Leapor's poem, like Duck's "Thresher's Labour" and Collier's *The Woman's Labor*, exposes the pastoral's deliberate obfuscation of rural labor and poverty,[3] but it does so using a markedly different strategy from that employed by either Duck or Collier. Whereas Duck and Collier put male and female laborers (respectively) back into the prospect from which they have been removed, Leapor depicts an aristocratic gentleman whose expectations of rural life, conditioned by the pastoral, are sorely disappointed by Mira's dirty linen, swarthy skin, and bad teeth; *real* experience of the repugnant female body, Leapor insists, demystifies pastoral literary conventions.

"Mira's Picture" is not by any means the first antiblason. Antiblasons are included in the first collection of poetry that eulogizes female body parts, Marot and Scève's *Blasons anatomiques du corps féminin* (1536).[4] Before the eighteenth century, antiblasons work, as parody always does, to better define that tradition. For example, in his poem "My Mistress' Eyes are Nothing Like the Sun," Shakespeare describes how unlike blason images his lover's body actually is, for the sake of succeeding better than his predecessors at praising her beauty: he de-idealizes for the sake of idealizing better, outdoing but not overturning the blason form. In contrast, antiblason poetry of the eighteenth century written by Jonathan Swift and Leapor questions the ideological investments of the form. It operates as that kind of literary history that engages in progressivist critique, the basic rhetorical structure of which is articulated in John Locke's *Essay concerning Human Understanding.*

Knowledge comes, Locke says, from "[o]bservation employ'd either about *external, sensible Objects; or about the internal Operations of our Minds, perceived and reflected on by our selves*";[5] the experience of observing provides a ground for "the taking away False Foundations" (*Essay*, "Epistle to the Reader," 10). Objective experience, experience of that which anyone would find to be existing in reality, is used by Locke to critique the ideas promulgated by past authorities,[6] just as the antiblason points to reality in order to critique literary conventions. Locke's critical, progressivist mode of analysis thus constitutes a "reflection on 'today' as difference in history and as motive for a particular philosophical task"—to take Michel Foucault's definition of Enlightenment discourse.[7] As an Enlightenment genre, the eighteenth-century antiblason deploys the rhetoric of experience to reflect on the adequacy of conventions; its "philosophical task" is to discover the reality hidden by traditional literary forms for the sake of overcoming their oppressive mystifications.

Contemporary histories of difference, whether feminist, post-Marxist, or new historicist, despite their desire to distance themselves from the positivism informing Enlightenment modes of critique, implicitly rely on the rhetoric of empiricism insofar as they presuppose the objectivity of their own pronouncements. Since writing antiblasons is, as shown in more detail below, an eighteenth-century way of doing a progressive, "new" history, analyzing one of its most debilitating pitfalls can elucidate a serious problem confronting those engaged now in recovering histories of difference through cultural artifacts that intrinsically exclude those histories.[8]

Although enabling a progressive questioning of exclusionary cultural forms, objectivity has its price. Demanding a "concordance between the mind of man and the nature of things," as Bacon does in describing the new science,[9] puts pressure on representation to become immediate—that is, for its own conditions to drop out of sight. *Tristram Shandy* tells us that Locke's *Essay* "is a history-book . . . of what passes in a man's own mind,"[10] but eighteenth-century writers collude in trying to forget that it is a "book," "an *account*" of the raw stuff of experience rather than that stuff itself. From Bacon to Sterne, history is being redefined so that rhetoric and conditions of representation are seen only as containers for actuality. But of course the rhetoricity of language continually reasserts itself, causing scientific writers a certain amount of anxiety, as evinced by the often-quoted passage from Thomas Sprat's *History of the Royal Society* in which he asks scientific writers to obviate "the mists and uncertainties [that come from] *Tropes* and *Figures*" by "return[ing] back to the primitive purity [of language], when men deliver'd so many *things* in almost an equal number of words."[11] Both Naomi Schorr and Jacqueline Rose have noticed that, when anxiety about representation runs particularly high in a given text, it turns misogynous; that is, it attempts to incite hatred of women by depicting the female body as disgusting.[12] The (post)modern era beginning with the Enlightenment might be defined by the intensity of anxiety over the sheer referentiality of discourse.[13] Depictions of the decaying female body are deployed to shore up this emerging, modern "representational epistemology," in which "to know reality is to have a correct [i.e., literal rather than figural, *actual*] representation of things."[14]

In "Mira's Picture," one can see the anxiety caused by an implicit claim to the referentiality of Leapor's discourse and, concomitantly, the use of misogyny to allay it. In her antiblason, Leapor uses the platform of realistic, experientially informed description as a method for attacking the way that aristocratic conventions represent laboring women. She describes the female body as disgusting as a way of asserting the greater objectivity of her own discourse in comparison with the aristocratic pastoral. "'Tis no great matter whether [Mira] has [teeth] or no / They look decay'd," Phillario exclaims: what difference does it make whether the nymph has teeth; they are rotting! While that sentence shirks responsibility for accurately depicting history (Mira may or may not have teeth), it simultaneously claims to do so: that they are pictured as rotting constitutes proof that these teeth are being accurately described—why would one describe teeth as decayed unless they actually are? The language of this poem is *able* to point to really existing teeth because they are rotting. Whether language can capture the "great matter"—the real world—that it points to "or no," is indeed a "great matter" since it reveals the oppressiveness of aristocratic pastoral form.

A logic becomes apparent in the protest made by "Mira's Picture" then, revealing a connection between feminist literary history and the antiblason tradition. Because misogyny sustains objectivity, and because progressivist discourse relies upon objective reality to demystify ideologically loaded misrepresentations of reality, misogynous representations are a particular temptation even for Enlightenment discourses that are themselves engaged in critiquing sexism. The trope of the repugnant female body has been used in the rhetoric of empiricism to ground its own objectivity and consequently has been a crucial component of progressivist discourses arising during the Enlightenment—including feminism itself. Reading Leapor's more explicitly feminist antiblasons shows that, unfortunately, the representational epistemology sustained by misogyny underpins feminist literary histories. In literary history, misogyny and feminism are interdependent: there is a temptation to misogyny in the writing of the a feminist literary history dedicated to recovering women's voices.

The Antiblason as Progressivist Literary History

The antiblason's critical power—and, as discussed below, that of feminism and new historicism—depends upon the visibility of its own literariness. We mistake antiblasons as mere statements of misogyny insofar as we do not notice that the speaker of the poem is a satiric persona. In both Leapor and Swift, the satiric persona is an object of attack: he is one of those "empiricks"—one of those "quacks, . . . mountebanks, enthusiasts, and theurgics"[15]—suspect for delivering such a misogynous outburst. The "Cassy" of Swift's "Cassinus and Peter. A Tragical Elegy," a speaker who no doubt observes the truth of Celia's bodily functions, is deeply suspect for being so interested in and affected by them; Swift is critiquing Cassy's empiricism, not Celia's body. Similarly, in "Mira's Picture," Phillario's desire to actually see the beautiful "rural nymphs" he has read about reveals that he too is a suspect "empirick," rather like the antiquaries who read classical texts as ethnographic descriptions rather than as art. Leapor's "The Visit" describes Mira begging entry into Artemisa's home that she might "'scape the penetrating Eye / Of Students in Physiognomy" (2:291). Empiricks such as Phillario and these physiognomists practicing their "body criticism"[16] can be seen as blasonneurs gone mad, trying to read the body to see whether Petrarchan sonnets are true.[17]

But satires that portray scientists as mere "empiricks" and mad blasonneurs rarely are read as critiquing their personae.[18] From Lord Orrery to Middleton Murry to Norman O. Brown, Swift's antiblasons have been connected to disturbances in his sexuality and his mind.[19] Critics who try to normalize Swift's message, to see it as "universal,"[20] often themselves purvey a certain amount of misogyny. For instance, according to Siebert, "critics agree that these [dressing-room] poems explode certain illusions surrounding romantic love": "A Beautiful Nymph" represents a lover's necessary "realization that even beautiful women stink."[21] It is difficult to find critics who notice that the female body does not in general seem to be the object of Swift's attack:[22] the picture of misogyny is too tempting.

One of the first readers of "Mira's Picture" obviously yields to the temptation of reading misogynous depictions literally. In the 1780s, a correspondent to the *Gentleman's Magazine* answers someone's query about "Molly Leapor" by describing her as "swarthy" and "crane-neck[ed]."[23] No longer a satire on gentlemanly ways of imagining reality, the poem is read by this historicist corresponding to the *Gentleman's Magazine* as accurately describing what Leapor looked like when she was alive. Distressingly, both the gentleman historicist who defuses the poem's political power on the one hand and Leapor herself on the other—*both* deploy the same rhetorical structure in their arguments: they both check literary figures against the real stuff of experience; they both take an empirical turn. But whereas Leapor uses ordinary experience to question the ideological stakes in conventional forms, and thus performs an act of demystification, the gentleman historian "confus[es] linguistic with natural reality."[24] The aristocratic gentleman's "historical" account of Leapor's body reduces a swarthy *figure* to a swarthy *body* by conceiving her discourse and his own as purely referential. What tempts him to defigure discourse, his and hers, is the titillating attraction of imagining a disgusting referent "beneath" the poem. Misogyny is not "naturally" titillating, but, at Leapor's particular historical moment and still in ours, misogyny has been eroticized.

The gentleman historicist who reports to us how Leapor actually looked is a historicist of the positivist kind—an "old" historicist—insofar as he tries to look through language to historical actuality by ignoring the rhetoricity of language. But nonetheless he writes to the *Gentleman's Magazine* out of a progressive interest in a laboring-class woman poet. There is a critical power to be found even in old historicism, but it seems nonetheless to differ crucially from the "new." "New" historicism may have roots in progressivist Enlightenment discourses, but it does not read texts as pictures looking out onto the world. And yet, any secure sense of the difference between old and new historicism disregards how difficult it is to avoid taking a referential view of language and a positivist approach to history. In "The New Historicism: Back to the Future," Marjorie Levinson describes how much of the old is in the new: "It is precisely our failure to articulate a critical field that sights *us* even as we compose *it*, that brings back the positivism, subjectivism and relativism of the rejected historicist methodology."[25] The resurgence of positivism comes from the new historicist's failure to sight himself in the field—that is, from the historicist's failure to see himself as using rhetoric to construct objectivity rather than seeing himself as an objective (impersonal, as good as absent) observer of reality.

Both new historicism and feminist historical materialism[26] turn toward an objective place called "experience" in order to attempt what Leapor is trying to do in her antiblason, that is, for the sake of demystification and critique. Unfortunately, if critics fail to see their own work as rhetorical, turning to experience in order to analyze the rhetoric of a past literary tradition ultimately (but not necessarily) subverts the political efficacy of their own criticism: like the gentleman historicist, they mistake the rhetoric used to critique for a description of an actual state of affairs. Because they share the empirical turn as method and then face the temptation to confuse methodological necessity with political reality, feminist materialists and new historicists risk importing into their accounts a narrative of the past that reads: "women, laborers, and colonized Others have disgusting, embrowned bodies."

Others have shown that misogyny is intrinsic to the world of experiment,[27] and that misogyny, classism, and racism are intrinsic to Enlightenment rationality.[28] Here the focus is different: this chapter shows that particular method used by literary historians writing during the Enlightenment, such as Leapor and the gentleman empiricist, and even afterward, such as Catherine Gallagher and Michael McKeon, for demystifying the classism and sexism of patriarchal literary conventions easily collapses into an epistemology that grounds the real in filthy femaleness. Mistaking the politicized deployment of experience, a rhetorical strategy, for reality, an extradiscursive thing, is no mere paradox; it threatens to disable feminist literary history. A critical turn toward "experience" is a rhetorical device that has been misrecognized as reality;[29] the device has been handed down to us from the antiblason tradition. The misogyny that is, consequently, inherent in this rhetorical strategy threatens to undermine efforts to retrieve women's protest and thereby threatens feminist literary history per se.

Misogyny and the Literary Assault on Empiricism

In Scriblerian satire against the new science,[30] Swift, Pope, and others insist that the empiricist's object of study is really the dead, decaying, and "embrowned" human body.[31] Thus, the empiricist Gulliver, like the "minute philosophers" described in book 4 of Pope's *Dunciad*, dutifully records the details of the disposing of his feces and urine in Lilliput[32] and in later Brobdingnag: "I hope the gentle reader will excuse me for dwelling on these and the like particulars, which, however insignificant they may appear to grovelling vulgar minds, yet will certainly help a philosopher to enlarge his thoughts and imagination, and apply them to the benefit of public as well as private life" (76). Envisaging the empiricist's truth as excrement is not only an assault on ideal versions of the empirical object; it renders the point of empirical pursuit as absurd as possible: it is not at all clear how Gulliver's record of his daily defecations can be used for "the benefit of public as well as private life"; why, Swift makes us ask, are the Minute Philosophers so hot in pursuit of grotesque details?

Swift's satire operates not by perverting empiricism but rather by overdramatizing it. The empiricist is just like Strephon of "The Lady's Dressing Room," who

Stole in, and took a strict survey
Of all the litter as it lay:
Whereof, to make the matter clear,
An inventory follows here.
(lines 7–10)

Like Strephon, the empiricist uses an ideal image or a descriptive term to cover a reality and render it attractive: Strephon takes an inventory of objects in the dressing room in order "to make the matter clear," that is, to clean it up. The "matter" is now not only attractive but also can now be accused of hiding behind or beneath it "[t]hose secrets of the hoary deep" (line 98), secrets that the empiricist can then seek to discover. He does discover them, in horror, horrified as much by what "really" attracted him as by the falsity of the image that hides the actual "fact" of excrement.

One thing that *Gulliver's Travels* does through its attention to excrement is to recognize the genre of the *Essay concerning Human Understanding*: Swift shows us that Locke's *Essay* is an antiblason that first appears to be idealizing body parts, as a blason would, but second uncovers a filthy underside to them (i.e., it de-idealizes them). Gulliver repeats, parodies, and mimics the moves made by Locke in his *Essay* in order to expose in empiricism this double movement. Gulliver in Brobdingnag discovers "that [his] sense was more acute in proportion to [his] littleness."[33] Locke imagines that an angel making its organs as small as possible would see minutiae independently of, and indeed as a replacement for, their total human significance: "What wonders would he discover, who could so fit his Eye to all sorts of Objects, as to see, when he pleased, the Figure and Motion of the minute Particles in the Blood, and other juices of Animals, as distinctly as he does at other times, the shape and motion of the Animals themselves" (2.23.13, 303). But the "wonders" Gulliver discovers upon becoming little are expressed in *Gulliver's Travels* in grotesque detail as several antiblasons on the breast. Swift thus informs us that there is a generic connection between Locke's *Essay* and Marot's *Blasons anatomiques du corps féminin*, of which the panegyric on "Le Beau Tétin" is the most famous.

In Brobdingnag, Gulliver is horrified to see the "monstrous breast" of a nurse giving suck in front of him and tells us so in a passage that might be called "Le Tétin Repugnant":

I must confess no object ever disgusted me so much as the sight of her monstrous breast. . . . It stood prominent six foot, and could not be less than sixteen in circumference. The nipple was about half the bigness of my head, and the hue both of that and the dug so varified with spots, pimples and freckles that nothing could appear more nauseous. . . . This made me reflect upon the fair skins of our English ladies, who appear so beautiful to us, only because they are of our own size, and their defects not to be seen but through a magnifying glass, where we find by experiment that the smoothest and whitest skins look rough and course, and ill coloured.[34]

"Experiment" with magnifying glasses reveals not wonders but monstrosities that make Gulliver nauseous, and reveals a fundamental difference between English men and "our English ladies": the "fair skins" of English women would really appear "varified with spots, pimples, and freckles," "ill-coloured"—no doubt "swarthy"—were we to see them up close. Gulliver's antiblason on the monstrous breast carefully distinguishes English men from English women by their swarthy skins.

Later, the monstrous breast is associated with decay that disgusts the miniature Gulliver at the same time that he fantasizes immersing himself in it:

One day the governess [of the miniature Gulliver's caretaker, Glumdalclitch] ordered our coachman to stop at several shops, where the beggars, watching their opportunity, crowded to the sides of the coach, and gave me the most horrible spectacles that ever an European eye beheld. There was a woman with a cancer in her breast, swelled to a monstrous size, full of holes, in two or three of which I could have easily crept, and covered my whole body. There was a fellow with a wen in his neck. . . . But the most hateful sight of all was the lice crawling on their clothes. I could see distinctly the limbs of these vermin with my naked eye, much better than those of an European louse through a microscope. . . . I should have been curious enough to dissect one of them, if I had proper instruments (which I unluckily left behind me in the ship) although indeed the sight was so nauseous, that it perfectly turned my stomach.[35]

The "European eye" magnifies the cancerous breast with a microscope precisely to turn the sight of decay into a titillating spectacle, into "the most horrible spectacle that ever an European eye beheld": Gulliver's fantasy of creeping into the holes of the cancerous breast, of being surrounded and engulfed by decay, is, Swift claims, what the empiricist really wants.

Scientific empirical researches, the allegedly unmediated acquisition of knowledge through the senses, have as their real object disavowal of one's own death. Empirical description fragments bodies and idealizes the parts so that the decay examined is not something that seems to happen to a person; the instruments of empiricism, microscopes and dissecting tools, are a means for shifting oneself out of the realm of decay. Because Gulliver left these "proper instruments" aboard his ship, Swift deploys the rhetorical "instruments" necessary for such disavowal by figuring the decaying body as female. But decay and with it death become by this very disavowal eroticized: a narcissistic identification with the disgusting female body allows the empiricist to immerse himself in it, as Gulliver does in the cancerous breast. Such an immersion in the abject female body is a source of erotic pleasure—here we can see "the murky source . . . of our loves."[36]

The decaying body that empiricism disavows and desires is not necessarily female—that is to say, empiricism is not necessarily misogynous—but it very often is. The empiricist wants to identify with but then at a crucial moment distance himself from decay. If the empiricist presumes himself to be male, then gendering the decaying body female allows him to distance himself from it by making it into a "her" and thus into an object of scopophilic desire. Gender difference allows for a dialectic of identification and disidentification.

But sometimes the dialectic does not work; sometimes gender difference is not enough to save the empiricist from an agonizing identification with dead and decaying matter. In moments of extreme instability, racial difference is mobilized for the sake of abjecting physical decay: Phillario and Corydon describe Mira's freckled face; the gentleman empiricist describes Leapor's "swarthy skin"; Swift describes the skin of a female "dug" as "so varified with spots, pimples and freckles" as to be "ill coloured." Disidentification can work through the figure of woman, who, Freud says, is "almost the same but not quite"; but sometimes, as Homi Bhabha says, such a dialectic requires someone who is "almost the same but not *white*."[37] Swarthiness as a signifier is ambiguous, pointing to what could be a racial or a class difference, since the lower classes had not yet "reformed" into adopting notions of cleanliness:[38] in any case, this sign of minimal otherness allows the empiricist viewer and reader to revel in the dirt with the Other with whom he identifies while simultaneously disavowing any identification. If repugnant gender difference is one of the mechanisms that make it possible for the empiricist blason to effectively represent a disavowal of and desire for bodily decay, why would a woman poet write an antiblason? What is to be gained for her?

The Instability of Parody as Critique

Use of the empirical turn is often a very effective mode of critique. Leapor's poem "Strephon to Celia. A modern Love-Letter" exposes the hypocrisy of upper-class discourses on "love"[39] by figuring "Celia" as uglier "in reality" than conventions of love poetry allow. Because Strephon is such a bad poet— "Yet I can hardly spell my Letter"—we can see that his blason is financially motivated rather than prompted by "real" love:

You need not wonder at my Flame,
For you are not a mortal Dame:
I saw you dropping from the Skies;
And let dull Idiots swear your Eyes
With Love their glowing Breast inspire,
I tell you they are Flames of Fire,
That scorch my Forehead to a Cinder,
. . . .
Your Cheeks that look as if they bled,
Are nothing else but Roses red.
Your Lips are Coral very bright,
Your Teeth—tho' Numbers out of spite,
May say they're Bones—yet 'twill appear
They're Rows of Pearl exceeding dear.
(1:104–6)

In order to critique the basis of upper-class love poetry, Leapor's poem veers toward the Swiftian grotesque blason. The fop speaker of this poem, like that found in Robert Gould's "The Playhouse,"[40] equates Celia with bird droppings that fall from the sky.[41] The poem almost disfigures Celia's face. In order to show that Strephon's descriptions of Celia's teeth as pearls and her cheeks as roses depend upon her "Five hundred Pounds a Year," the poem turns the "real" Celia's teeth into bones and almost depicts her face as if it were diseased—"bleeding."

Reading this poem, the reader is fairly secure that Strephon—and not Celia—is being parodied: we are witnessing Strephon's inept use of pastoral convention, not the emergence of Celia's "real" picture from rhetoric. Leapor clearly gains critical power through deploying the antiblason's misogyny— that is, what would be read as misogyny if we were to see the poem as a pure description of Celia. But often, revealing various ideologies to be class- and gender-specific by relying on the empirical turn—by showing that they fail to accurately describe experience—backfires.

In her country-house poem *Crumble-Hall*, Leapor overturns the conventions of that form described by Raymond Williams in *The Country and the City*. Usually the owners appear in a landscape and home devoid of laborers and servants: nature, these poems usually say, furnishes forth its riches of its own accord.[42] In contrast, Leapor absents the owners of the house and describes only the servants. When about to take in a prospect from the top of the house, "Mira" (Leapor's muse) is hurled into this "nether world" of the servants, where she records a "mournful" kitchen maid's lament to her husband Roger. Ursula's lament[43] begins by describing Roger, exhausted after a day's labor and a huge meal:

O'er-stuff'd with Beef; with Cabbage much too full,
And Dumpling too (fit Emblem of his Skull!)
With Mouth wide open, but with closing Eyes
Unwieldy *Roger* on the Table lies.
His able Lungs discharge a rattling Sound:
Prince barks, *Spot* howls, and the tall Roofs rebound.
Him *Urs'la* views; and with dejected Eyes,
"Ah! *Roger*, Ah!" the mournful Maiden cries:
"Is wretched *Urs'la* then your Care no more,
"That, while I sigh, thus you can sleep and snore?
"Ingrateful *Roger*! wilt thou leave me now?
"For you these Furrows mark my fading Brow:
"For you my Pigs resign their Morning Due:
"My hungry Chickens lose their Meat for you:
"And, was it not, Ah! was it not for thee,
"No goodly Pottage would be dress'd by me.
"For thee these Hands wind up the whirling Jack,
"Or place the Spit across the sloping Rack.
"I baste the Mutton with a chearful Heart,
"Because I know my *Roger* will have Part."
Thus she—But now her Dish-kettle began
To boil and blubber with the foaming Bran.
The greasy Apron round her Hips she ties,
And to each Plate the scalding Clout applies:
The purging Bath each glowing Dish refines,
And once again the polish'd Pewter shines.
(2:119–20)

In the anaphora "For you" and "for thee," Ursula says that she does all of her work only for Roger. Ursula attempts to transform her labor into what female labor will become for growing numbers of middle-class women: "mere epiphenomena of wifely devotion."[44] However, because Ursula and Roger work for the absent owners of Crumble-Hall, because Ursula works in the kitchen with Sophronia to feed not only Roger but "Grave *Colinettus*" and "surly *Graffo*," Ursula's lament "render[s] the contradictions of [bourgeois] romantic ideology, and its powerfully imaginary status *as* ideology, particularly obvious" (180): Ursula's repetition of "For you" and "for thee" is belied by her statement that she makes a dinner of which Roger will only "have Part"; she labors for pay, not "love."

In *Crumble-Hall*, Leapor parodies domestic ideology; she is trying to show that the ideal that represents women as working *only* for the love of men cannot be applied to women of the laboring classes such as Ursula. But here the parody slips out of her control: rhetoric and parody slip into realism and misogyny. Ursula's lament potentially tells us that the idea of romantic love *comes from* women; Ursula is stupid, the poem might be saying, to apply *her* notions of romantic love to that particular husband, to the Roger lying on the table, who resembles a stuffed pig, dressed and ready to eat. Leapor's portrait of Ursula can be read as locating this cultural corruption in female desires and demands.[45] It is difficult to tell in *Crumble-Hall* whether Ursula satirizes romantic expectations or whether conventional images of love in fact satirize Ursula (she is stupid to expect love from the swinish Roger) or satirize Ursula and Roger as laboring buffoons, "clowns" like the gravediggers in *Hamlet*, who cannot manage to get love right. Once again, critique can be recuperated as mere reiteration of the status quo: Ursula's mimicry, her repetition of bourgeois love with a difference, undecidably parodies either hegemonic ideals or Ursula herself.

As with Swift's antiblasons, Mary Leapor's love poetry potentially either reveals her own misogynous attitudes or criticizes social practices; in the case of *Crumble-Hall* in particular, whether she parodies or repeats the stylized laborer-as-buffoon is undecidable. Her biography makes it less undecidable. Because expressions of misogyny and classism would be less "natural" in her poetry than they allegedly are in Swift's, it is more obvious in her poems that the project of demystifying aristocratic ideals by relying on "experience" pulls her work in the direction of misogyny, that she is not *trying* to express misogyny but is rather forced to do so. Are we to read *Crumble-Hall* then as evidence of the inevitable failure of critiques launched from within literary conventions to undermine the classist and sexist bias of those conventions?

Leapor's Literary Criticism and Ours

The insight that the conscious desire to perform radical political actions can be co-opted because the forms of protest are always already contaminated is fundamental to new historicism. Although people have argued that the view of contaminated or co-opted protest comes from certain strands of Marxist theory[46] or from the Foucault of *Discipline and Punish*,[47] in Catherine Gallagher's view, the experience of that insight came to new historicists primarily from seeing the results of feminist activism. She recalls the moment when certain feminists arrived at this insight, after the failure of consciousness-raising to achieve its intended political effects: "Was it possible, we asked, that certain forms of subjectivity that felt oppositional were really a means by which power relations were maintained?"[48] This realization fundamentally altered feminist modes of interpretation: "[B]y focusing attention on our gendered individuation as the deepest moment of social oppression, some of us called into question the political reliability of our own subjectivity. We effectively collapsed the self/society division and began regarding our 'normal' consciousness and 'natural' inclinations as profoundly untrustworthy. We, along with our erstwhile political optimism, became for ourselves the objects of a hermeneutics of suspicion."[49] Gallagher here provides one of the most compelling accounts of the ideological formation of one's *own* subjectivity, a phenomenon of which naive feminism remains unaware. Similarly, the ideological construction of literary conventions renders possible, indeed likely, betrayal by liberatory discourses relying on those conventions, even if only to react against them.

This hermeneutics of suspicion has provided insight into exactly what compromises any project of demystification. Insofar as consciousness is ideologically constructed, it is untrustworthy; and in Leapor's work, insofar as her critique relies upon ideologically inflected conventions, it cannot help being antifeminist and classist. However, notice that the insight into individuation as fundamentally social provided by this hermeneutics of suspicion relies upon the very category of experience constructed by the eighteenth-century British empirical tradition; it too relies upon the rhetoric of experience that both enables and disables Leapor's protest against the oppression of women.[50] Because Gallagher relies on experience at the moment when she discovers the co-optation of modes of "subjectivity [that] felt oppositional," her "discovery" is like the gentleman historicist's revelation that Leapor really had swarthy skin: our oppositional subjectivities, she discovers, "really" are not oppositional. Such a "discovery" needs to be taken for what it is: the rhetorical *strategy* necessary for demystification, for analyzing what kinds of forces defuse or contain that oppositionality, should not be mistaken for *reality*—an empirical fact that subjectivity cannot be oppositional. To conclude that *Crumble-Hall*'s critique inevitably fails, then, is to mistake a rhetorical for a real predicament.

Moreover, the fatal moment when critics discover how opposition to hegemony has been co-opted by hegemonic forms—even though it does provide insight—puts us in an intellectually indefensible as well as politically reactionary role of dominance over the past writer whose articulation of protest we are trying to retrieve. Frederic Jameson has noticed that, in certain historicist accounts, "power"—and he is speaking of power in the sense of "power to contain protest"—often becomes an "increasingly total system or logic" that gives the critic herself complete mastery over the past. But if power indeed were so total, then where does the critic stand in order to see power operate? An epistemologically untenable mastery is purchased at the price of "fatalism," Jameson says: "Insofar as the theorist wins, therefore, by constructing an increasingly closed and terrifying machine, to that very degree he loses, since the critical capacity of his work is thereby paralyzed, and the impulses of negation and revolt, not to speak of those of social transformation, are increasingly perceived as vain and trivial in the face of the model itself."[51] In proclaiming power omnipotent, the critic does not simply *find* Leapor's protest contained but rather *enacts* that containment for the sake of achieving mastery.

In reading Leapor's antiblasons, how can we prevent the *mode* of critique—a mode that exerts a misogynous pull—from becoming the antifeminist conclusion that Leapor has no power to protest? In using theoretical insights into the functioning of power, how can we prevent the *mode* of critique—belief in "the attentive malevolence that turns everything to account"—from becoming a fatalist conclusion that the power to contain is omnipotent and resistance impossible?[52]

Some recent attempts to overcome this problem do not work. The desire for critical mastery will not be eluded by accounting for one's own position: self-disclosures have no effect on the critical work to which they are appended.[53] Nor can a feminist literary historian try to be hyperconscious, more conscious than Gallagher, for instance.[54] To avoid enacting dominance and containment, Bhabha says, we need to rediscover "a 'colonial' counter-modernity at work in the eighteenth- and nineteenth- century matrices of Western modernity":[55] we need to find those places where the countering of Enlightenment forms of oppression is visible. Historians of difference must ask how desires subversive of the existing social order can be represented in conventional forms that helped to build and sustain that order: we cannot see the blason and the pastoral as *only* instruments of the dominant ideology; if we do, we will fail to hear in these forms moments of protest or contestation, just as hegemonic forces always fail to hear protest against them. We are under an "ethical imperative," David Spurr asserts, to retrieve the "history of dissent" from colonial hegemony, a project "from which one is not excused by theoretical objections" to the possibility of other cultures adequately representing themselves.[56]

This "ethical imperative" is not a moral one but rather an imperative comprising an ethics of reading. Spurr is not advocating, as part of this ethic, a return to the naive view that historical and/or colonial others can unproblematically and directly represent themselves within literary and linguistic conventions that have until that moment sustained hegemony. Jean Howard describes this naive view among literary historians as analogous to naive feminists' sense of themselves as truly oppositional subjects, described by Gallagher above: in "the study of women as actors in history," "women's writing [is] expected *automatically* to yield evidence of resistance or of an alternative to patriarchal discourse."[57] Gayatri Spivak has uncovered just such "an unquestioned valorization of the oppressed as subject" in Foucault and Deleuze's "Intellectuals and Power."[58] In this account of class struggle, a sovereign subject of history mirrors a sovereign historian or theorist: by representing the oppressed as "self-knowing, politically canny subalterns, ... intellectuals represent themselves as transparent" (275); although explicitly claiming not to "speak for" subalterns, such rhetorical representations (*Darstellen*) do indeed politically represent subalterns (*Vertreten*) in the sense of appropriating their voices (275–77).

But if the naive view is epistemologically untenable, so is the allegedly more sophisticated, fatalist view of seeing historical and/or colonial others as unable to represent their political agendas within Western, hegemonic discourses, another approach to be abandoned in this ethics of reading. As S.P. Mohanty has shown, cultural criticism's belief in the unknowability of the Other posits epistemologically an extreme relativism that is both philosophically and politically problematic. Grounded philosophically in a now-defunct postivism,[59] such fatalism involves politically the constriction of diverse interests to "debilitatingly insular spaces" (15): if "you"—i.e., the Other—cannot represent yourself to me in hegemonic Western discourses, "I cannot—and consequently need not—think about how your space impinges on mine, or how my history is defined together with yours. If that is the case, I may have started by declaring a pious political wish, but I end by denying that I need to take you seriously" (14). The "pious political wish" that started the intellectual's declaration as to the theoretical impossibility of representing resistance to hegemony would be the refusal to appropriate the other's voice. But in fact both the naive theorist who does appropriate the other's voice by claiming to have "found" it, as if the critic's and the writer's discourses are transparent, *and* the sophisticated theorist who claims not to be able to find such a voice—both of them effect the same foreclosure: the subaltern goes unheard. It is for this reason that Howard wants "to promote an historical analysis that, on the one hand, refuses naivete about what produces difference and enables an oppositional subjectivity and, on the other hand, refuses a fatalism about the possibility of seeing, even within dominant discourses, the traces of genuine social struggle."[60] What is needed is a critic who refuses to represent—to herself stand for—interests of the oppressed but also refuses to declare those interests illegible, a critic who takes part in the oppressed group. Only through partisanship, only by "think[ing] about . . . how my history is defined together with yours"[61] can we avoid enacting an epistemologically untenable critical mastery either through proclaiming our own transparency, the naive view, or our own impermeability, the fatalist one.

For the historian, partisanship must involve granting as much agency to the subject of the past as one imagines oneself to have: both subjects are situated in a context that gives symbolic acts a historically specific significance, but both subjects' symbolic actions are not limited to a simple reiteration of that context. The literary critic has to be able to envision in literary traditions and forms the possibility of contradictions and ruptures interrupting their ideological work. Paradoxically, the critic's own ideologically suspect projection is *interrupted* rather than facilitated, as one might expect, by the admittedly partisan effort to grant historical others this limited kind of discursive agency. To think about how discursive agency can be recovered through partisanship is precisely not to efface the requisite "critique of ideological subject-constitution within state formations and systems of political economy" erased by the naive view;[62] rather it is to extend that critique to one's own discourse. To insist upon the capacity of historical others to represent themselves in the ironic spaces of what are sexist, classist, and racist modes of representation, ideally, leads to heightened awareness of how those conventions determine criticism as well, as has happened here. That Leapor's feminist and anticlassist critique of the oppression of country-house laborers can be recuperated as a misogynous depiction of Ursula is a result of her reliance upon the rhetoric of empiricism as a strategy for demystification; but to read *Crumble-Hall* as evidence that protest is inevitably contaminated is to join the gentleman empiricist's camp and partake of its epistemological blindness by mistaking rhetoric for the real.

Conclusion: Misogyny and Patriarchy

In the picture of the sonnet lady, figure 2,[63] we can see once again that the "experience" used to demystify aristocratic conventions presents us with a degraded, disfigured female body. The picture portrays in mimetic images all of the figures used in blason poetry: cupid sits on her brow, her breasts are globes, her eyes suns, her hair nets and hooks to catch hearts, her lips coral, her teeth pearls. This picture originally appeared in 1654, in John Davies's English translation of *Le berger extravagant* by Charles Sorel. *The extravagant shepherd* satirizes Lysis for falling in love with his own rhetoric; Anselme draws Lysis this picture to show him how ugly the woman described by such rhetoric "really" is.[64] She is hideous, a monster. The attempt to turn rhetoric into description has a misogynous effect, serving in Sorel's tale as *remedia amoris*. This picture illustrates for us that there is a difference between metaphors and mimetic images, figures and pictures, language and reality. But it is tempting to see this picture as just a picture of a monster rather than as a satire on literalizing readers.[65]

Misogyny is a most effective means for forgetting literariness. Thus, in a

Figure 2. The sonnet lady, from [Charles Sorel] *The extravagant shepherd; or the history of the shepherd Lysis* [trans. John Davies] (London: T. Newcomb, 1654). Reprinted courtesy of the Division of Rare and Manuscript Collections, Cornell University Library, Ithaca, N.Y.

recent feminist and Marxist argument entitled "Historicizing Patriarchy," Michael McKeon describes and celebrates the very "empirical turn" analyzed here as it occurs in Mandeville's *The Fable of the Bees*. "Mandeville, in 1723," McKeon writes, "unmasks as an acculturation the apparent naturalness of female modesty."[66] "The brilliance," he continues, of Mandeville's analysis of "modesty" in Remark C of the *Fable* "is characteristic of an age that may justly be seen as witnessing the birth of the sociological imagination, which demystifies what appears given by recognizing it as, not natural, but social or cultural. What must be recognized as well, however, is the flip side of this insight: its dependence on a knowledge of what is *truly* given, without which the demystification loses all coherence (303). McKeon rightly notices that "what is *truly* given" for Mandeville is a modern and oppressive conception of "gender difference" (300). But McKeon misses the virulent misogyny in Mandeville's "brilliant" analysis of the sociocultural; as in the long tradition of medieval misogyny preceding it, Mandeville's text identifies "women with the illusory."[67] According to Mandeville, women represent themselves as "virtuous" through the practice of "modesty." But underneath that veneer, Mandeville says, women are *really* "Savage Monster[s]" who will do anything, even employ a "killing wet-nurse,"[68] to protect their reputations: "The same Woman that Murders her bastard in the most execrable manner, if she is Married afterwards, may take care of, cherish, and feel all the tenderness for her Infant that the fondest Mother can be capable of. . . . Common Whores, whom all the World knows to be such, hardly ever destroy their Children . . . ; not because they are less Cruel or more Virtuous, but because they have lost their Modesty."[69] Mandeville later expands these views in *A Modest Defence of Publick Stews*, a pamphlet that describes women's bodies as "blown" or spoiled meat:[70] the reality Mandeville unmasks is the filthy female mind and body. The objective, impersonal stance necessary for sociocultural critique requires unmasking repugnant difference.

McKeon might have noticed the role misogyny plays in "the birth of the sociological imagination," had he looked at the figures that are used by Mandeville to represent "what is *truly* given"—the figure of woman as savage monster. Describing Remark C as "brilliant" imports some of Mandeville's misogyny into McKeon's own account. Both McKeon's and Mandeville's texts try to be analytic and devoid of figures. As in the picture of the sonnet lady, misogyny accompanies and shores up the two texts' claims to be objective, to accurately depict reality.[71] But objectivity has its value: Mandeville's Remark C is recognizing cultural forms as constructed rather than natural and eternal. Does demystificatory power such as that found in Mandeville's text—and McKeon's as well—always require misogyny as its price?

At a certain moment, Leapor is indeed able to expose interest in oppressive conventions without unconsciously taking on the interests, contrary to her own, inhering in the empirical method of demystification. Leapor's poem "Man the Monarch" recognizes and tries to overcome how repugnant gender difference has been marshaled to define monarchy in Sir Robert Filmer's *Observations Concerning the Original of Government, Upon Hugo Grotius* (1652), used with Filmer's *Patriarcha* to represent the Tory position in favor of absolutism, and in John Locke's *Two Treatises on Government* (1690), a Whig attack on Filmer's work that favors constitutional monarchy.[72] Not surprisingly, although they are opponents, both Filmer and Locke use the unquestioned naturalness of woman's subordination to man in order to prove what government can or cannot be. They both say, in effect, We know that God and/or Nature wants women to be powerless; we can decipher God's/Nature's intent simply because we know that no edict of God's would grant power to women. Thus Filmer reiterates throughout his *Observation Upon Grotius* that the power of kings comes from the commandment "honor thy father and thy mother,"[73] completely free of any apprehension that this commandment could support a dyarchy rather than a monarchy. Locke calls him on the use of this commandment by pointing out that the "Apocriphal Words," "*and Mother* . . . are always left out."[74] But unfortunately, Locke restores the missing apocryphal words to the commandment upon which Filmer wishes to base the divine right of kings only in order to show that the fifth commandment is not about political power: "*Honour thy Father and Mother* cannot possibly be understood of Political Subjection and Obedience" because Mothers could not possibly be granted political power by God (65, 188). Leapor's "Man the Monarch" fantasmatically reconstructs the dyarchy that Filmer ignores and Locke pronounces impossible. "Nature" explicitly designs woman to rule with man, Leapor says, until

> [Man] view'd his Consort with an envious Eye;
> Greedy of Pow'r, he hugg'd the tott'ring Throne;
> Pleased with Homage, and would reign alone;
> And, better to secure his doubtful Rule,
> Roll'd his wise Eye-balls, and pronounc'd her *Fool.*
> (2:10)

"Man the Monarch" shows why "mother" got left out of political rule in the first place.

In addition to the eruption of the words "and mother" back into Filmer's *Upon Grotius* and *Patriarcha*, Filmer's patriarchal system is interrupted by the notion of matriarchal lineage when he attacks Grotius's radical use of a rhetorical structure and legal device, the "negative pregnant":

[Grotius] tells us he "rejects the opinion of them, who everywhere and without exception will have the chief power to be . . . the people's, that it is lawful for them to compel and punish Kings as oft as they misuse their power." And "this opinion," he confesseth, "if it be altogether received, hath been and may be the cause of many evils." This cautelous rejection [by Grotius of the people's right to revolt against unjust monarchs] qualified with these terms of *everywhere, without exception,* and *altogether,* makes but a mixed negation, partly negative and partly affirmative (which our lawyers call a negative pregnant). Which brings forth this modal proposition, *that in some places with some exception, and in some sort, the people may compel and punish their Kings.*[75]

Here the negative form is "pregnant," as a mother would be, with the power to disrupt the monarchical power of Filmer's text: Grotius has not pictured a democracy, but his negative pregnant leaves space for its possibility; the revolutionary power of this space is pointed to by the word "pregnant," a word that brings up the dependence of patriarchy on matriarchs. Interestingly, in the 1679 and 1696 editions of *Upon Grotius,* there is a misprint: instead of the current legal term "negative pregnant" (*OED*), "negative repugnant" has been substituted; "repugnant" could mean simply "opposed," but it could also mean calling forth antipathy or disgust.[76] It might be possible, for either an eighteenth-century or a twentieth-century reader of *Upon Grotius* well enough aware that "negative *pregnant*" is the correct legal term, to see this misprint as fortuitous: repugnant or aversive descriptions of the female body, one might begin to think, are pregnant with possibilities excluded from conventional discourse.

In "Man the Monarch," Leapor again makes use of blason conventions to describe the beautiful woman that Nature has made. After making the being she favors more than men, Nature grieves to see woman become merely "A Set of useless and neglected Charms" (2:9). Female charms are useless; but surely, as the blason form being used by Leapor at this moment obstreperously asserts, such charms are not neglected in lyric poetry, where they are incessantly described as things (coral lips, teeth that are pearls). Some other kind of female charms, charms not described by the blason, are neglected. In woman's present dejected state, Leapor says, "*Then* her pale Lips no pearly Teeth disclose" (2:9, emphasis added). Notice the difference between Leapor's teeth and the female teeth that appear in Mandeville's Remark C: "[T]he Modesty of Women is the Result of Custom and Education. . . . [N]otwithstanding this, the most Virtuous Young Woman alive will often, in spite of her Teeth, have Thoughts and confus'd Ideas of Things arise in her Imagination, which she would not reveal to some People for a Thousand Worlds."[77] "In spite of her Teeth" is a figure, of course, meaning literally "despite her opposition"; Mandeville sees through those teeth to the filthy thoughts hidden by custom and education. Here misogyny sustains his demystification, as it sustains Leapor's own *feminist* demystification quoted at the beginning of this chapter, "Mira's Picture," in which Mira's teeth "look decay'd with Posset, and with Plumbs, / And seem prepar'd to quit her swelling Gums." In "Man the Monarch," Leapor's line works differently than it does in Mandeville's Remark C and "Mira's Picture": in the line "Then her pale Lips no pearly Teeth disclose," woman dejectedly shows the world *no* pearly teeth, teeth she may indeed have. An experiential demystification of the ideal would say that a woman's teeth are not pearls— they are really decayed with Posset—or that her modesty is not genuine— she is really a hypocrite. The undecidability of the line, whether it says that the teeth are or are not pearls, moves us away from an ideal picture without substituting a picture of decay. Leapor effectively resists the misogynous pull of such demystifications: woman does not disclose her pearly teeth, but she does not *not* have them, either.

In Leapor's poem "Man the Monarch," we find not a negative pregnant— in which case the line would tell us that her teeth are not "everywhere, without exception, and altogether" pearls—but rather what we might call a pregnant negative: this mouth contains no pearly teeth; what it does contain is part of a woman's body that is imperceptible, unknowable, not pictured. If we take "Teeth" in the figurative sense in which Mandeville uses it, the oppressed woman's mouth contains no opposition, but it does not *not* contain it either. The line "Then her pale lips no pearly teeth disclose" is pregnant with that which radically disrupts a misogynous and classist empiricism. Do we have a better way now than the negative pregnant to put Grotius's formulation of how opposition is possible under democracy? Or a less sexist way than the pregnant negative to write the female body?

In this reading of "Man the Monarch," Leapor impregnates a repugnant rhetorical structure by using it to depict indescribable, pearly-or-not teeth, and thereby criticizes an oppressive ideal image without stepping into an empirical reality that degrades the female body. Leapor is elsewhere: not in the world where teeth are pearls and not in the world where they are bones, but in an as yet only ironic space between the two where the female body is neither idealized nor degraded. The space of negativity, pregnant with disruptive power that does not slip into yet another empirical positivity, is the space that feminist, historicist discourse needs continually to recover.

The historicist insight as to the always already co-opted nature of opposition is crucial in debunking a view of the subject as capable of simply declaring her own conscious resistance to the misogynous, classist culture in which she lives, and in debunking oppositional histories that operate without attention to the effect of literary conventions on the kinds of ideas that can be articulated within them. However, the contemporary literary historian's fatalist vision of a historical text's necessary co-optation is itself just as much a product of those conventions as is the alleged containment of past protest. Thus, if it is necessary for historians of difference to avoid simply seeing assertions of protest as efficacious, it is equally necessary to avoid seeing such protest as always already undercut by inherently misogynous conventions. This analysis attempts to displace the desire for critical mastery offered by both views onto a partisan interest in recovering a limited kind of agency, in discovering the means by which feminist interests might be articulated within discourses designed to render them inaudible. Leapor uses the negative pregnant as a figure and as a strategy—a strategy of denegation—for speaking within hegemonic discourses; similarly, this essay has tried to be not *not* oppositional. Both of those tactics are ways of confronting the problem that misogynous representations surface frequently in demystificatory discourses such as feminism. These tactics require attention to figuration: insofar as the oppression of women has been used to support the emergence of a realist bias in which discourse is seen as primarily designed to accurately picture reality, feminist interests and rhetorical analysis are allied. In short, feminist literary historians need to find something else and something more that can be said by the women writers of the past despite those realist, misogynous conventions—in the very "elsewhere," the space opened up by rhetoric, that all literary conventions contain. It may seem that this argument expects feminists to be able to do very little in working toward overturning oppressive social structures—mere textual analysis! As Marge Piercy puts it in her feminist novel *Small Changes*, "This waiting has teeth."[78]

In the three previous chapters, I looked at popular literature that either uses inartistic means for keeping textual indeterminacy open or flatly tries to close it down. Insofar as they do none of those things, Mary Leapor's poems could have been canonized along with the works of Pope and Swift, but they were not. The next chapter attempts to answer the question, Why not?

5

Misogyny and the Canon

The Character of Women
in Anthologies of Poetry

Alexander Pope opens his "Epistle to a Lady" by quoting Martha Blount, who says, famously, "Most women have no characters at all." "Character" can mean personality or moral fiber, but it can also refer to printed letters on a page, as Pope punningly points out in some verses on his publisher. He praises the character of the bookseller Bernard Lintot, especially as it appears on the title page of Lintot's publications:[1]

> His Character's beyond compare;
> Like his own Person, large and fair.
> [Other booksellers] print their Names in Letters small,
> But *LINTOTT* stands in Capital;
> Author and he with equal Grace
> Appear, and stare you in the Face.[2]

If character is print, then Blount's aphorism means that most women have not published their writings in print. But "character" is also more than a printed letter of the alphabet to Pope: it is aesthetic value. In introducing the third volume of the Pope-Swift *Miscellanies*, Pope insists that there is "a character in every piece" of poetry included in his collection.[3] In his usage of it, then, the word "character" conjoins issues worrying Pope and his contemporaries: the proper place for women's writing, the nature of printed matter, and aesthetic value. With regard to the latter, Pope defines aesthetic character in order to distinguish Swift's and Pope's poems from those written by "[t]he Mob of Gentlemen" who, Pope says in "To Augustus," spread "Like twinkling Stars the Miscellanies o'er."[4] The word "gentlemen" is meant ironically because coupled with the word "mob": a rabble of hacks, Pope says, writes characterless poetry.

Critics have long noticed that Pope and Swift were under pressure to distinguish themselves from the mob[5] once membership in a coterie of gentlemanly writers no longer safely established their authority.[6] "To Augustus," like book 4 of *The Dunciad*, is about "distinction" in the way that Bourdieu means it: "[s]ocial subjects distinguish themselves by the distinctions they make."[7] What accompanies aesthetic pleasure, John Guillory says, "is the pleasure of *distinction*,"[8] a pleasure felt at the moment of having "the denied experience of a social relationship of exclusion."[9] In "To Augustus," Pope asserts the aesthetic value of his work over the value of works by a mob of poetasters and gets pleasure in a sublimated form by ejecting a group of people from his class.

It may seem that, in "To Augustus" and *The Dunciad*, Pope successfully excludes hack writing from the canon and thereby cordons off popular, mass-produced literature from the realm of "High" literature or "the field of restricted production" in Bourdieu's terms.[10] But not all lists of great works are canons—Pope's list at the end of "An Essay on Criticism" is not—even though lists are always exclusive. Pinning the merely mechanical reproduction of printed characters upon a class of men is part of Pope's attempt to reassert a distinction between high and low literature based on membership in a coterie at a moment when that basis is being eroded.[11] It is precisely in order to establish the aesthetic as a realm independent of matter, to establish an abstract notion of "the literary work" that exists independently of any particular material reproduction of it,[12] that social and gender distinctions are marshaled throughout the eighteenth century—not just by Pope. This chapter will show that the medium of the anthology at its emergence established canonical poetry and canonical authors in contradistinction to popular literature written by a mob of men and poetry written by excessively embodied women.[13] The anthology repeats over and over again, in its format and various prefaces, the ideas implicit in Pope's use of the word "character": the mob writes characterless poetry, and women are loose, characterless people who do not write great works at all.[14] Anthologies bestow authority upon "prominent" writers by canonizing a certain kind of style that is possible to achieve only by members of an intellectual class. By imagining promiscuous physicality as female, literary history was able to enlist gender in the continuous project of conceptually segregating printed from aesthetic character.

The argument presented here is not that men of the trading classes and women were excluded from the canon because of what they wrote. Critics on both sides of the issue of canon reform agree: establishing canonical literature may have entailed politically motivated exclusions, but the meaning of "great" literature cannot on that account be reduced to the promotion of a politically conservative agenda.[15] Furthermore, such arguments are sometimes out-and-out misleading: if women writers were excluded because of an antifeminist, politically conservative bias, then feminist critics are in the impossible position of having to discover that unknown early modern women writers had radical political views, which is adamantly not true.[16] Margaret Ezell has successfully shown that women who wrote before the nineteenth century can be seen as having been "silenced" only if one believes that only canonical and/or commercially successful texts count as "public" writing, a view not shared by early modern women writers.[17] The problem with seeing early modern women writers as downtrodden by having been excluded and/or seeing them as responding to being excluded from the canon is that there was no such thing as a canon at the moment when seventeenth- and eighteenth-century women were writing.

It is only at the *end* of the eighteenth century that the word "literature" begins to designate fictionalized works of art in poetry and prose,[18] the word "canon" begins to be used to designate a list of literary texts,[19] and the notion of literary period comes into existence[20]—all necessary ingredients for transforming a list into the canon. Trevor Ross has recently modified an earlier argument that had pushed canonizing back in time: "something happened," he says, "in the late eighteenth century to the way works were valued."[21] Many things happened at that time: by the end of the eighteenth century, Thomas Warton and Samuel Johnson had written the literary history necessary for canonizing; and during the late eighteenth and early nineteenth centuries, French, German, and English writers articulated the aesthetic ideal of "pure poetry" necessary for forming a canon.[22]

However, investigations into the emergence of the modern notion of canonicity cannot afford to confine themselves to the history of ideas alone. Frank Kermode says about Harold Bloom's book on the canon that "his preoccupation with agonistic contests has rather obscured Bloom's view of how tradition works."[23] This true statement applies equally to Kermode: to see canon formation as happening via "spokespersons," as Kermode does (9), also obscures how tradition works. Matthew Arnold's direct statements about what constitutes great poetry did much less to establish the canon than did Thomas Ward's collection of poems in which the essay first appears: Arnold says in his general introduction that "Chaucer is not one of the great classics";[24] Ward's volumes, like hundreds of other collections, include much of Chaucer's work; obviously the collections prevail.

Production practices, Thomas Bonnell argues, create the canon: "Printing and publishing were key—[and] not [merely the publishing of] lists [of valuable writings], but [the publishing of] poetic works, huge collections that represented the complete works of dozens of poets."[25] Bonnell rightly asserts that it is crucial to analyze printing practices and marketing techniques when talking about the emergence of the canon. However, the huge multivolume collections do not present us with *the* canon as we know it: they were far too inclusive, containing myriad unknown male poets. As Guillory puts it, what "we conventionally recognize as 'the canon' [is comprised of] only those works included in such survey courses or anthologies as the Norton or the Oxford."[26] There is no canon of great English poetry until literary history is produced in a particular form by a specific medium: the anthology properly speaking, which does not come into existence until the early nineteenth century. The anthology is distinct from miscellaneous collections published throughout the eighteenth century.[27] The miscellany manages a specific kind of desire, "curiosity"; the canonizing anthology promotes a new kind of desire for works with aesthetic character.

The figure of gender is crucial in establishing the difference between mere curiosities and great works of art. Women writers' works appear scattered throughout the miscellany,[28] but when the anthology comes into existence, women writers are excluded from the canon it creates.[29] It is not that compilers of anthologies hated women. Misogyny is not a "natural" feeling; it is a long-standing but not eternal mode of establishing difference, via affect, that has been harnessed to perform various kinds of ideological work during various periods; it is interesting not in itself but in terms of what gets displaced onto it. During the eighteenth century, the textual media that frame literary works figure woman as "matter" in order to establish the conditions necessary for the exchange of great works of art.

Establishing a canon of British poetry requires constructing poetry in a way that differs from commodifying popular fiction. In order to become part of a tradition, the poem has to be a commodity written not by a nobody, as a novel must be,[30] but by a somebody: the poet's identity plays a crucial role in establishing a tradition of national poetry. And yet somehow, despite being tied to a particular physical body, canonical works must be exchangeable, words available as if owned by *no body*. The poet and his oeuvre need to be identities that are peculiarly embodied and disembodied at the same time. This chapter will show that women were excluded from the canon because the female body has been enlisted in a complex mechanism for figuring the oeuvre of great male poets as simultaneously immaterial and hypermaterial: monumental.

The first section of this chapter shows that women writers are excluded from anthologies. The second section shows that what has been defined as, and even feels like, great poetry can in a very real sense be seen as sublimated class warfare.[31] The last sections show that abjecting the female body from the conception of high, canonical literature is what performs the cultural work, continually necessary, of idealizing the all-too-material canonical text and thereby maintaining its exchangeability.[32] Only by charting this simultaneous embodiment and disembodiment of the high poet, endowing him with "character" in the sense of aesthetic value and simultaneously discounting character as printed matter—only by tracking that process can we see what transforms a list of poets into a canon. After determining what stimulates desire for canonical texts, we can begin to decide whether the canon is worth fighting to preserve in the face of some very substantial threats to it both from within the discipline and from without.

The Exclusion of Women Writers from the Anthology and British Poetic Literary History

Alexander Dyce introduces his 1827 anthology of women poets, *Specimens of British Poetesses*, by attacking recent publications for excluding women from literary history. In compiling this anthology of women poets, he says, "we feel an honest satisfaction in the reflection, that our tedious chase through the jungles of forgotten literature must procure to this undertaking the good-will of our country-women."[33] Dyce's lament is sadly too true: women poets were excluded completely from the fifty-eight volumes of writings to which Samuel Johnson appended his prefaces (1779–81), from John Bell's multivolume collection (1789–94), from Robert Anderson's (1792–5), and from Alexander Chalmers's of 1810.[34] But the multivolume collections did not themselves exclude women because it is primarily anthologies of poetry that established the canon as we know it. The fact of women writers' exclusion from anthologies and from canonical literary history is not verifiable *statistically*. For one thing, late-eighteenth- and early-nineteenth-century teaching collections do include women poets, as Ian Michael's research well shows.[35] However, these collections were not attempting to establish canonical literary history for the bourgeoisie, as were anthologies. Instead, they were directed toward children, who would gradually move up to disciplinary anthologies,[36] and toward people of modest means, as is stated explicitly in one of Vicessimus Knox's editions, abridged so as to be "adapted to the Convenience and Finances of all."[37] For another thing, if one does not distinguish miscellaneous from anthological form, one cannot see the exclusion of women from canonizing discourse.

Many of the volumes being produced late in the eighteenth century and early in the nineteenth are in fact still miscellaneous in form. These volumes are loaded with women authors,[38] more of them statistically than ever appear in early-eighteenth-century miscellanies such as the Dryden-Tonson collections or the mid-to-late-century collections comprising the Dodsley group. But the moment a collection claims to be representing British poetic literary history, and the moment it simultaneously organizes authors in anthological form, or at least gets close, women are excluded. The most fully developed examples are William Hazlitt's *Select Poets of Great Britain* (1825);[39] *The British Anthology; or, Poetical Library* (1824),[40] which looks most like the Norton; and John Aikin's *Select Works of the British Poets with Biographical and Critical Prefaces* (1820).[41] Anthologies concerned to delineate poetic literary history do one of the following: they exclude women poets completely, as do Hazlitt and Aikin; they include so few by comparison to male poets that they in fact emphasize the absence of women poets rather than their presence;[42] they include women in a section of the collection that is no longer anthological but miscellaneous in form;[43] or, finally, they include only contemporaneous women poets, proclaiming that no earlier "examples of female genius" could be found.[44] Women poets do not appear in the volumes presenting British poetic history.[45] As this chapter shows, representing women poets as forgotten is integral to the anthology medium: they took up the burden of representing the material body in order to help solve the difficult problem of establishing the poet as one who has an immortal body that transcends time. As can be seen in metaphors used by collectors to describe the poems they select, gender plays a crucial role in the process of immortalizing poetry as a body.

The Shift from Miscellany to Anthology Form: Use of the Body Metaphor

Excerpts of lines of poetry published in rhyming dictionaries before the eighteenth century were read by members of the merchant and trading classes in order that they might adopt coterie language and thereby raise their status.[46] The very early collections functioned like "the schoolboy's gradus" that John Aikin complains of at the end of the eighteenth century, providing "tropes and figures" to be used over and over again, "hackneyed combinations of substantives and epithets," as Aikin calls them.[47] Since rhyming dictionaries were simply a source for combinations of words, it mattered little how correctly an editor quoted the poem being excerpted that contained such combinations. But in the preface to Thomas Hayward's 1738 collection of excerpts of poetry, *The British Muse*, William Oldys tells us that this collection, unlike previous ones, is preeminently concerned with the integrity of what it quotes. Oldys insists upon a poem's integrity by figuring the excerpt of poetry as a body: the difference between the "sublime" beauties that Hayward has collected, Oldys says, and those collected by earlier compilers of beauties is that earlier collections "mutilate," "mangle," and "maim" what they quote.[48] To "mangle" a passage, if you remove the body metaphor, is simply to misquote it. *The British Muse* does not want to provide us with inaccurately quoted excerpts that other writers are then free to themselves misquote. If the compilers of rhyming dictionaries did not misquote the passages they compiled, they certainly gave others the license to do so, to pillage those passages for ideas or phraseology without recognizing the author as the owner of those particular words. The words of an unmangled quotation are not usable by artisans but are rather whole entities that deserve to be admired as sublime in their own right.

Like Hayward's *British Muse*, the large, six- to twelve-volume miscellaneous collections published from 1748 to 1783, the series of collections that begins with Dodsley's *Collection of Poems* (1748),[49] differ from, on the one hand, the coterie-productions produced by Tonson, Lintot, Dryden, Pope, and Swift—and, on the other, the rhyming dictionaries that taught people how to become members of such coteries. Guided in design by "gentlemen,"[50] Dodsley's collection contains a large number of poems by and to peers (approximately half), thus maintaining close associations with elite culture.[51] They present this culture to "the gentry and professional classes" comprising their readership. Dodsley's volumes and the supplements to them present aristocratic tastes to class-climbers of the emerging bourgeoisie.[52] That is, the editors and writers do not simply perform membership in a coterie but instead project class struggle onto the aesthetic.

Containing "lords, ladies, gentlemen, and others,"[53] the Dodsley group of miscellanies actually foregrounds those "others"—if not Dodsley himself (a former servant turned into a gentlemanly publisher), then others such as the businessman poet Matthew Green (who is in Dodsley and Pearch explicitly identified as "of the Custom House,")[54] as well as Thomas Gray, the "son of a scrivener."[55] If Boswell can be believed, Dodsley took the businessman Green to epitomize the author collected in his miscellanies,[56] thus again giving center stage to the not-yet-genteel poet. When Gray says that he is happy to have his elegy appear in the 1755 edition of Dodsley's collection, volume 4, because of the "company" he keeps in that volume,[57] Gray is talking undecidably about the aesthetic value of the poems alongside his own (as Suarez presumes) and about the social value of appearing with so many aristocrats (another possible interpretation). In the company of the names presented in these volumes, Gray and Green can be seen as performing their entry into what William Mason called in his discussion of "the poetical class," a cultural aristocracy.[58]

One can see in titles of collections published throughout the eighteenth century a split between, on the one hand, mirthful (often vulgar) and pornographic (often aristocratic) collections,[59] and, on the other "serious" melancholic poetry.[60] As an attempt to represent "high" culture,[61] Dodsley's collection focuses on serious, melancholy poetry. Ever since Milton's *Il Penseroso*, writing "melancholy" poetry is a way of proclaiming oneself a serious poet. Melancholy poems such as Matthew Green's *The Spleen*, one of the most famous of a really astounding number of such poems,[62] contain "digressions" on the desire for fame as a poet; and, if *Rambler* number 8 is any indication, ambition can be seen as a primary cause of the disease. If the desire for fame as an author causes melancholy, it is only by addressing melancholy that one can become an author. The central figures of these collections, Elizabeth Carter,[63] Thomas Gray, Matthew Green, and William Collins,[64] achieve poetical status through writing to or about melancholy. These poets are from humble beginnings (Collins's father was a "hatter") or remain members of the professional classes who get published in Dodsley along with a number of peers by writing poetry; these volumes, then, are the place where they perform what is necessary to move up in class. The "eminent Hands" of the earlier-century Tonson and Lintot collections have ceded to the "several Hands" mentioned in the titles of the Dodsley group, not because class has been forgotten but because eminence has been transferred from a quality in the hands and body one is born with to an achievement one can make through writing melancholy poetry and thereby tracing one's poetical lineage back to Milton. Dodsley, Pearch, and Nichols offer, to members of the emerging middle class, professional immortality through entering into "the poetical class."

During the thirty years throughout which the Dodsley group begins and continues to be published, obsessively collecting among themselves every "fugitive piece" of "merit,"[65] we can see a shift in the function of poetry. Editors since Elizabeth Cooper had begun to realize that printed texts were not ephemeral if mass produced.[66] The editor of one of the Dodsley group collections, George Pearch, says that he wants to prevent poems from "perish[ing] into oblivion," thus metaphorically equating poems with living bodies.[67] In contrast to earlier miscellanies such as Hayward's *British Muse*, then, midcentury miscellanies such as the Dodsley group imagine not excerpts as whole bodies but rather single poems as whole bodies as a way of proffering poetry as a form of immortality. The voluminous midcentury collections of contemporaneous writers[68] therefore seem to be participating in the education of the rising middle class—but not *only* on the side of consumption, not *only* by offering that class the stuff it needs to read. Instead, these collections are participating in the education of the new men by stimulating their desire to produce poetry. Promising their productions an eternal place in a collection is one way of getting them to write and to desire to assimilate the education that they need to write. "[E]ternal life is one of the most sought-after social privileges," Bourdieu points out,[69] and these collections promise eternity metonymically, as it were, to poets via preserving their poems.

The anthology figures not single poems but an author's oeuvre as a whole, living body, thereby changing the basis upon which one would secure immortality. Henry Headley's *Select Beauties of Ancient English Poetry* of 1787 is among the first anthologies proper, containing a retrospect of dead poets classed by period. Headley represents in terms of the body his anxieties about interfering with a dead author's self-representation by excluding poems from an author's oeuvre: he feels a "melancholy reluctance," he says, about "thus playing the anatomist"; he does not want to cut up or mutilate, as an anatomist would, the body of poems that an author has accumulated during his lifetime.[70] Headley excuses what he sees as his own propensity for including too much poetry by saying that he did not want to consign authors to "the horrors of perpetual oblivion" (x): "With the '*disjecti membra Poetae*' before me, let me be pardoned then, if I have sometimes, as I fear I have, listened to the captivating whispers of mercy instead of the cool dictates of unsentimental criticism: often I have exulted to find an unexpected latent beauty, which on a first perusal had escaped me, that might countenance the preservation of a doubtful passage, which I had just doomed to its former oblivion" (xi). By worrying about the "*disjecti membra Poetae*," Headley compares poetry to the body of Orpheus.[71] Past poetry had been "doomed" to oblivion before a collector of poetry such as Headley arrived to resurrect the body. The "captivating whispers" of poetry are not so much directed at Headley as they are at his readers, who can, from perusing Headley's collection, now imagine a similar kind of salvation at the hands of future collectors, should they decide to write. Headley's fully anthological work whispers to people that they might achieve a new kind of status distinct from the old status determined for poets by the social relations in which they existed, and having that status is connected with having a whole body, unlike the torn-up body of Orpheus. In the headnote to Queen Elizabeth (the only woman included in the collection), Headley disparages her poetry by saying, "[L]ittle else can now be gratified by the perusal of Elizabeth's poetry than mere curiosity": "Dead Queens rank but with meaner mortals."[72] What collections of poetry whisper, then, which is so captivating, is the promise to establish an eternal status—a poetic rank—that is independent of contemporaneous socioeconomic relations, of any material conditions of existence, those material conditions here associated with a dead woman's body.

The way the body metaphor functions in Headley's anthology differs from the way it functions in Pearch's miscellany. Whereas Pearch equates a poem with a body, in the passage from Headley's preface it is not clear exactly what unit of poetry is being equated with a body: it might be a "beauty," an excerpt of a poem, or a set of poems by a single author, "select specimens of prominent excellence,"[73] as he puts it, or, finally, all the poems in the collection itself. In the first case, a sentence or two is being envisioned as a body; in the second it is an author's oeuvre, figured as the Orpheus-like body of the author himself; in the third, it is the body of "ancient English poetry" that could be potentially torn up. Headley's collection therefore adopts the body metaphor used by Hayward, equating lines of poetry with a body and so making quotations inviolable, but rejects that used by Pearch, which sees an individual poem as a living body, substituting for the latter two other equations: body with oeuvre, body with the nation's poetry.

What is at stake in metaphorically equating with the body the correctly quoted excerpt, the author's oeuvre, and the nation's poetry? More importantly, how do these three equations shape a mere list of poems into a canon? This question can be answered by examining two specific examples of poets whose canonical status has been determined by these body metaphors, Thomas Gray and Matthew Green.

First, why view the *excerpt* of poetry as a body? Oldys tells us that there is a difference between a "mangled" excerpt and a correctly quoted or "sublime" one. From the 1740s on, when Oldys was writing his preface, it was no longer possible for poets to use rhyming dictionaries in quite the same way. That is, the sublime beauty or excerpt perfectly preserved in a collection could no longer be directly imported by would-be poets into their own poetry. By midcentury, or a bit later, straight repetition of a combination of words had come to be firmly counted as plagiarism—a shift that was felt by Pope, Roger Lonsdale points out, but actually first catches up to Gray, the canonical tradition's most aggressively "allusive," "borrowing," or "plagiarizing" poet, depending upon one's point of view.[74] Guillory points out that Gray's "Elegy in a Country Churchyard" is itself like a commonplace book.[75] But something saves the poem from being merely mechanical repetition of past poets' words, like a collection of their poetry, and instead transforms it into one of the quintessentially canonical poems (85–99). Gray's "Elegy" features in Dodsley's 1755 *Collection of Poems* (volume 4), along with Matthew Green's *The Spleen*.[76] We can tell what constitutes the aesthetic character of Gray's poem by contrasting it with Green's, which did not get canonized by later anthologists who selected from among the mass of poems reprinted by the Dodsley group.

The first thing to be said about the difference between a Gray and a Green shows us how the first metaphor discussed, excerpt as body, works in tandem with the third, nation's poetry as body, to characterize canonical literature. Businessmen poets such as Green either ignored their predecessors, whom they did not have time to read, or used a rhyming dictionary—which is to say, quoted words and phrases mechanically, exactly. Insofar as authors are seen as owners of property,[77] to quote exactly is to rob someone of the riches of their words. But if anthologies of beautiful whole poems are coming into existence as part of a nationalist project showing the progress of letters in England up to the present time, authors' words are not reusable because they are monuments to the past. To "embody" an author for literary history will mean to constitute his body out of words. Quoting an author's words exactly, *mechanical repetition*, would reveal them to be disembodied, detached from any one speaker, and would thus let the "original" speaker die.

Gray's "Elegy" does not copy past poets exactly: it is a commonplace book written by someone such as Johnson or Hazlitt, who unadvisedly trusted his own memories for quotations; in some ways, it is almost like a dictionary, using the words from a previous passage but reworking them in a different syntax and disposition. In 1808 Egerton Brydges insisted that one could "'trace almost all the ingredients of [Gray's] pathetic and sublime compositions home to their sources,'" but says that, although the "'particles' of thought" are borrowed, "'the combination [of them] is his own.'"[78] Why does stirring "not quite identifiable literary memories"[79] produce the sublime for Gray's readers? Insofar as those particular words are seen to embody an author, repeating the words out of sequence, *misquoting*, would be like tearing off bits of his body, as indeed Oldys envisions it. Misquoting literary words is represented as a kind of sparagmos or scattering of an earlier canonical author's body parts. But there is a third alternative: slight misquoting—more properly called *sublime* misquoting—the practice of quoting one word of an author's phrasing in one line, another a few lines later. What is sublime about slight misquoting is the near miss of completed aggression: the original author is not allowed to die. His words are not simply misquoted, not scattered, and not thereby proven to be infinitely usable, infinitely detachable, like the *disjecti membra* of a dead body. Rather, the poet's words are used in separate lines: the lines are close enough together to evoke memory of the older poet's passage, but not so close together that they either repeat or blatantly misquote, either inhabit or tear up, the past poet's body.

Businessmen poets who write, as Aikin puts it, "hasty effusions" rely on rhyming dictionaries; they do not correctly quote past poets, as the compilers of beauties do, but pillage artifacts. Aikin describes the difference between a canonical and a businessman poet in his discussion of Green, who is actually, Aikin says, like neither:

[Green] had not, like a GRAY or a COLLINS, his mind early fraught with all the stores of classic literature; nor could he devote months and years of learned leisure to the exquisite charms of versification or the refined ornaments of diction. He was a man of business, who had only the intervals of his regular employment to improve his mind by reading and reflection; and his poems appear to have been truly no more than hasty effusions for the amusement of himself and his particular circle of friends. . . . But nature had bestowed on [Green] a strong and quick conception. . . . No man has ever thought more copiously or with more originality; no man ever fell less into the beaten track of common-place ideas and expressions. That cant of poetical phraseology, which is the only resource of an ordinary writer, and which those of a superior class find it difficult to avoid, is scarcely anywhere to be met with in [Green].[80]

Although not a Gray, whose mind is stored with literary memories, Green is actually better than the average "hasty" writer because original. "Ordinary" businessmen poets repeat the words of past poets exactly; in contrast, those of a "superior class," viz. canonical poets, pay homage. Green does neither, and so, despite Aikin's best efforts, does not become a canonical poet, as determined by his inclusion typically in anthologies.

The difference between Gray and businessmen poets is that, whereas they use a rhyming dictionary, Gray's mind, by virtue of having the time to read intensely, has actually *become* a rhyming dictionary. What the contrast between Gray and Green shows us is that the difference between Gray and the businessmen poets is *not* one of sheer originality: Gray must fill his mouth with the words of past and present poets, but he must do so without mechanically repeating them for the sake of securing himself in a "superior class." Such an instance can be seen in some notorious lines in the "Elegy":[81]

> Full many a gem of purest ray serene
> The dark unfathomed caves of ocean bear:
> Full many a flower is born to blush unseen
> And waste its sweetness on the desert air.[82]

Suvir Kaul has connected those lines with a passage comprising Belinda's lament in *The Rape of the Lock*: after the "rape," she wishes that she had "un-admir'd remain'd," gone to a place where she could "keep my Charms conceal'd from mortal Eye, / Like Roses that in Desarts bloom and die."[83] The only actual word repeated in Gray's lines from the "original" is "desert," Gray's "blushing unseen" standing in for Pope's "un-admir'd remain'd," "Charms conceal'd," and "bloom and die." Gray has obviously made use of Pope's poetic idea. But he has *not* repeated mechanically the words of

Pope's poem: one could not find such an idea digested under the head of rhyming dictionary: would it appear under "deserts," "blooming," or "neglect/unmerited"? One sees that a few more words of past poets are repeated in Gray's stanza if one looks up "gem" in Johnson's dictionary, where Cowley is quoted: "Stones of small worth may lie *unseen* by day; / But night itself does the rich *gem* betray."[84] In relying on Pope and Cowley, Gray reveals himself as one who has spent as much time with literature as did Johnson, and who therefore has what are distinctively literary memories. The aesthetic character of Gray's "Elegy" consists in manifesting that he has had time to be in intimate relation with past poets, time available only to members of a leisure or educated class.[85]

Conceiving of an excerpt as a body, as early miscellanies and anthologies both do, is a way of denying access to the creation of canonical poetry by distinguishing between those who will mechanically repeat what they can get from rhyming dictionaries and those who will artfully sublimate their borrowings from passages not to be found under the "heads" of rhyming dictionaries. What is the difference between metaphorically equating a poem with a whole body, as midcentury miscellanies do, and imagining author's oeuvre and national literature as whole bodies, as anthologies do?

If a poem is seen as a body, then an author can become immortal by writing one poem. Collections published during the time when the numerous volumes of the Dodsley group were produced were too radically democratic, allowing any and every businessman a share of cultural capital, purchasable with only one or two poems: since an author's poems are sometimes grouped together but also often scattered throughout miscellany collections, a newcomer to the world of literature might not easily recognize the difference between a Green and a Collins.

Anthologists want to distinguish between poets such as Green, "whose performances," Aikin says, "have not *mass* enough to fill a considerable space in the public eye,"[86] and poets having a larger oeuvre because they have had, by birth or employment, more time to write. Thus Headley attacks Johnson for including the "rabble" who appear in *The Works of the English Poets*; he quotes Pope's "To Augustus" in order to distinguish the mob from canonical poets: "To have shed *their twinkling radiance, the miscellanies o'er*, was the highest honour many of those, who are [in Johnson's volumes] adopted as legitimate and established Poets, could affect; to a more conspicuous and dignified hemisphere they had none of the slightest pretensions."[87] The rabble of businessmen poets shed a "twinkling radiance," emanating from single poems scattered throughout miscellanies. The rabble kept out of the canon are businessmen like Green, but not simply because they write single poems. Despite devoting their lives to letters, Gray and

Collins did not produce a noticeably larger number of poems than Green did, and in fact the small output of Gray and Collins is scattered throughout miscellanies. However, because their language reveals that they have invested huge amounts of time reading literature, they can be seen as creating an oeuvre, a whole body, and can take their places as "legitimate" poets who exist in "a more conspicuous and dignified hemisphere." The oeuvre is a celestial body; its hemisphere is the British canon.

Bourdieu's work documents the rise of an intellectual class distinct from and at war with the bourgeoisie: whereas upper-middle-class business magnates assert dominance by procuring economic capital, the intellectual class asserts its ascendency by accruing cultural capital.[88] When literature came into existence, it was quintessentially the bourgeois object insofar as knowing literature was seen as a means for rising up into the upper middle class.[89] In the face of the maddening tendency among eighteenth-century businessmen to prefer writing poetry to reading it, there came to be a mechanism for distinguishing bourgeois readers of literature from intellectual producers of it. One method for keeping the occasional poet out of the class of literati, for separating high from popular poetry, was the practice among canonical poets of sublime misquoting that gives to an author a divine body.

Does the preceding account necessarily invalidate analyses of aesthetic pleasure as independent of economic determination such as Kermode's or Knapp's? For Guillory, it does not. The "articulation of aesthetic discourse," which certainly *is* a move in a game on the part of one class of "cultural dispossession" of another class, is not coterminous with nor "identical to aesthetic experience": "the aesthetic disposition tends to recognize objectified (that is, culturally certified) [i.e., *canonical*] forms, but not aesthetic experience itself, which falls silent before the monuments of culture."[90]

As shown below, such monuments are built and made available for nationalist identification. Ideals—especially collective ones—are not simply formed; they take a great deal of cultural work to produce and sustain. The body metaphor does its real work in enabling the anthology to produce the author's oeuvre and the nation as ideal images available for identification to members of the British middle class, to an "imagined community."[91] These two identities were produced by the emergence of two kinds of collections during the late eighteenth and early nineteenth century, a new kind of miscellany and the anthology proper, each of which manages two antithetical kinds of readerly desire.

Curiosity versus Identity

Rhyming dictionaries always collected the works of past poets, but most early-eighteenth-century miscellanies collect poems by contemporaries, the collections edited by Elizabeth Cooper and Thomas Hayward being two exceptions. But by midcentury, there begin to appear miscellaneous collections that attempt to reproduce books and manuscripts from past ages. William Oldys's *Harleian Miscellany* (1744) and Thomas Percy's *Reliques of Ancient English Poetry* (1765) are two early examples of antiquarian collections; George Ellis's miscellaneous collection (1790) and Robert Southey's *Specimens* (1807) are later examples.[92] Like the early-eighteenth-century coterie productions, the new, antiquarian kind of miscellany refuses to metaphorically equate the form of collections with any kind of organic entity for specific, structural reasons. In the introduction to *The Harleian Miscellany: or a Collection of Scarce, Curious, and Entertaining Pamphlets and Tracts*, Samuel Johnson explains why he, Oldys, and Osbourne decided not to distribute "the great Heaps of Pamphlets" in Sir Robert Harley's library "according to their Subjects or their Dates." If we do so, he says, "we shall preclude ourselves from the Advantage of any future Discoveries; and we cannot hope to assemble at once all the Pamphlets which have been written in any Age, or on any Subject."[93] The miscellany presents only part of a collection and presumes, in its structure, that collecting will be continued.[94] The miscellany does not therefore contain a whole body. In his 1807 volume, *Specimens of the Later English Poets,* itself a miscellany in form, Robert Southey distinguishes the anthology, or a collection of living flowers, from the "*hortus siccus,*" the miscellany that collects almost everything printed within a certain period of time in order to gratify the curiosity of "historians," "philologists," and "antiquarians."[95] Because it contains inorganic matter—it is a "dried bouquet"—the antiquarian miscellany need not claim to constitute a whole, and so collecting can continue indefinitely.

The continuous collecting of antiquities is driven by a very particular kind of desire: curiosity. In the preface to *Reliques of Ancient English Poetry* of 1765, Thomas Percy repeats the word "curiosity" constantly, as if it were a nervous tick. Curiosity is for him a desire of the historian-compiler,[96] an attribute of historical knowledge (xviii), an ancient relic such as a poem (xviii), and a kind of intensity pervading the curious work done examining ancient customs (xix). Freud would call it "polymorphously perverse."[97]

What a curious person desires is twofold: first, he or she wants to know material history. Remember that Headley regrets including Queen Elizabeth's poetry in his collection because it is inferior in quality to the other poems but gratifies the reader's "curiosity"[98] to know more about history. Southey's *Specimens* (1807) is designed, he says, to "exhibit specimens of every writer whose verses . . . find their place upon the shelves of the collector" because the works of such "indifferent Poets. . . . characterise their age more truly" (iv)—they give us not poetry but history. Headley, Southey, and numerous critics today say about "minor" women's poetry that it is only good enough to read out of curiosity about what things were like during the time, but we can put this another way: what makes a poet "inferior" is being an object of curiosity. The desire to see women as sexual objects prods critics to see their poetry as mere curiosities: as can be seen from Matthew Arnold's attempt to clean off the word "curiosity"[99] and Freud's work on the sexual enlightenment of children,[100] the curious person desires, second, to see sexual bodies.

In contrast to the curiosity-promoting antiquarian miscellany that can never be filled, the anthology tries to collect all of literary history envisioned as a whole body. William Hazlitt tells us in his *Select Poets of Great Britain,* the first full-blown, fully modern anthology published in 1825,[101] that he is intent "to offer the public a *Body of English Poetry,* from Chaucer to Burns, such as might at once satisfy individual curiosity and justify our *national* pride."[102] Although Hazlitt says that his volumes "satisfy curiosity," the character of that desire is altered by the change from continuous collecting to a completed form. The completed form is not only the form of the nation but also the author's oeuvre.

Unlike the compiler of a miscellany who, even if he or she does print several poems by one author often scatters them throughout the volumes,[103] the compiler of an anthology wants us to have a complete, whole representation of an author's oeuvre. The anthology must, as George Ellis's preface to his 1790 collection *Specimens of the Early English Poets* proclaims, "characterize the manner of the several authors" it prints:[104] it must produce a character that has aesthetic value or a characteristic style, but no material character—aesthetic character must not be bound to any particular printed edition of the author's works.

Seeing the text as an ideality separable from any material instantiation of it is one way of commodifying it. A text reducible to the common value of human labor in the abstract is simply consumable: like a Harlequin romance, one reads it and throws it away. But canonical texts are not simply consumable. As (cultural) capital, they are consumed for the sake of producing surplus value, and that value does not accrue to the purchaser but rather "flow[s] back to its initial point of departure."[105] The surplus value that literary works produce for the author and the oeuvre when that very author and oeuvre are consumed as commodities is immortality: author and oeuvre have to be abstracted and monumentalized at the same time.

We can see the attempt to distinguish author from material body even in the form of the anthology's table of contents. Eighteenth-century miscellanies include many kinds of address with multiple elements: Mr., first-name, Sir, Lady, anonymous, and so forth. But anthologies list patronymics only (e.g., "Chaucer," "Spencer," "Shakespeare," "Milton," "Dryden"), unless the poet is a woman, in which case the first name or "Mrs." is used, or a peer who for some reason needs to be identified as such, in which case "Sir" is added: the table of contents of Croly's collection contains all patronymics except "Sir William Smith," "Charlotte Smith," and "Mrs. Hemans." Anthologies give us a list of single, last names; one becomes aware of the name designating a social and material (i.e., historical) body only if the poet is a woman or an aristocrat whose title it is important to note. By contrasting embodied and disembodied names, the anthology distances from the great authors the materiality that threatens to undermine the author's status as transcendent of time.[106]

And the anthology has other ways of immortalizing the canonical author by ejecting materiality. The last editions of Dodsley and Pearch and the first editions of Nichols, collections in the Dodsley group, provide for the first time footnotes about the author. From the frontispiece to volume 1 of Nichols, which is indeed the head of a poet (fig. 3), one might wonder why it does not contain headnotes. Once footnotes get moved, transformed into headnotes, a collection has fully achieved anthological form. The editors of anthologies moved the Dodsley group's footnotes to the head of a selection of an author's works, now consolidated in one place in the collection, just as one might erect a tombstone over a body. In fact, the headnotes often quote tombstone inscriptions. Further, Dryden's portrait (fig. 3) resembles Samuel Johnson's (fig. 4), which is a portrait of Johnson's head standing on a funerary monument. The anthology provides a sort of idealized graveyard, the poet's works consolidated into a body under a tombstone-like headnote. But that body is not dead, as is manifested by its organic integrity, its wholeness. Hazlitt explicitly attacks miscellaneous collections for presenting readers with "a numberless quantity of shreds and patches" rather than a quantity and quality of works sufficient to represent an author's whole oeuvre.[107] Hazlitt alludes to Hamlet's epithet for Claudius, "A King of shreds and patches" (3.4.103), which clarifies Hazlitt's view: a body of poetic works without an organization and headnotes connecting them to both national poetic history and to the author is like an illegitimate king, a king of shreds and patches. The poet's works as constructed by Hazlitt's anthology must be an imaginary whole just like the imaginary nation, or the king's second body.[108]

Once established, the whole body of a poet's works can then be identified with by "a large and a respectable *body* of the public," as Headley designates his readers.[109] Numbers of people forming a body will identify with numbers of authors and their works constituting a body of national poetry. In contrast to the objective of "grasping" of (sexual) objects, curiosity's end, the identificatory fusion promoted by anthologies will be "respectable."

Figure 3. Frontispiece from [John Nichols, ed.] *A Select Collection of Poems: With Notes Biographical and Historical* (London: 1780-82). By permission of the British Library, 238.e.15.

We often say that the canonical and bourgeois object, high literature, had to be moralistic to please the bourgeoisie. But then we also say, contradictorily, that aesthetic considerations are separate from moral ones.[110] It is true that if one compares early-eighteenth-century aristocratic miscellanies with later anthologies, a middle-class moralism seems to inform the anthology-compiler's principles of selection. Unlike Hazlitt's or Headley's collections, Dryden's *Miscellanies* contain sexually explicit, seductive poems.[111] The bawdy collection *Deliciae Poeticae; or Parnassus Display'd*, is written by "Philomusus," and this lover of the female muses is meant not at all in the transcendent but rather in the physical sense.[112] Many miscellanies are therefore *Academy of Compliments* volumes,[113] designed to further one's amorous exploits, and many more are entitled *The Ladies Miscellany*, early in the century designating collections designed to seduce women,[114] only much later designating those designed to instruct them in virtue.[115] Curll's 1718 *Ladies Miscellany*, Benedict tells us, promises to give readers "many

Figure 4. Frontispiece from *A Dictionary of the English Language*, 5th ed., corr. (London: Strahan et al., 1773). Courtesy of the Langsam Library, University of Cincinnati.

curious tracts." Fifield D'Assigny's *Ladies Miscellany: or, a curious collection of Amorous Poems* (1730) promises us "curious poems on love and gallantry." In both cases, what arouses curiosity is "prurient poetry."[116]

For literature to come into existence as an ideal object, the desire to identify with an ideal body of words must be differentiated from curiosity at material bodies. Headley, remember, has already given us a clue as to how that differentiation will be established. He excludes all women poets from his collection except Queen Elizabeth, and then distinguishes her poetry with this headnote: "[L]ittle else can now be gratified by the perusal of Elizabeth's poetry than mere curiosity."[117] Gender will be the figure that distinguishes titillating curiosity (curiosity over the sexual body) and antiquarian desire (curiosity over a material past, or dead bodies) from an interest in canonical literature. My claim is this: canonical knowledge is produced by the abjection of carnal knowledge (in all senses of the term) from the field of literary pleasure.

Expelling the Female Body and Aestheticizing the Text

A long history of medieval, Jacobean, and Augustan misogyny informs Hazlitt's seemingly gender-neutral claim, in his introduction to *Select British Poets*: "To possess a work of this kind ought to be like holding the contents of a library in one's hand without any of the refuse or 'baser matter.'"[118] Hazlitt has told us that his collection is built upon the same plan as Vicessimus Knox's *Elegant Extracts* but that it "has been compressed by means of a more severe selection of matter" (i). The "'baser matter'" excluded from a view of Britain's "natural preeminence" (ii) in the field of poetry is women's writing: Knox's volume of poetry contains women writers, whereas Hazlitt's does not. The 1809 collection *Specimens of British Poets* inserts into the British canon only three poems by women, two women who are not designated by their real names but by the names Swift calls them in his poetry: "Stella" (Esther Johnson) and "Vanessa" (Hesther Vanhomrigh). The presence of women writers who featured in Swift's poems as virtuous points to the absence of Swift's grotesque Celias and Corinnas. None of Swift's dressing-room poems appear in the collection, and the frontispiece to volume 2 is a scene from "The Rape of the Lock" by Henry Fuseli: Pope's clean lady of the boudoir contrasts implicitly with Swift's disgusting female figures who are deliberately pointed to as absent. Crucially, the filthy female body of immoral women is absent from anthological space.

Even Colman and Thornton's *Poems by Eminent Ladies* calls attention to the physical embodiedness of the women poets represented in their collection, who, they say, "are a standing proof that great abilities are not confined to the men, and that genius often glows with equal warmth, and perhaps with more delicacy, in the breast of a female."[119] The principle of genius becomes *more* embodied for poetesses than poets in the offhand remark "perhaps with more delicacy," which calls attention to the physical difference between male and female breasts. This remark rivets the abstract interiority metonymically designated by the word "breast" in the case of men to physical mammary glands, the weight of a whole poetic tradition working to incarnate the female Tétin.

After apologizing for the omission of women poets from his volumes covering the earlier periods of poetic literary history, Hall celebrates the fact that he is able to include "many" women poets in the volume covering his own century. Later, twentieth-century anthologies forget the women poets who for Hall were timeless and transcendent. Croly's 1828 collection leaves out Mary Leapor, who is contained in Southey's 1807 *Specimens*; Samuel Hall's 1836 collection leaves out Charlotte Smith, contained in Croly's 1828 collection; twentieth-century canonizing anthologies forget Mary Tighe altogether. Through these publishing practices, women's poetry is being metaphorically equated with perishable bodies that are seen as living only during or slightly after the women's actual lifetime. Each anthology kills off through forgetfulness the previous period's women poets, poets declared "eternally" great by their own generation. In that way, women keep taking on the body and dying with it so that male poets can have eternal life.

What hollows out the image of the poet, allowing it therefore to be inhabitable by every member of the nation, is the absence of body, the fact that indeed headnotes are like tombstones marking what is and is not a body. The anthology must be an idealized graveyard: tombstones, the anthology's headnotes, must forever signify a body of words that is not decaying. The anthology renders the image of the poet, and with it, the image of the nation immortal by attaching bodily remains to the figure of woman and then walling women out. Given the tradition of misogyny, it is not surprising that women would be called upon again to perform the task of representing mortal flesh. It is because women are equated with the material that a forgetting of and disgust with women poets underwrites canon formation itself.

Canonicity and Character: The Ethics of Revision

The foregoing analysis of the character of canons answers a question posed by Frank Kermode: What gives canonical poetry its "consuming relevance"?[120] Certainly, what counts as "high literature" is determined by denying various social groups access to processes of production and therefore to cultural capital. Moreover, misogyny helps to construct figuratively the canonical object in such a way as to make it a fit object of desire. Exclusions based on class and gender may not play a part in those conscious or unconscious considerations that go into valuing literature, but they do play a part in constructing for the early modern subject the desire to consume high literature and therefore in structuring the media that determine what is available for consumption. If indeed such exclusions ground the possibility of canonizing, then canon *reform* is not possible. That is, "opening" the canon up to those excluded from it can only mean that the canon as such will disappear.[121] The current teaching collections that have added things to the canon, in other words, present us not with a new canon but with something else.

Lawrence Grossberg says that cultural studies is not about canon reform, that it is work carried on in ignorance of a canon.[122] Critics are worried about abandoning canonical knowledge, along with its requirement that we correctly quote past poets as a way of knowing them, in the face of forces such as information technology[123] and the rise of a professional-managerial class that wishes to abolish bourgeois forms of capital.[124] Nonetheless, it may be that the discipline of cultural studies is constituting a new kind of cultural artifact, the object of a new kind of desire. Stephen Greenblatt has described that new desire as the "wonder" that will replace "the spirit of veneration" with which canonical works are usually approached. The quintessentially bourgeois object, available for nationalist identification, will be given up for love of an object imbricated in a resonating nexus of texts,[125] or even better, for love of "the complex social practices that shaped, and still shape, the absorbent surface" of the canonical text.[126]

Cheryl Walker has argued that feminists need to hang onto the conception of author, an ideal "character."[127] But, as shown above, women poets cannot have the character of the canonical author because that character is erected as an ideal by abjecting from it the body figured as female. But if a new desire reshapes our disciplinary object and with it the discipline itself, then my counterargument contains good news for those of us who wish to read and teach women poets, to have them as an object of academic desire. If we will soon no longer desire venerable cultural monuments, then it is a good thing, is it not, that early modern women poets have no canonical character at all?

6

Transcending Misogyny

Anna Letitia Barbauld
Writes Her Way Out

Until 1994 Anna Letitia Barbauld appeared in twentieth-century teaching anthologies of Romantic poetry only in a headnote to the *Rime of the Ancient Mariner*.[1] David Perkins quotes a passage from Coleridge's *Table Talk* dated 31 May 1830:

> Mrs. Barbauld [1743–1825, poet and essayist] once told me that she admired the Ancient Mariner very much, but that there were two faults in it,—it was improbable, and had no moral. As for the probability, I owned that that might admit some question; but as to the want of a moral, I told her that in my own judgment the poem had too much; and that the only or chief fault, if I might say so, was the obtrusion of the moral sentiment so openly on the reader as a principle or cause of action in a work of pure imagination.[2]

Barbauld here serves to epitomize the anti-romantic, didactic reader, anticipating the Victorian reading of Romantic writers that moralized Wordsworth and devalued those to whom it could not ascribe moralistic intent.[3] But it was not only Barbauld's allegedly anti-aesthetic, straight-laced moralism that irritated her contemporaries. Charles Lamb actually cursed her in 1802, P.M. Zall tells us: "Damn them! I mean the cursed Barbauld crew, those Blights and Blasts of all that is Human in man and child."[4] Preferring John Newbery's *Goody Two Shoes* (1766) to Barbauld's *Hymns for Children*, Lamb attacks Barbauld and her "crew" for their soul-killing rationalism. And finally, Henry Crabb Robinson records his profound irritation with Barbauld for not sufficiently distinguishing Wordsworth from "all sorts of pretended poets. Mrs. Barbauld prefers to all others the idyll—the return of a brother who finds his brother and friends all dead."[5] Presumably, the poems by "pretended poets" that Barbauld prefers resemble Wordsworth's "The Brothers": they are poems about how one's life depends upon participation in a community.

The qualities that make Barbauld unfit to judge and thus also produce "great art," then, qualify her to be a Dissenter: moralism, rationalism, and anti-individualism (a communitarianism of some sort). Thus, the critics among Barbauld's contemporaries are quite possibly discriminating against her as much on religious as on artistic grounds: even if they believe themselves to be sympathetic to the principles of Dissent, Coleridge, Lamb, and Robinson do not want Barbauld's dissenting principles to mix with art.[6] What is most disconcerting about such a mixture, as is especially visible in Robinson's comment, is that, because of her adherence to rationalist principles of equality, Barbauld does not have a properly "reverential attitude" toward texts and authors. That attitude has been called "a legacy of Romantic aestheticism": indeed, reverence stimulates the desire to consume the literary canon that emerged, as the previous chapter shows, precisely during the time in which Barbauld established her career as an author, the period we know as Romantic.[7] Chapter 5 demonstrates that poets attempting to write "serious" literature during the eighteenth century most often wrote melancholy poetry, imitating and competing with Milton's "Il Penseroso"; that the aura of canonical literary works comes from a sense of sublimity produced by (as expressed in chapter 5) the near miss of completed aggression when one poet uses a previous poet's words in a scattered way so as to appear to be almost stealing them but not quite; and that the abjection of women poets subtends the idealizing process that renders canonical texts and authors transcendent of place and time. This chapter shows that, because of her particular religious beliefs, Barbauld is able to reject the melancholy affect, the aggressive individualism, and the disgust with women's bodies that produce a Romantic reverence for male-authored texts.

Such a rejection is bad, of course, insofar as it ultimately renders her poetry—as far as canonizing anthologies are concerned— perishable and noncanonical. It is good insofar as it enables her to write great poetry, as defined by the introduction to this book, without imagining herself as disembodied: disgust with women's bodies, the bodies and texts of women writers, was not merely a mechanism carried on by editors and introducers of canons, but it was endemic to cultural production of the period;[8] it threatened a woman writer's relation to her own words. Barbauld probably did not look at canon-producing male authors and consciously decided not to do what they did, and she may or may not have consciously thought about her culture's attitude toward women's bodies and texts. However, Barbauld did in fact develop an aesthetic of her own, contrary to the emerging dominant one of high Romanticism, because of her religious beliefs as a Dissenter—in particular because she was intellectually engaged with Joseph Priestley. Her aesthetic is independent of her consciously held beliefs: Barbauld's religious views were not identical to Priestley's notoriously materialist ones. However, the sense of beauty impelling her literary production is discernibly influenced by materialism and dissent. Barbauld's knowledge of Priestley's materialist views gave her access to a fantasy underlying and stimulating her poetic productivity in the face of ideologies designed—if not to shut it down—then at least to devalue it as ephemeral cultural material.

In "To Mr. S.T. Coleridge," "To Lord Byron," and "[A Rebuke to Robert Southey,]" then, Barbauld is not simply a scold, as "rebuke" in the title given by others to the latter poem implies. An anti-Victorian aestheticism that stringently distinguishes religious views from poetic truth has blinded us to a crucial feature of poetic production among those for whom morality and poetry were not mutually exclusive. In "high romantic poetry," male poets establish their voices as transcendent and eternal, Susan Wolfson says, through erecting a gender hierarchy in which the feminine is seen as immanent and worldly.[9] Through a sense of her own superior religiosity, a sense of having greater purity of soul than Byron and thus of being more worthy than he is to translate or imitate Hebrew poetry, Barbauld is able to overturn that hierarchy and to establish herself as equally transcendent. She is able to do so because, for Barbauld, a soul's purity does not come *despite* but *because of* its connection to the body—to materiality, coded as feminine in a culture attempting to perform a secular version of the transubstantiation ritual (see the introduction, pp. 6-7).

This chapter elucidates Barbauld's beliefs about the purpose and effects of poetry, her Christian views as discernible from treatises and poems, and finally the crucial sense of superiority she was able to establish based on those views. She attacks high Romantic poets primarily for being melancholy, herself refusing melancholia because she was, to use her own words for it, "sure" and "secure" in the knowledge of salvation. Instead of promoting endless mourning, she wants to impart to her readers a sense of the certainty of salvation. Her attacks on Coleridge, Byron, and Southey consist in attempts to bring them into a community of the saved. Hers is a superiority, then, that does not depend upon beating others out in a competition, but, on the contrary, upon building up a community of superior beings. The sense of superiority that enables Barbauld to establish her own authority as a poet is part of a religious system of beliefs that includes a purposeful aesthetic: poetry saves souls.

There is no such thing, any good Kantian critic would say, as a functional aesthetic: the aesthetic is, by definition, disinterested. Barbauld's Christian beliefs, one wants to say, are anti-aesthetic, are about life rather than art, ethics rather than aesthetics. However, her system is better seen as an aesthetic that provides an alternative to that which grounds production of the canon. Looking at her system as offering a possible alternative allows us to see features of the Romantic aesthetic that produced, features otherwise invisible.

Barbauld sees her poetry as superior in three ways to that written by male Romantic poets. First, it does not promote the melancholy, to which she objects, on both religious and political grounds, because she sees it as the internalization of feudal, courtly relationships. Second, her poetry is speaking on behalf of a community rather than an individual. And finally, the fantasy underlying her poetic production is that there are no souls apart from bodies.[10] Because transcendence does not involve escaping but rather refining the material, being a woman poet—and thus, according to the stereotype, more sensual, more embodied, more material than men—does not disqualify her for greatness. To elucidate Barbauld's ideas as an Enlightenment thinker is not necessarily to condone them. It is not necessary to believe that poetry is part of God's plan for salvation, nor that community can be established on the basis of communion (a dangerous belief, in light of twentieth-century fascism!)—it is not necessary to believe these ideas in order to appreciate what they did for Barbauld as a writer. It is her vision of God as overturning all hierarchies, and her fantasy that spirit is not distinct from matter but rather matter refined, that enables Barbauld to establish herself as simultaneously female and transcendent and thereby to assume an authoritative poetic voice.

As seen in chapter 4, Mary Leapor makes use of conventional literary forms to launch her critique of social oppression, the critique potentially disarmed insofar as we misread her use of conventions as traditional rather than innovative. Although Barbauld too relies on conventional forms such as the meditative descriptive poem and Juvenalian satire, she judges both her own poetry and poetry written by others (Robinson's "pretended poets") in accordance with an alternative to various idealist Romantic aesthetics:[11] hers is a dissenting aesthetic.[12] Barbauld's dissenting aesthetic enabled her to write her way out of the trap, depicted in the previous chapter, of being an immanent, material, only-historically-significant woman poet. But the way out only works to promote her *own* sense of poetic authority, not to procure for her canonical status. That is, Barbauld wrote her way out of sexist oppression for *herself* but not into the canon, which of course was out of her control. Regardless of her aesthetic principles, the dialectic of abjection and idealization carried on by miscellanies and anthologies rendered her body of words specifically female, and thus mortal.

Poetry and Salvation

In his *Memoirs*, Joseph Priestley takes credit for having instigated Barbauld's writing career when he was a tutor at Warrington Academy: "Mrs. Barbauld has told me that it was the perusal of some verses of mine that first induced her to write anything in verse, so that this country is in some measure indebted to me for one of the best poets it can boast of."[13] Priestley's influence on Barbauld extends to his theology, to his vision of an end to "the corruptions of Christianity" through enlightenment: "The gross darkness of that night which has for many centuries obscured our holy religion, we may clearly see, is past; the morning is opening upon us; and we cannot doubt but that the light will increase, and extend itself more and more unto the perfect day."[14] Exactly how this all-conquering empire of light will accomplish this task, Priestley says in the preface to his first volume on air, is by putting an end "to all undue and usurped authority in the business of religion, as well as of science." In the same preface, Priestley also says that for tyrants to "patronize polite literature [is to cherish] an enemy in disguise."[15] Thus, Priestley believes that reform would be accomplished by radical leveling and that poetry was part of that process.

It was certainly odd to see poetry and science as allies at this time, but as M.H. Abrams points out, many of the Dissenters opposed mainstream Romantic thought on precisely that issue. In his *Essay on the Application of Natural History to Poetry* (1777), John Aikin (Barbauld's brother) insists that "nothing can be really beautiful which has not truth as its basis."[16] And so in his attack of "the cursed Barbauld crew," Lamb says that because of Barbauld's books for children, "Science has succeeded to Poetry no less in the little walks of children than with men."[17] If there is something scientific about Barbauld's poetry and prose, it comes from the participation of her writings in the program Priestley imagines. For Priestley, "all truth had religious value."[18] He is interested in refining religious thought as one would gold: "the thorough examination of everything relating to Christianity . . . has been the 'refiner's fire' with respect to it."[19] "Refining fire" is one metaphor that Barbauld might have obtained from Priestley, either in his juvenalia or in his conversation, although as shown below, she reworked it to develop her own aesthetic system. It is important to note here that Barbauld participated at Warrington in conversations with people who saw poetry as having revolutionary potential in furthering truth and therefore in improving religion and morality.

Melancholia: Internalized Feudalism

Coleridge once said, "the generation of the modern worldly Dissenter was thus: Presbyterian, Arian, Socinian, and last Unitarian,"[20] and he saw Priestley as the author of modern Unitarianism. Although possibly not yet a subscriber to Socinianism during his time at Warrington, Priestley, like most of Warrington Academy, was Arian,[21] the distinction between the two consisting, Ira Brown says, in beliefs about Christ: Arians saw Christ as divine but not deity, whereas Socinians saw Christ as human (Brown, 14 n. 10). Barbauld reveals that she has at least moved into Arianism by the time she wrote her pamphlet addressed to Gilbert Wakefield on the value of public worship (1792). There is a hint in Barbauld's "Answer to Wakefield" that she might also be a Socinian insofar as she seems at moments to equate Christ with other great religious thinkers, thus emphasizing his humanity.[22] However, in *The Georgian Chronicle*, Betsy Rodgers quotes Lucy Aikin's letter to Dr. Channing, conveying memories of the religious atmosphere at Warrington and providing the name "Free Dissenters" for the religious attitudes at Warrington:

> Long before my time, however, my kindred—the Jennings, the Belshams, my excellent grandfather Aikin, and his friend and tutor Doddridge—had begun to break forth out of the chains and darkness of Calvinism, and their manners softened with their system. My youth was spent among the disciples or fellow-labourers of Price and Priestley, the descendents of Dr. John Taylor, the Arian, or in the society of that most amiable of men, Dr. Enfield. Amongst these there was no rigorism. Dancing, cards, the theatre, were all held lawful in moderation: in *manners*, the Free Dissenters, as they were called, came much nearer the Church than to their own stricter brethren, yet in *doctrine* no sect departed so far from the Establishment.[23]

No matter what her particular form of dissent—whether it be Arian or Unitarian—Barbauld opposes Calvinism in doctrine no less than manners by asserting her belief in a radically egalitarian God. The Calvinist idea of God, "so incompatible with . . . justice and benevolence," she says in her "Answer to Wakefield," must come from seeing "the Deity" as "likened to an absolute monarch," most of whom are tyrants (2:464): "These features of human depravity have been most faithfully transferred to the Supreme being. . . . That error can neither be salutary nor harmless, which attributes to the Deity injustice and cruelty. . . . Let those who hold such tenets consider, that the invisible Creator has no name, and is identified only by his character; and they will tremble to think what being they are worshiping" (2:465–66). Calvinists worship the devil, Barbauld implies. For God to have the character of God, he must be completely just and not cruel. She attacks people like Price for debasing themselves to God because she sees the impulse to do so as the same impulse that drives a courtier to debase himself to a king (2:467): the true God would not promote a tyrant's inequities. She says that Price is "not to think that virtue is one thing here, and another in Heaven" (2:467–68). The "standard of moral feeling" must not be "totally different from those ideas of praise and blame, merit and demerit, upon which we do and must act in our commerce with our fellow creatures" (2:469). That is, we must treat everyone justly as our equal and so must feel in our relationship with God that we are treated with the same justice. Calvinistic beliefs that one is either saved or not independently of anything, at the arbitrary whim of God, come from living under an unjust government, the system of absolute monarchy. Depraved ideas of human commerce promoted by monarchy "have been sublimed," she says, "into all the tremendous horrors of Calvinistic faith" (2:465).

What are those horrors exactly? They were minutely detailed in what Priestley calls in his *Memoirs* "books of experience" (Brown, 6): religious conversion narratives. In a collection of Methodist pamphlets of this type, these conversion narratives have a conventional plot: a religious person becomes obsessed with the idea that he is not saved, falls into the deepest melancholia, contemplates suicide, and then is saved by the "experience" of God's grace descending to let him know that he is indeed saved for eternity.[24] Priestley himself underwent such a depression and because of that abandoned the Calvinistic doctrine of his parents (Brown, 6–7). Barbauld attacks Price and other Christians for indulging in the self-hatred promoted by the Calvinist notion that we are all vile sinners, but some of us, the elect, will be saved, no matter what we do: "Above all, it would be desirable to separate from religion that idea of gloom which in this country has but too generally accompanied it. . . . [T]he cause must be sought, partly in our national character, which I am afraid is *not* naturally either very cheerful or very social . . . and partly to the colour of our religious systems. . . . [N]o one, I will venture to assert, can believe in ["the insufficiency of virtue to escape the wrath of God"] . . . and yet be cheerful" (2:463–64).

It is for failing to banish such horrors from their thought that Barbauld attacks many prominent male poets. "The idea that all [human beings] are vile," Barbauld says, leads to "the debasing terrors of a [Samuel] Johnson, or of more blameless men than he" (2:468). It is precisely because of her antipathy for melancholia that Barbauld opposes Wakefield's desire to replace public worship with private: "The metaphysical reasoner, entangled in the nets of sophistry, may involve himself in the intricacies of contradictory syllogisms till reason grows giddy . . . ; but when he acts in the presence of his fellow-creatures, his mind resumes its tone and vigour, and social devotion gives a colour and body to the deductions of reason. Berkeley, probably, never doubted of the existence of the material world when he quitted his closet. Some minds, . . . through a timorous and melancholy spirit remain always in a perplexed and doubting state, if they rest merely on the conclusions built upon their own investigation" (2:444–45). Hume's *Treatise of Human Understanding* follows the same plot pattern as the one appearing in this quotation: a metaphysical reasoner falls into skepticism and despair, emerges from his study, engages with people, feels the passions attendant upon human interaction, and cannot even remember the speculations that led him to doubt and despair. In Hume's account of overcoming despair as well as in Barbauld's description of it, interactions with people give one's apprehension of the world the "colour and body" necessary to make material existence convincing.

Barbauld sees Coleridge as falling into the same dangers as Berkeley and Hume. Thus, in her poem "To Coleridge," Barbauld tells Coleridge that "sickly hesitation and blank fear / [and also] Indolence" haunt the grove of "deep philosophy."[25] She warns him: "Not in the maze of metaphysic lore / Build thou thy place of resting; lightly tread / The dangerous ground, on noble aims intent" (133, lines 34–36). She ends her poem by exhorting him to participate in "Active scenes":

> And fair exertion, for bright fame sustained,
> For friends, for country, chase each spleen-fed fog
> That blots the wide creation—
> Now Heaven conduct thee with a Parent's love!
> (133, lines 40–43)

That Barbauld believes Coleridge's hesitation and indolence to come from a kind of Calvinistic self-hatred is implied by the language of the poem, which is identical to the language of her attack on Calvinism in her pamphlet advocating public prayer. The poem addressed to Coleridge opens, in Dantesque fashion, by telling us that

> Midway [up] the hill of Science, after steep
> And rugged paths that tire th'unpractised feet
> A Grove extends, in tangled mazes wrought,
> And fill'd with strange enchantment: . . .
> . . . . unearthly forms
> Glide thro' the gloom, and mystic visions swim
> Before the cheated sense.
> (132, lines 1–9)

Calvinism's "gloom," Barbauld says in the "Answer to Wakefield," "darkens" religion with "superstition" (2:468–69), a superstition that can be eradicated only by replacing Romantic ideas with radically egalitarian ones: "The age which has demolished dungeons, rejected torture, and given so fair a prospect of abolishing the iniquity of the slave trade, cannot long retain among its articles of belief the gloomy perplexities of Calvinism" (2:470). Calvinism is tempting, Barbauld says in her poem to Southey. She tells him that she too enjoys indulging in Romantic melancholy:

> How does my pensive soul, in these lone scenes,
> Remote from mortal tread, delight to dwell
> Where I on Nature, and on Nature's God,
> In calm repose, can meditate profound!
> (195, lines 37–40)

But, as in the case of Berkeley, Hume, and Coleridge, she admonishes Southey for staying alone, for not emerging at least on Sunday and worshiping publicly:

> Nor would I, Southey, for the world forgo
> This dearest privilege to man allow'd,
> Due, as the Sun each Sabbath day shall shine,
> To meet, with kindred man, the Parent God.
> (196, lines 80–83)

Barbauld believes herself to be better fit to engage a poetic program than either Coleridge or Southey because of her ability to renounce the pleasures of melancholy: "Tho' sweet as fabling poets ever sung, / Mine ear thy warbling Philomel [will] forgo / . . . / To raise with man a nobler strain of praise" (196, lines 62–65).

For Barbauld, poets who indulge in melancholy and represent that indulgence in their poems lead people astray: "The idea that all are vile . . . is an idea as consolatory to the profligate, as it is humiliating to the saint" (2:468). And it is for such profligacy, it seems, that she enjoins Byron not to translate biblical ideas as he has attempted in *Hebrew Melodies*: "Touch not the harp of Jesse's son, / . . . / Those springs to thee are closed" (170, lines 1, 9).

Community

It is clear that, for Barbauld, melancholy can be cured by coming out of the closet and joining with people to worship God. But in what sense can her poetry be seen as part of public worship whereas poetry by Coleridge, Southey, and Byron cannot? Or how is her poetry unaffected by melancholy? Barbauld's poems, she believes, participate in community, while poetry of the high Romantic male poets does not. As mentioned in the previous chapter, poets wrote their own versions of "Il Penseroso" in order to stake out a place in the canon, to proclaim their genius. As Adam Phillips puts it, "The Romantic concept of genius—the apotheosis of originality—was itself a kind of elegy for a lost community."[26] Coleridge, Southey, and Byron represent melancholy solitude; she represents a way out of melancholia and back into community. How does she avoid the trap of solitary genius?

First, she insists that good poems must participate in a community. Public worship is important, she says, because people's feelings constitute "one common flame." In public worship one finds "the electric fire of correspondent feeling" (2:419–20): correspondence comes from people—not, as in Wordsworth's "glad preamble," from the breeze. Barbauld defines "Social Worship" (2:448) as a group of people who are communing their thoughts and feelings to each other. Her poetry attempts to be such a flame: in "Corsica," she tries to paint a picture of Paoli and the heroic liberators of Greece that will inspire imitation, which Barbauld represents as kindling a fire: "What then should Britons feel? should they not catch / The warm contagion of heroic ardour, / And kindle at a fire so like their own?" (21, lines 15–17). Poetic kindling will inspire heroic action. A poet cannot write without such fire, she says to Byron: "Forbear—til time shall bring the hour / Thy softened heart shall feel a power / To touch thy lips with fire" (170, lines 13–15). A softened heart, a heart not hardened by sin, will write poetry that arouses the fire of correspondent feeling, will make people want to stop sinning. But how does poetry help people to stop sinning?

Barbauld wants her poems to cure the English people's Calvinistic melancholia. In her pamphlet on public worship, remember, Barbauld attacks Price for public self-debasement. "When," she asks, "will Christians permit themselves to believe that the same conduct which gains them the approbation of good men here, will secure the favour Heaven hereafter?" (2:466–67). Such security is necessary to avoid committing the sins of either profligacy (if I am not saved no matter what I do, who cares if I sin?) and of falling into melancholy despair and isolation. So her poetry attempts to promote security, as can be seen in two of her hymns. One of them, speaking to people who are "the salt of the earth," ends with "your reward is sure" (128, line 64); another ends "Sinner, come! for here is found / . . . / Rest eternal, sacred, sure" (122, lines 17–20).

In an early poem, Barbauld represents herself as coming out of timidity into this security. In "An Address to the Deity," a very young Barbauld represents herself "trembling" and having a voice too "feeble" to write this poem (4, lines 2–3). But then, suddenly, "As by a charm, the waves of grief subside" (4, line 13):

> Thus shall I rest, unmov'd by all alarms,
> Secure within the temple of thine arms,
> From anxious cares, from gloomy terrors free,
> And feel myself omnipotent in thee.
> (5, lines 69–72)

To be free to write poetry, and to be free from sin, one must imagine that God is both just and imitable (2:466). One must feel secure and feel a sense of one's own power because of that justice. Thus she says in her "Answer to Wakefield" that public worship abolishes "the invidious distinctions of wealth," teaching "the poor man" that he is fundamentally equal: "He rises from his knees, and feels himself a man. . . . Every time social worship is celebrated, it includes a virtual declaration of the Rights of Man" (2:448). And such is true for women reading her "Address to the Deity" as well: Barbauld feels herself "omnipotent in thee" as a fledgling poet because she knows that a just God eradicates hierarchies, whether of class or gender. Her claim to omnipotence is a virtual declaration of the rights of woman. Barbauld is consequently sure that she is saved, and secure against melancholy.

As to melancholy feelings, solitude is necessary for moments of penitence when one indulges in "those humiliating feelings," Barbauld says, but one must not get addicted to such feelings. The passion for self-humiliation should not be cultivated, whereas joy should. Joy will impel a person to "seek for fellowship and communication": "The flame indeed may be kindled by silent musing; but when kindled it must infallibly spread. . . . Joy is too brilliant a thing to be confined within our own bosoms" (2:428). For Barbauld, people must dwell on the fact that they are saved, cultivate or "kindle" joyous feelings, and then be driven to spread those feelings publicly like fire.

A moment in one of her poems in which she stimulates joy, and with it communicative, anti-melancholic desire, is also a moment when she describes the kind of community her poems seek to build. "Corsica" prophesies of the troubles in Greece that "virtue [will] triumph" (25, line 146), which unfortunately does not come true. The poem recognizes the error of her prophecy: "So vainly wish'd, so fondly hoped the muse" (26, line 184). But then, the poem says, such hopes were not so fond or foolish after all:

> Not with the purple colouring of success
> Is virtue best adorn'd: th'attempt is praise.

There yet remains a freedom, nobler far
Than kings or senates can destroy or give;
Beyond the proud oppressor's cruel grasp
Seated secure; uninjur'd undestroy'd;
Worthy of Gods; The freedom of the mind.
(26, lines 195–201)

Here mental freedom is more than just the expression of an Enlightenment ideal. Barbauld sees her poem as "a prayer for [the] success" of the Greek rebels, whose actions are themselves a type of "praise." To act justly is to imitate God and so to praise him. Through the power of poetry as "a contagious fire," her readers will be inspired to imitate Paoli's heroism, knowing that actions taken in the world to promote justice are rarely if ever successful. Her readers are thus members of a community that looks very Kantian to me: they live in a kingdom of ends. It does not matter what happens when one performs heroic actions designed to imitate divine justice—in fact, the result *cannot* matter, or there would be other reasons for acting than the desire for justice itself. Members of this community do not care about the ends; they act for the sake of the action itself, which is both an enactment of justice and itself a prayer of praise.[27] Instead of offering melancholy words in private, people must offer their public actions as a prayer. Barbauld's poem is a call to the action that is public prayer.

Barbauld was able to distinguish her poetic voice from Coleridge's, Byron's, and Southey's, then, because her verse promoted and took part in publicity.[28] Her poems attempt to cure melancholia in readers, rather than to induce it, and to give them a sense of "security." Relieving themselves of melancholia means seeing God as both just and imitable. Melancholic poetry imagines a despotic God and, like the Calvinist religion on which melancholy poetry is based, it inures people to injustice:

We often boast . . . of the purity of our religion, as opposed to the grossness of the theology of the Greeks and Romans; but we should remember, that cruelty is as much worse than licentiousness, as a Moloch is worse than a satyr. . . . When will [Christians] cease making their court to their Maker by the same servile debasement and affectation of lowliness by which the vain potentates of the earth are flattered? When a harmless and well-meaning man, in the exaggerated figures of theological rhetoric, calls himself the vilest of sinners, it is in precisely the same spirit of false humility in which the courtier uses degrading and disqualifying expressions when he speaks of himself in his adulatory addresses to his sovereign. (2:466–67)

In contrast to debasing oneself before God, which teaches one political self-deprecation, having self-confidence, feeling that sinlessness is possible to achieve, she believes, will enable readers to participate in a community of people who all act in accordance with justice.

It has been argued that the reverence eighteenth-century critics such as Thomas Warton felt for the authors they began to canonize displaced passions generated by feudal social structures onto the structure of literature as a discipline.[29] High Romantic literature was produced in the wake of Warton's canonizing efforts so that poets were conscious, for the first time in literary history, of writing poems that would reach posterity in the form of a canon.[30] Barbauld argues that Romantic melancholy poetry, deriving its sublimity from one's passionate self-debasement or annihilation before a greater power, promotes feudal, politically retrograde passions.[31] In contrast, her poems, like public worship, are a "virtual declaration of the rights of men." According to Barbauld's aesthetic, all great poetry—Wordsworth's "The Brothers," for instance—draws readers into participating in a community of ends according to passionately loved principles of equality and justice. In denigrating Romantic melancholy, Barbauld rejects feudal forms of self-prostration transferred by eighteenth-century literary critics and Romantic poets to the aura surrounding canonical works.

The Transcendent (Female) Body

But establishing her poetic voice as distinct from high Romantic poets was not enough to transform Barbauld's poetic voice from "feeble" to strong. There was during the late eighteenth and early nineteenth centuries a misogynous movement to separate women from great poets. This movement was not explicitly an attempt to quash women's genius, nor merely a response to the high visibility and popularity of women poets documented by Marlon Ross and Stuart Curran.[32] As shown in chapter 5, establishing a canon of male authors whose works were conceived of as transcending time required pinning historical specificity and materiality on women. Vicessimus Knox explicitly recognized in 1793 that there was a systematic attempt to exclude women poets in general, and Barbauld in particular, from the first disciplinary anthologies, that is, from anthologies that attempted to establish the canon as we know it, Hazlitt's *Select British Poets* being a prime example.[33] As noted in chapter 5, Hazlitt claims to have revised Knox's *Elegant Extracts* by removing from it inferior poetry, which he calls "baser matter," and Barbauld's poetry is one of his excisions.[34]

But Barbauld's religious ideals protect her from herself seeing her own poetry as basely embodied. The blason tradition of poetry, itemizing parts of women's bodies, works to embody women. As we have seen in chapter 4, women poets such as Mary Leapor were able to put embodying blason and antiblason poetry to feminist uses. Barbauld puts the form to religious uses that have feminist effects. During the Restoration, blason poetry often took the form of love songs. Barbauld's poem "The Origin of Song-Writing," gives us a sense of how she will deploy the genre. The poem describes Cupid as having disobeyed his mother Venus and the female Muses. Venus instructs the Muses:

> Teach him to spell those mystic names
> That kindle bright immortal flames;
> And guide his young unpractis'd feet
> To reach coy learning's lofty seat.
> (47–48, lines 51–54)

The phrase "spell . . . mystic names" recalls Barbauld's "Address to the Deity," in which God helps her to overcome melancholy and effectively write poems by teaching her to "read his awful name, emblazon'd on high / . . . / [and to see] the mystic characters . . . / Wrought in each flower, inscrib'd in every tree" (5, lines 57–60). Basically, then, Venus wants the Muses to teach Cupid to write poems the way that God has taught Barbauld to write poems.

Unfortunately, Cupid—"the sly insidious child"—steals the Muses' power but abjures the goal of "kind[ling] bright immortal flames":

> Now no more the slacken'd strings
> Breathe of high immortal things,
> But Cupid tunes the Muses lyre,
> To languid notes of soft desire.
> (48, lines 61–64)

It is tempting to see Barbauld as here insisting that songs are about physical love, whereas hymns are about spiritual. But elsewhere Barbauld defends writers who use the language of passionate love to address or speak about God: "Love borrows the language of Devotion, for the votaries of that passion are fond of suing those exaggerated expressions which suit nothing below the divinity; and you can hardly address the greatest of all Beings in a strain of more profound adoration than the lover uses to the object of his attachment."[35] What is wrong with the language of love is not that it expresses physical desire, but that it is addressed to the wrong being: one should express one's undying love only to God. The distinction between what Cupid ought to write about and what he does write about, then, is not the distinction commonly made between spirit and flesh, but rather a new one: "The Origin of Song-Writing" differentiates hard, disciplined, controlled desire—desire actively directed to God—from a desire that is "soft" or "languid"—desire passively suffered, directed to the wrong object.

At first glance, it seems as though Barbauld is inveighing in her hymns against having any physical feeling at all. For instance, in hymn 8, a voice from "a crowd of Pilgrims" cries out:

> We purge our mortal dross away,
>   Refining as we run;
> But while we die to earth and sense,
>   Our heaven is begun.
> (124, lines 33–36)

This stanza sounds fairly puritanical, as if one's job were to forgo physical appetite and seek spiritual reward. But "dying to earth and sense" is for Barbauld, I would argue, less a matter of forgoing the physical than it is of refining it. Barbauld's songs, for example song 4 ("When gentle Celia first I knew"), are cautionary tales about what happens to people who have not trained themselves to desire the right thing. After forgoing a passion for Celia that has been shaped by "Reason and taste" for a passion for Chloris springing from unrefined appetite, the speaker despairs: "Oft shall I curse my iron chain" (43, lines 3, 25). The poem ends with his friends watching him drift out to sea, lost, until he finally commits suicide or, as the song says, "And foundering yields to fate" (44, line 42). This song is designed to frighten the reader away from the melancholy passion that Cupid offers, back toward the rational love of a just God. But combining "reason" with "taste" as missing controllers of passion suggests that reason does not supplant or oppose the sensual but rather refines it.

That religious sentiment refines rather than extinguishes sensuous passion is suggested by the flame imagery pervasive in her work: in hymn 6, "Pious Friendship," she tells us that the "union sweet [of] according minds" is a "generous flame within" that "Refine[s] from earth and cleanse[s] from sin" (90, lines 2, 7–8). In contrast to refining (hard, disciplined) passion, the lovers in the songs who passively accept rather than actively form their own physical appetites are enthralled to cruel lovers. Worshiping God does not involve forgoing physical passion, but it does require forgoing completely passive physical pleasure, including a masochistic desire to grieve uncontrollably. Sheer appetite is sinful, then, only because it puts one person in thrall to another, encouraging the psyche to revert to a melancholy, masochistic, feudal subservience. Barbauld's theology includes the notion that good spiritual love does not supplant sinful physical appetite, but, on the contrary, represents desire in its highest, most refined form. In "An Address to the Deity," when God tells her his name, she suddenly "feel[s] that name my inmost thoughts controul / And, ... / ... the waves of grief subside" (4, lines 11–13). God's name reworks her passion so that, instead of the masochistic sublime thrill of "gloomy terrors," she "feel[s]" the intensely passionate exultation of being "omnipotent in thee" (5, lines 71–72). Wisdom is not separate from pleasure, even from physical pleasure, but an outgrowth of it.[36] For Barbauld, spirit is not distinct from matter, but a form of it—and, specifically, passion formed by God's name: words, poetry.

It is interesting to speculate that some of Barbauld's views may have their origin in Priestley's infamous materialism, derived, apparently, from his understanding of David Hartley's *Observations on Man.* Willey tells us that Priestley adopted Hartley's "necessitarianism" but warns against confusing it with Calvinist notions of predestination.[37] In Calvinism, nothing one does while alive will affect the state of the soul after death; that state is predetermined. The doctrine of necessity, under which scientific laws are laws, would seem to preclude willful action as well: elements impinging on one's mind in the environment cause one to think, feel, and (re)act a certain way. According to Priestley, "the doctrine of necessity" insists upon "the necessary influence of motives to determine the choice."[38] But for Priestley, Willey says, although "[people's] conduct follows necessarily from their motives," the motives themselves are not determined by environment alone: "you can supply [people], by persuasion, with even better and better motives."[39] Learning rhetoric, or the art of persuasion, helps one to form good word bodies that impinge upon the senses graphically or aurally, stimulating people to act.

Barbauld's "Address to the Deity," as shown above, describes things in the world as God's writing:

> I read his awful name, emblazon'd high
> With golden letters on th'illumin'd sky;
> Nor less the mystic characters I see
> Wrought in each flower, inscrib'd in every tree;
> In every leaf that trembles to the breeze
> I hear the voice of God among the trees;
> (5, lines 57–62)

Barbauld expresses a similar idea in "A Summer Evening's Meditation":

> ... he, whose hand
> With hieroglyphics elder than the Nile,
> Inscrib'd the mystic tablet; hung [the stars] on high

To public gaze, and said, adore, O man!
The finger of thy God.
(81, lines 31–35)

McCarthy and Kraft see such passages as stating "a traditional idea of nature as the 'writing' of God, as in Sir Thomas Browne's *Religio Medici* (1635): 'The Finger of God hath left an inscription on all his works.'"[40] Significantly, "An Address to Deity," where Barbauld first expresses the idea that nature is God's writing, is perhaps the second poem she wrote, inspired by a sermon Priestley gave to ministers at Wakefield. In it, he says that a "truly and perfectly good man . . . lives, as it were, constantly *seeing him who is invisible*. He sees God in every thing, and he sees every thing in God. . . . His whole life will be, as it were, one act of devotion."[41] Devotion consists in reading the world properly as the words of God, a material incarnation of divine spirit.

As mentioned above, Barbauld admonishes "metaphysical reasoner[s]" such as "Berkeley" and Coleridge to go into church for public worship where divinity is incarnate in the congregation: there, "slow hesitating doubts vanish in a moment"—there one cannot doubt "the existence of the material world" (2:445), which leads one to doubt the existence of God as well. Those people who are capable of "abstruse reasoning" are in fact on the same level as "the multitudes" whom Barbauld urges the metaphysical thinkers to help: "As for the multitude, . . . so much do they require the assistance of some object within the grasp of their senses, that it is to be doubted whether they could be at all persuaded of the existence of a spiritual invisible power, if that existence was not statedly acknowledged by some act which should impress the reality of it upon their minds, by connecting it with places, persons, and times" (2:445–46). It is God who provides the material places, persons, and times, but only proper education and self-discipline stimulate the reading capacities necessary for seeing material reality as God's words. It is precisely that kind of capacity that is cultivated by Barbauld's *Hymns in Prose*, designed for children: "God is in every place; he speaks in every sound we hear, he is seen in all that our eyes behold: nothing, oh! child of reason, is without God: let God, therefore, be in all thy thoughts."[42]

Just as Priestley and Barbauld believe that the spirit of God is nothing separate from the material incarnations that constitute God's writing, Priestley sees the spirit of people as nothing separate from their bodies. In his "Disquisitions on Matter and Spirit," Priestley argues against dualism. One cannot possibly imagine what heaven and hell consist in without sensation, and one cannot imagine sensation without a body, he argues, so it is much more consistent to imagine the indelible union of body and spirit than to believe that the spirit hops from one body to another, from mortal to immortal. Barbauld's "Summer Evening's Meditation" instantiates such an idea, since her "soul," "longing to behold her maker," meditates on God by moving through the universe in a very physical way, passing planets named as landmarks (83, lines 111–12). Her "contemplation" is rather like Jodi Foster's voyage in *Contact*, with Barbauld's special effects deployed rhetorically rather than visually as she ascends to the edge of the universe. She evokes a physical sense of God's "presence," aurally available as the "tongue in every star that talks with man / And wooes him to be wise" (81–83, lines 18, 101, 49–50). Barbauld imagines her own death at the end of the poem, "the hour [that] will come," as a moment "[w]hen all these splendours" imagined earlier in the poem "bursting on my sight / Shall stand unveil'd, and to my ravish'd sense / Unlock the glories of the world unknown" (84, lines 119–21). Barbauld will die not by shedding her sense, not by sailing up out of the body that allows her to have sensations. Rather, death for her is ravishment, sensation brought to the highest degree of pleasure.

It is the pleasure offered by beautiful, truthful words—like the pleasure offered by the sights and sounds of astounding natural objects that are God's words—that for Priestley and Barbauld forms the glue holding together spirit and body, meaning and matter. "[E]very body," Priestley says, "as *solid* and *impenetrable*, must necessarily have some particular *form* or *shape*; but it is no less obvious, that no such *figured thing* can exist, unless the parts of which it consists have a mutual attraction, so as either to keep contiguous to, or preserve a certain distance from each other. The power of attraction, therefore, must be essential to the *actual existence* of all matter, since no substance can retain any *form* without it."[43] Physical desire or "attraction" holds material particles together into a form, and it is this desire that we call "soul," although, according to Priestley, it is nothing independent of matter. Every "figured thing," be it the stars (according to Barbauld, God's "lamps" that speak wisdom with their "tongues"),[44] the words of a poem, or the body or face of a human being (its "figure"), has soul because of (and not despite) its physical attractiveness.

For Barbauld, the way that one monitors one's words, just as one channels the body's physical desires, via "reason and taste," determines the soul's state, which consists in the quality and degree of attractiveness and ravishment (pleasure given and pleasure received). As shown in the previous chapter, anthologies of great poetry produced during the Romantic period exclude women writers almost completely. But teaching anthologies designed for young children and the poor such as William Enfield's *The Speaker* and Knox's *Elegant Extracts* did contain women writers.[45] The reason for this is expressed in pedagogical essays as well as anthologizing practices. Women writers were seen as best at using language not for intellectual or spiritual gratification but for sensual enjoyment that young children could indeed appreciate, just as they enjoy baby talk and cooing sounds made by their mothers. According to Richard Lovell Edgeworth, children enjoy "the beauties of . . . Barbauld" when young; they can thus learn to like poetry at an early age and later move on to seriously thoughtful and rational readings.[46] Given the difference between the contents of teaching collections and canonizing anthologies, discussed in the previous chapter, edited by Hazlitt, Campbell, and Aikin, this culture expected children to graduate from reading poetry that pleases *physically* (that is beautiful in sound), a feature of all verse including that written by women and inferior male poets, to poetry that stimulates one *intellectually* and *spiritually*, as does poetry written by the great male masters. Because Barbauld does not believe that the sensual and the spiritual are separate, she does not subscribe to this division of labor. Insofar as the spirit is refined by refining sensations, by redirecting one's attractions in accordance with "reason and taste," inculcating bad taste is spiritually dangerous. For that reason Barbauld wrote her *Hymns in Prose for Children* (1781): children should not read "verse till they are able to relish good verse";[47] they should not be physically stimulated until able intellectually to actively determine the direction of their physical pleasure.

The belief that body and spirit are not distinct entities enables Barbauld to claim for women higher moral authority *as* sensual beings, deeply—even physically—affected by language that they read and write. Women are capable of being governed by reason, she says in "On Female Studies," and, because they are trained to be virtuous, they are diverted from developing tastes that will misguide their souls: "the broader mirth and more boisterous gayety of the other sex are to [women] prohibited."[48] Although most writers, including Wollstonecraft, see sensibility's connection to physical sensuousness as putting it "on the brink of vice" if not "curbed by reason,"[49] Barbauld does not see physical passion as antithetical to spiritual growth; for her reason is not "a curb" on passion but a directional device, directing women away from the bawdy (bad taste) and toward great art (good taste). She aligns a rationally and tastefully directed sensibility with a chastity that nonetheless unabashedly procures inordinate amounts of pleasure:

[T]he purity and simplicity of heart which a woman ought never, in her freest commerce with the world, to wear off, her very seclusion from the jarring interests and coarser amusements of society, fit her in a peculiar manner for the worlds of fancy and sentiment, and dispose her to the quickest relish of what is pathetic, sublime, or tender. To you, therefore, the beauties of poetry, of moral painting, and all, in general, that is comprised under the term of polite literature, lie particularly open, and you cannot neglect them without neglecting a very copious source of enjoyment. ("Female Studies," 41–42)

She is not saying, "stay simple, pure, and secluded so that you save your soul by not being tempted by bodily desires." She is saying, "stay simple, pure, and secluded so that your bodily desires do not get corrupted by being sexualized and your pleasure reduced." "Polite literature," *more* attractive than the bawdy jokes one hears in "commerce with the world," provides "a very copious source of enjoyment." Cultivating the mind, she says, "will open to you an inexhaustible fund of wonder and delight" ("Female Studies," 43). And Barbauld speaks here not only of the passive pleasures of reading and acquiring knowledge. She directs women to "love and cultivate" their native language: "know all its elegancies, its force, its happy turns of expression, and possess yourself of all its riches" ("Female Studies," 42).

Because for Barbauld sensibility is not a spiritual liability, a force to be curbed or contained, because for her it is good to seek as much pleasure as one can get, women have the advantage in cultivating their souls: "But of all reading, what most ought to engage your attention are works of sentiment and morals. Morals is that study in which alone both sexes have an equal interest; and in sentiment yours has even the advantage" ("Female Studies," 43). Thus Barbauld's belief in the materiality of the soul transforms women's sensitivity from a vice into a virtue and allows her to see her own writing as, if more sensuous than writing by men, *not* on that account less serious, less spiritually significant, less capable of saving souls.

However, the adequation Barbauld makes in her theology between receiving and giving pleasure, between attraction and ravishment, produces what often look like antifeminist ideas in her writing, as in the paragraph ending the first letter of "On Female Education": "[A well-educated woman] will seem to know everything by leading every one to speak of what he knows; and when she is with those to whom she can give no real information, she will yet delight them by the original turns of thought and sprightly elegance which will attend her manner of speaking on any subject" ("Female Studies," 43). Such advice looks masochistic, as does the line in her poem "To a Lady, with some painted Flowers" that scandalized Mary Wollstonecraft, "Your best, your sweetest empire is—to please" (77, line 18). These passages could in fact be passionately advocating the very ideal of feudal subservience that she protests against in Coleridge and Southey, the masochistic passion of courtly service now mapped onto gender. And it is indeed the case that economic rationalists such as Adam Smith, liberal theorists such as Locke, and rational Dissenters, all present theories that founder when confronted with "the economic problem" of masochism. Barbauld wants to deny that people are necessarily attracted to masochism, for which she condemns melancholy poetry, and perhaps her repressed masochism returns here. But in "On Female Education," pleasing men with your words is represented as coeval with being pleased by them. And "To a Lady" makes the activity of pleasing men not an arduous task requiring self-debasement, but women's "sweetest empire," only the sweetest of perhaps many empires. Pleasing is represented as a way of getting pleasure, but the tasks involved in pleasing also procure pleasure on their own. Barbauld's requirement that women please, antifeminist though it is,[50] does not actually participate in a masochistic affective economy, rather, it rewrites that economy in a way that is radically egalitarian: one gets pleasure by pleasing others in ways that please oneself. In her poem "On a Lady's Writing," Barbauld describes a woman's physical bearing—her body, her manners—as identical with her writing: "the same graces o'er her pen preside / That form her manners and her footsteps guide" (70, lines 5–6). Refining the figure one makes in society and figuring spiritual truths in one's poetry are identical tasks. Being an admirable figure and making great poetic figures are the same, and both accomplishments give pleasure to viewers and readers as much as to oneself.

To imagine the physical beauty of the female body as just like the beautiful words of the poet is to see materiality as transcendent and to reconceive women's writing: no physical necessity consigns it in advance to the category of "baser matter"; women's writing *can* become the passionate but spiritually efficacious utterances of the "virtuous few" whom she describes in her hymn "Ye are the salt of the earth." One of the people she describes as "Salt of the Earth" is Lafayette; others are the Polish people who, fighting for freedom in 1794, were defeated by Russian troops. But some are female: they are "Angels of love" who tend the sick in hospitals and the dying in prisons. All of these people, male and female, are encompassed by the word "you" in the hymn that addresses them. These people are also great writers:

> Whene'er you touch the poet's lyre,
>   A loftier strain is heard;
> Each ardent thought is your's alone,
>   And every burning word.
> . . . .
> Your's is the writing on the wall
>   That turns the tyrant pale.
> (127–28, lines 25–28, 35–36)

The "writing on the wall" that great writers repeat is a repetition of God's own mystic and burning words—the spiritual fire whose physical form is attraction to and attractiveness of bodies (natural objects, words, people). These contagious, fiery words say that all people are radically equal. Tyrants will pale at such news because, of course, they are not behaving as if people were equal. And some poets, whose strain is not as lofty—perhaps Coleridge, Southey, Byron—write verse in a melancholic mood that is based on a sense of inequality, of one's own vileness. The radical equality of all people includes female as well as male people: gender indeterminacy in this hymn comes from Barbauld's vision of the radical equality of women whose attachment to words is simultaneously physical and spiritual, and who therefore can be as writerly as anyone else.

Abjection

As chapter 5 has shown, anthologies and miscellanies of poetry collectively abject women for the sake of establishing male writers as transcendent. One Romantic writer discusses indirectly the poetic productions—"performances" as they are called throughout the eighteenth century in introductions to collections of poems—that must be rendered transcendent through the process of abjection. Charles Lamb's "On the Tragedies of Shakespeare" (1811) is an essay notorious for exemplifying Romantic sentiment against theatricality. However, while arguing that Shakespeare's texts need to be read rather than seen in performance, Lamb mentions in passing how much he detests the kind of memorization of Shakespeare's soliloquies made possible by "*Enfield Speakers* and, such kind of books."[51] In his essay, Lamb ruminates on the difference between a text written by an author and the innumerable productions of that text in print, between the ideal "text" and its material instantiations: just as audiences might prefer one performance by an actor to any other performance, or indeed to silently reading words on the page, Lamb fears that readers might desire a particular reproduction of a text but not others. Lamb wants readers to desire the abstract "text" rather than its embodiment as a commodity not produced by an author, but rather by publishers and printers. He is also simultaneously worried that these commodities are not consumable, that desire might come to rest in any one of them and end circulation. Lamb assaults anthologies like William Enfield's *The Speaker*, connecting them with the performances his essay disdains:

> How far the very custom of hearing any thing spouted, withers and blows upon a fine passage, may be seen in those speeches from *Henry the Fifth*, etc., which are current in the mouths of school-boys from being to be found in

Enfield Speakers, and such kind of books. I confess myself utterly unable to appreciate that celebrated soliloquy in *Hamlet*, beginning "To be or not to be," . . . it has been so handled and pawed about by declamatory boys and men, and torn so inhumanly from its living place and principle of continuity in the play, till it is become to me a perfect dead member. (113)

How exactly is Lamb figuring here the reproductions of "To be or not to be" in anthologies and in readers' mouths, two related kinds of performances or productions? Is the soliloquy imagined to be an embryo aborted from the play figured as a female body, or is it here imagined to be the phallus and the play castrated by its reproduction in various kinds of print? Undecidably both. The body that emerges when Lamb is discussing the canonization of Shakespeare through anthologies is maybe male, maybe female. Here we see the collapse of the distinction between abstract, ideal text and printed or performed material instantiations of it, a distinction mapped onto sexual difference, which is also collapsing via the process of abjection:[52] the body here cannot quite be pinned on women and thereby ejected from the idealized "text." Lamb spends the rest of the essay trying to disembody the text by insisting that the reader is a completely bodiless entity when reading. But here, as he looks at what anthologies do, their precarious albeit practical methods for sustaining texts as abstractions begin to break down. That breakdown is signaled by the eruption into his essay of an indeterminately gendered, abject body. Only the virulent, sadistic kind of misogyny will reestablish the distinction between male ideal text and female printed matter, described above in chapter 5). Cursing the Barbauld crew will help, especially if one sees Barbauld as a "bare" "bald" female body: Coleridge, Southey, and Lamb called Barbauld "Mrs Bare-bald" and "Mistress Bare and Bald" in retaliation for a bad review of Lamb's *John Woodvil* that the three erroneously attributed to Barbauld.[53] Gender indeterminacy has to be violently resolved so that embodiedness, materiality, and mortality can be pinned on women. Sadism directed by early Romantics at Barbauld served the purpose of shoring up unstable distinctions.

The Fantasy Underlying a Dissenting Aesthetic

Gender indeterminacy can be violently resolved through virulent misogyny; left unresolved, it produces the literariness that allows for multiple points of identification within a work, stimulating readerly play. What makes Barbauld's poems "To Mr C[olerid]ge" and "A Summer Evening's Meditation" great poetry is a certain ambiguity about the material, produced in accordance with the dissenting aesthetic adumbrated above. In her poem to

Coleridge, Barbauld tells Coleridge that those who remain "enchanted" by the grove of metaphysics do so in order to escape mortality:

> . . . . Here each mind
> Of finer mold, acute and delicate,
> Rests for a space, in fairy bowers entranced;
> And loves the softened light and tender gloom;
> And, pampered with most unsubstantial food,
> Looks down indignant on the grosser world,
> And matter's cumbrous shapings.[54]
> (132–33, lines 25–32)

Barbauld is here accusing idealists and metaphysicians (and Coleridge) of distinguishing themselves from matter through engaging in their spiritualizing, subtilizing melancholia. But she calls this melancholy enchantment "unsubstantial food." Cox suggests that "unsubstantial food" contrasts with maternal nourishment and is therefore perhaps gendered male.[55] Since the food described is food for the soul, Barbauld's phrase says that melancholia is spiritually insufficient. But she is also calling it unsubstantial, i.e., not material. Melancholia is spiritually insufficient because not worldly, not material enough. But then Barbauld continues: "Youth belov'd / . . . / be this Circe of the studious cell / Enjoyed, but still subservient" (133, lines 32, 37–38). The studious cell is a Circe—a woman who enthralls you by gratifying sensual desires. Is melancholy loitering in the wood of metaphysics an attempt to distance oneself from or immerse oneself in the physical? Is it masculine and transcendent, or feminine and immanent? Undecidably both.

"A Summer Evening's Meditation" similarly establishes a rich kind of gender ambiguity. Like Coleridge's ruminations in "Frost at Midnight" written some twenty-one years later, Barbauld's meditations are stimulated by a "stranger," but Barbauld's stranger is not a piece of ash on the grate; rather, it is internal:

> At this still hour the self-collected soul
> Turns inward, and beholds a stranger there
> Of high descent, and more than mortal rank;
> An embryo God; a spark of fire divine,
> Which must burn on for ages, when the sun,
> (Fair transitory creature of a day!)
> Has clos'd his golden eye. . . .
> (82, lines 53–59)

This fire is not exactly immaterial—it is rather unformed matter, an embryo. But this spark is contrasted with the sun, matter that will ultimately burn out because only material. It is significant that this ephemeral burning matter is gendered "he," though there is a classical precedent, given the connection of the sun with Apollo. God is gendered "he" as well, so both divine and material fires are masculine. What Barbauld finds when she goes to the outer reaches of the universe out of "longing to behold her Maker" (83, line 111) is "The desarts of creation, wide and wild; / Where embryo systems and unkindled suns / Sleep in the womb of chaos" (83, lines 95–97). It is seeing this womb that stimulates the speaker's astonishment, the sublime awe that checks her flight. Is God female, a womb full of embryos? God may be "he" or "she," but, in any case, it is God for whom she "ripens," God who will "ravish" her (84, lines 119, 121). The image of a womb that ravishes gives this poem its power and depth.

The same kind of gender indeterminacy that operates here makes Lamb's essay on Shakespeare's tragedies great literature as well, but the two textual moments spring from different sources. Barbauld's education as a Dissenter, and in particular that education received from Priestley, informs a fantasy underlying her poetry and prose. The fantasy that materiality refines itself into transcendence allows her to value women's bodies and women's words as simultaneously material and transcendent. Although probably not connected to any consciously held materialist theology on Barbauld's part (that is, she may have seen Priestley's doctrines as extreme), a fantasy of sublime materiality promotes the gender ambiguity in these poems that sustains their literariness, that enables them to offer a play of identifications (see the introduction, pp. 12-14). The playful ambiguity in Lamb's text, though promoting great writing, is rendered intolerable to him by the nature of his ideological task: to distinguish an author's text in the abstract from any material production of it, be it a printed book or a theatrical performance. Because this play is intolerable, Lamb must pay—or I should say that women in general (Barbauld in particular) and schoolboys (or lower-class men trying to learn to speak well in order to raise their status—these people must pay, since it is Lamb's misogyny and his classism that allows him to disavow such ambiguity: women poets are bare and bald; declamatory boys and men handle and paw words, embodying them in a thoroughly disgusting performance; great, transcendent male poets like Shakespeare have no truck with either.

An Alternate Aesthetic, Rejected

It is her vision of religious faith as overcoming gendered hierarchies, expressed indirectly in her hymn "To the Salt of the Earth," and her sense of her own work as superior to Southey's and Coleridge's because based in joy rather than melancholy, community rather than solitude, that enables Barbauld to produce poetry. We need to read her concern with the state of writers' souls, then, less as narrow-minded morality antithetical to the spirit of poetry and more as a principle of poetic production. Through her relation to God, Barbauld is able to assume an embodied but nonetheless transcendent poetic voice. Not sharing her aesthetic views, however, literary history has excluded her from the canon until 1994.

The previous chapter argued that seeing poetry written by male poets as transcendent depends upon the abjection of woman. Disciplinary anthologies that do not contain women poets, together with antiquarian miscellaneous collections and teaching anthologies that do contain women, collectively perform abjection: antiquarian collections pin historical specificity onto female poets; teaching collections such as Knox's *Elegant Extracts*, insofar as they are informed by pedagogical theory in which children should be taught to love poetry by first being exposed to the most beautiful because most sensuous kind, pin the materiality of language on women; by excluding women poets found in the other two kinds of collections, disciplinary anthologies encourage their readers to project their own mortality onto the women poets found elsewhere, thereby constituting a canon of immortal (male-authored) verse.

Priestley, as we have seen, saw Barbauld as one of Britain's greatest poets, as did her brother John Aikin. John Guillory sees Barbauld herself as "at the vanguard of the anthologizing movement by which English literature was given a canonical form" because he sees Enfield's *Speaker* as "the Adamic ancestor of the Norton Anthology."[56] But, in addition to the fact that *The Speaker* was deliberately designed to teach elocution, which the Norton is not, the tables of contents of Norton anthologies before 1993 resemble much more closely William Hazlitt's *Select British Poets* or John Aikin's *Select Works of the British Poets* than they do any of the collections used in schools.[57] Sadly, even Barbauld's staunchest supporter, her brother, who encouraged her to publish the notoriously maligned poem "Eighteen Hundred and Eleven" because of its brilliance—sadly, even he did not include her poetry in his anthology of canonical verse.[58] The need to embody and materialize women poets and thereby render them immanent is structural and so strong that it can prompt Arthur Symons to respond in the following way to Wordsworth's statement that the only poem he ever envied anyone for writing was Barbauld's "Life": "The last lines . . . are not less than an inspiration, a woman's . . ."[59] Symons has to locate her lines physically in her body, to limit their scope so that they are seen not as stimulating universal feelings, the provenance of canonical verse, but instead evoke sentiments that are only "a woman's."

Melancholy poetry, a poetic type antithetical to Barbauld's own poetic practice, dominates the canon.[60] But her critique of that kind of poetry, that it may instill in its readers a politically dangerous passion for subservience, has been revived in a powerful way recently by critics during a moment when women poets such as Barbauld and Leapor are being rediscovered, and the canon, sustained by a misogynous structure, is breaking down. Terry Eagleton, for example, persuasively argues that the aesthetic promotes bourgeois hegemony.[61] However, such criticism will not have its intended salutary effect if we see it as applying to "the aesthetic" rather than to one aesthetic theory among many.

Conclusion

In the preceding chapters, I have shown that there was, during the course of the eighteenth century, a shift in the affective economies informing both reading and writing practices. Early writers such as Dryden, Swift, Pope, and Otway try to keep open the play of textual indeterminacies. One way to preserve literariness is to ensure that readers and auditors will be induced, willingly or not, to identify with multiple positions in the text. In early-eighteenth-century satire, misogynous portraits that implicate the misogynous voyeur (satiric persona and reader) in what are allegedly only the disgusting woman's crimes make satiric persona, reader, and satiric object all at moments identifiable with each other, thereby keeping the play of identifications in the text mobile and indeterminate. In early she-tragedies, excessively pathetic portraits of a raped and murdered female figure attempt to dissuade the audience from disidentifying with her, despite her sufferings. Both satire and she-tragedy, then, fuel a sadomasochistic reading economy in which the reader identifies with both active and passive positions in a scene of humiliation.

As the century progresses, however, we see more virulent forms of misogyny in the structures of texts and in reading practices. Later texts try to prevent readers from identifying with the figure of woman in misogynous representations, and indeed, an emerging belief that women are essentially different from men abets the process. Lillo's *London Merchant* and Mandeville's *Modest Defence of Publick Stews* both contain misogynous representations that sadistically immolate the figure of woman, Mandeville's text going so far as to turn her into a rotting carcass. These texts encourage a sadistic reading economy, in which we wholly disidentify with and deanimate a female figure who is seen as wholly other because literally referring to female anatomy. Eighteenth-century literature has not been completely successful at inculcating such reading practices, but they everywhere contaminate our reading processes. As the attempt to recover Mary Leapor's work shows, even feminist literary critics wishing to recover women's protest within conventional discourses that circumvent dissent sometimes read as misogynists.

I hope to have shown that the fate of misogyny and literature are intertwined. As I have argued in chapter 6, misogyny and literature have since the inception of the discipline of English literature been connected, and they are still connected. We can see that connection in the disciplinary changes currently under way: the dismantling of the canon and of literary sexism go hand in hand. But this book has shown that misogyny and literature are connected in another crucial way as well. What makes misogyny virulent is the refusal to understand language's fundamental literariness. Misogynous texts use the figure of woman to abject sexual desire and materiality from the realms of both proper business and great literature. That abjection works only insofar as the texts in which it occurs are not read as literary but as referential discourse. The misogyny that forecloses on the literariness of texts consists in imagining that representations of women are about a real-world referent rather than about the sometimes conflicting functions that representations must serve: ideology, demystification, abjection for the sake of erecting ideals. As readers, we can recover these contradictions only by being willing to see gender as a figure, not a thing. Recovering literariness and denaturalizing sexism turn out to be compatible tasks.

I will end this book by pointing to a passage from Swift's *Gulliver's Travels* in which, I believe, he insists that two kinds of oppression—sexism and classism—are connected to newly emerging attitudes toward language. Swift connects oppression to the belief that language performs fundamentally anti-rhetorical tasks. Gulliver is visiting the Grand Academy of Lagado, the school of languages, where he finds projectors who are working on "a scheme for entirely abolishing all words whatsoever. . . . An expedient was . . . offered," Gulliver says,

> that since words are only names for *things*, it would be more convenient for all men to carry about them such *things* as were necessary to express the particular business they are to discourse on. And this invention would certainly have taken place, to the great ease as well as health of the subject, if the women in conjunction with the vulgar and illiterate had not threatened to raise a rebellion, unless they might be allowed the liberty to speak with their tongues, after the manner of their forefathers; such constant and irreconcilable enemies to science are the common people.[1]

Swift treats Gulliver ironically here, himself taking the side of "the common people." Science has determined that words must refer to things. Women

and the poor, he implies, *ought* to rebel against such so-called "progress."
But why should it be specifically "women in conjunction with the vulgar
and illiterate" who rebel against progress, rather than everyone? Swift saw
a connection between reducing language's figurative power, on the one hand,
and misogyny and class oppression on the other. From Swift's vignette, and
from the evidence and arguments presented in this book, it is possible to
say: dismantling misogyny and preserving literary play depend upon each
other. I hope further to have convincingly shown here that misogyny is not
necessary. If the disgust aroused by representations of women's bodies is in
any sense a "real" feeling, it is nonetheless not disgust *at* women. Disgust
allegedly aroused by women's bodies comes in fact from the stench of social
inequity.

Notes

―――――•――――――

Introduction

1. Fredric Bogel pointed out to me the significance of "dizened." Laura Brown notices the curious absence of the female body from Swift's scatalogical satire, that the locus of his disgust is commodities adorning women rather than the female body itself ("Reading Race and Gender: Jonathan Swift," *Eighteenth-Century Studies* 23.4 [summer 1990]: 427–29).

2. Jonathan Swift, "A Beautiful Young Nymph Going to Bed. Written for the Honour of the Fair Sex," in *Jonathan Swift: The Complete Poems*, ed. Pat Rogers (New Haven, Conn.: Yale Univ. Press, 1983), 453–54.

3. Mary Douglas, *Purity and Danger: An Analysis of the Concepts of Pollution and Taboo* (London: Ark Press, 1984).

4. One of the most promising trends in current analyses of misogyny, begun by Peter Stallybrass and Allon White in *The Politics and Poetics of Transgression* (Ithaca, N.Y.: Cornell Univ. Press, 1986), requires asking what kinds of anxieties generated by social, economic, and political changes are displaced onto representations of misogyny in eighteenth-century literature. In her "Nets and Bridles," Ann Rosalind Jones answers that question by arguing that the excoriation of lustful women in early modern conduct manuals expresses anxiety over the new, bourgeois upstart, the rising class defined by class mobility ("'Nets and Bridles': Early Modern Conduct Books and Sixteenth-Century Women's Lyrics," in *The Ideology of Conduct: Essays on Literature and the History of Sexuality*, ed. Nancy Armstrong and Leonard Tennenhouse [New York: Methuen, 1987], 39–72). In *The Ends of Empire: Women and Ideology in Early Eighteenth-Century Literature* (Ithaca, N.Y.: Cornell Univ. Press, 1993), Laura Brown has shown that anxieties over trade and empire have been displaced onto the female figures in Swift's scatalogical satire.

5. In the first book-length analysis of misogyny, *The Troublesome Helpmate*, Katharine M. Rogers was constrained to define it in terms of an individual author's pathology (*The Troublesome Helpmate: A History of Misogyny in Lit-*

erature [Seattle: Univ. of Washington Press, 1966]). More recent feminist critics, from Sandra Gilbert and Susan Gubar's *Madwoman in the Attic: The Woman Writer and the Nineteenth-Century Literary Imagination* (New Haven, Conn.: Yale Univ. Press, 1979) to Felicity Nussbaum's *The Brink of All We Hate: English Satires on Women 1660–1750* (Lexington: Univ. Press of Kentucky, 1984) and Ellen Pollak's *The Poetics of Sexual Myth: Gender and Ideology in the Verses of Swift and Pope* (Chicago: Univ. of Chicago Press, 1985), have gone beyond Rogers in seeing misogynous representations as systematic and as performing important kinds of ideological work.

6. Karl Marx, *Capital: A Critique of Political Economy*, vol. I, trans. Ben Fowkes (New York: Vintage Books, 1977), 884–86; Raymond Williams, *The Country and the City* (New York: Oxford Univ. Press, 1973), 39.

7. Lawrence Stone and Jeanne C. Fawtier Stone, *An Open Elite? England 1540–1880* (Oxford: Clarendon Press, 1984), 7.

8. C.B. MacPherson, "Capitalism and the Changing Concept of Property," in *Feudalism, Capitalism, and Beyond*, ed. Eugene Kamenka and Ronald S. Neale (London: Edward Arnold, 1975), 104–24.

9. Frederick L. Nussbaum, *A History of the Economic Institutions of Modern Europe* (New York: F.S. Crofts, 1933), 196, 207.

10. Frances Elizabeth Baldwin, *Sumptuary Laws and Personal Regulation in England* (Baltimore: Johns Hopkins Univ. Press, 1926).

11. Marx, *Capital,* 886.

12. According to Norma Landau, one problem with a Marxist narrative is that it cannot account for capitalism taking so long—the whole eighteenth century—to "triumph" ("Eighteenth-Century England: Tales Historians Tell," *Eighteenth-Century Studies* 22.2 [winter 1988–89]: 210–11). Work done by J.G.A Pocock can help to explain the delay. For Pocock, both classical and early modern civic humanists contend that healthy government can result only from private virtue (*Politics, Language, and Time: Essays on Political Thought and History* [New York: Atheneum, 1971], 90–91). Pocock argues that Harringtonian civic humanism, with its ambiguous attitude toward entrepreneurial economic activity (91, 140), persists as a vibrant public discourse until the late eighteenth century (144) despite the new arguments launched by Bernard Mandeville and Adam Smith about the public benefits of private selfishness. According to Landau, such civic humanism provides ideological and political resistance to or ambivalence about high finance; it takes a long century, in this account, for capitalist values to supplant civic virtues as the predominating ideal (215). On Hirschman, see note 24 below.

13. Neil McKendrick, John Brewer, and J.H. Plumb, *The Birth of a Consumer Society: The Commercialization of Eighteenth-Century England* (Bloomington: Indiana Univ. Press, 1982).

14. Marx, *Capital,* 151–52. Marx does not say, although he implies through the logic of his argument, that Aristotle and Greek society saw slaves as fundamentally human: Aristotle cannot abstract human labor as value because some

human labor is valuable (paid) and some is not. The implication here is that capitalist slave-owning societies must in fact see slaves as inhuman in order to effectively commodify labor: in that case, human labor is paid and subhuman labor is not. Such a conclusion is borne out in fact. It is true, biological racism was not full-blown at the outset of industrial capitalism to establish the necessary difference between human and slave labor (see Nicholas Hudson, "From 'Nation' to 'Race': The Origin of Racial Classification in Eighteenth-Century Thought," *Eighteenth-Century Studies* 29.3 [spring 1996], 247–64). Until racist theories could denigrate Africans as not human, abjection, I argue in this book, established necessary differences between women and slaves to prevent new democratic theories from granting political power and freedom to either group, and to allow distinguishing between their labor and human labor in the abstract.

15. Stallybrass and White, *Politics and Poetics of Transgression,* 88–89.

16. Julia Kristeva, *Powers of Horror: An Essay on Abjection,* trans. Leon S. Roudiez (New York: Columbia Univ. Press, 1982); Julia Kristeva, *Tales of Love,* trans. Leon S. Roudiez (New York: Columbia Univ. Press, 1987).

17. Lacan calls "the mirror stage" "the triumphant assumption of the image" (*Écrits* [Paris: Seuil, 1966], 185; quoted in Jean Laplanche and Jean-Baptiste Pontalis, *The Language of Psychoanalysis,* trans. Donald Nicholson-Smith [New York: W.W. Norton, 1973], 251).

18. Sigmund Freud, "Repression," in *The Standard Edition of the Works of Sigmund Freud,* James Strachey, gen. ed., 24 vols. (London: Hogarth Press, 1953–1966), 14:150.

19. Neil Hertz, *The End of the Line: Essays on Psychoanalysis and the Sublime* (New York: Columbia Univ. Press, 1985).

20. Jonathan Swift, *A Tale of a Tub* (1704), in *Gulliver's Travels and Other Writings,* ed. Louis A. Landa (Boston: Houghton Mifflin, 1960), 324.

21. "[T]he borderline patient. . . . is a metaphysician who carries the experience of the impossible to the point of scatology" (Kristeva, *Powers,* 54). Instead of arguing that Swift is a borderline patient, I want to suggest that, if he were writing now, he would look like one. I want to understand what historical conditions would make Swift look like a borderline patient to us now.

22. René Girard, *Violence and the Sacred,* trans. Patrick Gregory (Baltimore: Johns Hopkins Univ. Press, 1977).

23. On philosophical discourses, see Fredric Bogel, *Literature and Insubstantiality in Later Eighteenth-Century England* (Princeton, N.J.: Princeton Univ. Press, 1984); for discourses constituting political economy and concepts of fiction necessary both to money and credit, see James Thompson, *Models of Value: Eighteenth-Century Political Economy and the Novel* (Durham, N.C.: Duke Univ. Press, 1996); and Colin Nicholson, *Writing and the Rise of Finance: Capital Satires of the Early Eighteenth Century* (Cambridge: Cambridge Univ. Press, 1994); for discourses constituting notions of fiction and authorship, see Catherine Gallagher, *Nobody's Story: The Vanishing Acts of Women Writers in the Marketplace 1670–1820* (Berkeley: Univ. of California Press, 1994).

24. Albert O. Hirschman, *The Passions and the Interests: Political Arguments for Capitalism before Its Triumph* (Princeton, N.J.: Princeton Univ. Press, 1977), 9–12.

25. John Goodridge, *Rural Life in Eighteenth-Century English Poetry* (New York: Cambridge Univ. Press, 1995), 6; John Barrell, *The Dark Side of the Landscape: The Rural Poor in English Painting* (New York: Cambridge Univ. Press, 1980), 8–9.

26. Barbara Benedict rejects the distinction traditionally made between anthologies that give us the canon of great literature as it has evolved through time, on the one hand, and, on the other, miscellanies that collect poems relevant to the moment of publication and often published in the miscellanies for the first time (*Making the Modern Reader: Cultural Mediation in Early Modern Literary Anthologies* [Princeton, N.J.: Princeton Univ. Press, 1996], 3–4). As I argue in more detail in chapter 5, however, Benedict rejects the distinction partly because her study of poetry collections ends at just the moment when disciplinary anthologies come into existence, at the beginning of the nineteenth century. Miscellanies look no different from anthologies to her because she examines none of the texts that I define below as anthological.

27. See chapter 5, note 45.

28. Terry Eagleton, *The Ideology of the Aesthetic* (Cambridge, Mass.: Basil Blackwell, 1990), 25.

29. John Guillory, *Cultural Capital: The Problem of Literary Canon Formation* (Chicago: Univ. of Chicago Press, 1993), 19–20.

30. On literature as interrogative, see Susan Wolfson, "Questioning 'The Romantic Ideology': Wordsworth," *Revue Internationale de Philosophie* 174.3 (1990), 429–47. By saying that language is never sheerly ideological, I do not mean that there is anything that exists "outside" of ideology, only that there is always something in excess of it in any text.

31. This important point has been made at various moments by Margaret Ezell, *Writing Women's Literary History* (Baltimore: Johns Hopkins Univ. Press, 1993); and Donna Landry, *The Muses of Resistance: Laboring-Class Women's Poetry in Britain, 1739–1796* (New York: Cambridge Univ. Press, 1990).

32. Pierre Bourdieu, "The Market of Symbolic Goods," reprinted in *The Field of Cultural Production: Essays on Art and Literature,* ed. Randal Johnson (New York: Columbia Univ. Press, 1993), 112–44; Guillory, *Cultural Capital,* 327.

33. Barbara Herrnstein Smith, *Contingencies of Value: Alternative Perspectives for Critical Theory* (Cambridge, Mass.: Harvard Univ. Press, 1988), 10.

34. "The aesthetic is going to come back: the question is, on what terms?" Cora Kaplan, panel discussion, Miami Summer Institute, Miami Univ., Oxford, Ohio, 6 June 1998.

35. See Susan Wolfson, "'Romantic Ideology' and the Values of Aesthetic Form," in *Aesthetics and Ideology,* ed. George Levine (New Brunswick, N.J.: Rutgers Univ. Press, 1994), 192; and George Levine, "Introduction: Reclaiming the Aesthetic," in Levine, *Aesthetics and Ideology,* 1.

36. Mary Sidney Watson, "When Flattery Kills: Barbauld and the Anthologies," paper delivered at the Annual Meeting of the Modern Language Association, Chicago, 28 December 1995.

37. In "Literary Critics as Intellectuals: Class Analysis and the Crisis of the Humanities" (in *Rethinking Class: Literary Studies and Social Formations*, ed. Wai Chee Dimock and Michael T. Gilmore [New York: Columbia Univ. Press, 1994]), John Guillory notices that the literature is disintegrating as a disciplinary object at the moment when the bourgeoisie no longer needs knowledge of literature as a class marker, when instead knowledge produced by the university is serving a new professional-managerial class of people, who perhaps want initiation into technical vocabularies rather than signs for demonstrating knowledge of high culture to be manipulated for the sake of moving up in class: the professional-managerial class might want more to read theory than literature. Guillory questions whether the critique of the canon within the discipline of English is progressive or simply serving the needs of a new task master—not the bourgeoisie this time, but a newly emerging class (114–15).

38. Valuing Barbauld's poetry for reasons other than political is something that Lisa Vargo is trying to accomplish in "The Case of Anna Laetitia Barbauld's 'To Mr. Coleridge,'" *Charles Lamb Bulletin*, n.s., 102 (April 1998): 55–63.

39. See notes 44 and 62 below.

40. D.W. Winnicott, *Playing and Reality* (New York: Routledge, 1982), 47.

41. Judith Butler, *Bodies That Matter: On the Discursive Limits of Sex* (New York: Routledge, 1993), 267 n. 7. Butler quotes Jean Laplanche and Jean-Baptiste Pontalis, "Fantasy and the Origins of Sexuality," in *Formation of Fantasy*, ed. Victor Burgin, James Donald, and Cora Kaplan (London: Methuen, 1986), 26–27.

42. "Freud passes from [considering] fantasy to the question of how subjects tie themselves ethically to each other and enter a socially viable world. . . . Fantasy is not therefore antagonistic to social reality; it is its precondition or psychic glue" (Jacqueline Rose, *States of Fantasy* (Oxford: Clarendon Press, 1996), 3).

43. Butler, *Bodies That Matter,* 105.

44. Thus, Steven Knapp defines "literary interest" as "an interest in representations that construct new compositions of thought and value out of preexisting relations between words and objects and the responses associated with them. . . . [E]ncountering [such] complex scenarios is likely to increase a reader's self-consciousness about her ethical and political dispositions. . . . A person who discovers, by reading literature, the conflicts, inconsistencies, and overdeterminations among her own dispositions is a person who can read *herself* as an instance of descriptive representation. . . . [L]iterary interest. . . . give[s] an unusually pure experience of what liberal agency . . . is like" (*Literary Interest: The Limits of Anti-Formalism* [Cambridge, Mass.: Harvard Univ. Press, 1993], 89, 101, 103). Although later in that book Knapp finds himself "unhappy" with the historicism by which he connects literary interest to the expe-

rience of liberal agency, he does here and perhaps even by the end of his book maintain that literary interest comes from the experience of identifying with multiple dispositions, which makes possible seeing one's own disposition as an identity, as representative rather than merely particular (139–140). Implicit in Knapp's account, then, is that the literary allows for multiple identifications and disidentifications.

45. Diana Fuss, *Identification Papers* (New York: Routledge, 1995), 4.

46. Butler, *Bodies That Matter,* 99.

47. Roger Chartier reminds us that structures in a text never absolutely determine reading practices (*The Order of Books: Readers, Authors, and Libraries in Europe between the Fourteenth and the Eighteenth Centuries* [Stanford, Calif.: Stanford Univ. Press, 1994], 23).

48. "[Samuel Johnson] had a love and respect for Jordan, not for his literature, but for his worth" (James Boswell, *The Life of Samuel Johnson*, ed. Claude Rawson [New York: Everyman, 1992], 32).

49. See Jürgen Habermas, *The Structural Transformation of the Public Sphere: An Inquiry into a Category of Bourgeois Society*, trans. Thomas Burger (Cambridge, Mass.: MIT Press, 1991). According to Habermas, during the early eighteenth century there emerges "the thoroughly bourgeois idea of the freely self-actualizing personality." According to this conception, a person is no longer what he is simply by virtue of his present status, his place in a hierarchy; on the contrary, present and future status are determined by attributes of his personality (13).

In summarizing the work done by Lawrence Stone, David Cressy, and Keith Wrightson on social change in Renaissance England, Mary Beth Rose defines "social mobility" as "a perceived fluidity among social ranks and classes and instability in the determination of social status" (*The Expense of Spirit: Love and Sexuality in English Renaissance Drama* [Ithaca: Cornell Univ. Press, 1988], 47). See pp. 44–51 of *The Expense of Spirit* for her full summary.

On the rise of the middle class and its connection to the notion of social mobility, see Ian Watt, *The Rise of the Novel: Studies in Defoe, Richardson and Fielding* (Berkeley: Univ. of California Press, 1957); Ronald S. Neale, "The Bourgeoisie, Historically, Has Played a Most Revolutionary Part," in Kamenka and Neale, *Feudalism, Capitalism, and Beyond,* 85–102.

On the shift from a status to a class society, "class" being only a function of self-consciousness as class, see Eric J. Hobsbawm, "Class Consciousness in History," in *Aspects of History and Class Consciousness*, ed. Istvan Meszaros (New York: Herder and Herder, 1971): "For the purposes of the historian . . . class and the problem of class consciousness are inseparable. Class in the full sense only comes into existence at the historical moment when classes begin to acquire consciousness of themselves as such" (6). See also E.P. Thompson, "Eighteenth-Century English Society: Class Struggle without Class?" *Journal of Social History* (May 1978): 133–65: "Class and class-consciousness are always the last, not the first, stage in a real historical process" (149).

50. Ann Rosalind Jones, "'Nets and Bridles,'" 39–72.

51. Fuss, *Identification Papers*, 2.

52. Guillory, *Cultural Capital*.

53. Raymond Williams, *Marxism and Literature* (New York: Oxford Univ. Press, 1977), 129.

54. Thomas Laqueur, "Orgasm, Generation, and the Politics of Reproductive Biology," *Representations* 14 (spring 1986): 4–5. Kristina Straub argues that, although gender ambiguity became "intolerable when associated with a male" around the time that boys stopped playing women's parts on the British stage (after 1660), "the cross-dressed actress of the early to mid–eighteenth century seems to constitute a historical possibility for pleasure in sexual and gender ambiguities" (*Sexual Suspects: Eighteenth-Century Players and Sexual Ideology* [Princeton, N.J.: Princeton Univ. Press, 1992], 127). That is, as the demand for fixing identity emerges, the figure of woman seems to be a last refuge for ambiguity. From the mid–eighteenth century on, however, the identity of woman becomes fixed in opposition to man (see note 55).

55. Katharine Eisaman Maus, "'Playhouse Flesh and Blood': Sexual Ideology and the Restoration Actress," *ELH* 46 (1979), 595–617; Thomas Laqueur, *Making Sex: Body and Gender from the Greeks to Freud* (Cambridge, Mass.: Harvard Univ. Press, 1990).

56. Butler, *Bodies That Matter*, 105.

57. I show in detail in chapter 4 that there is a kinship between the misogynous antiblason, such as Swift's "To a Beautiful Young Nymph," and progressive Enlightenment discourse including feminism, but that this kinship is historical rather than necessary.

58. For instance, Jones begins her argument in "Nets and Bridles" by showing that the sudden eruption of the more virulently misogynous representations she analyzes cannot be seen as a reaction to what women were doing historically; they were not, she says, at that moment demanding or seizing more power. And a recent analysis of misogyny in Swift and Pope by Marilyn Francus similarly begins by denying that misogyny was historically justified ("The Monstrous Mother: Reproductive Anxiety in Swift and Pope," *ELH* 61.4 [winter 1994]: 829–52): misogyny, both Jones and Francus implicitly argue, *could* have been a natural response to historical circumstances. Similarly, Brown's analysis begins by noting that Swift's attack on "Celia" "clearly exceeds [her] own poor power to offend" ("Reading Race and Gender," 427). That is, she does have some power to offend, and what we need to analyze is the *excessive* sense of offense, not any and all misogyny. That misogyny is at least partly "natural" is thus an assumption shared even by the best recent analyses of it, including Mary Beth Rose's important work, *The Expense of Spirit*, 70–71.

59. Georg Lukács, *Realism in Our Time: Literature and the Class Struggle*, trans. John Mander and Necke Mander (New York: Harper and Row, 1962), 68.

60. Fuss, *Identification Papers*, 8; Butler, *Bodies That Matter*, 103.

61. Kristeva, *Powers*, 9–15, 53–54.

62. This kind of pleasure produced by literariness, pleasure that comes from indifferentiation and loss of identity, has been described by Roland Barthes in "The Death of the Author": "[W]riting is the destruction of every voice, of every point of origin. Writing is that neutral, composite, oblique space where our subject slips away, the negative where all identity is lost" (*Image / Music / Text*, ed. and trans. Stephen Heath [New York: Hill and Wong, 1977], 142).

63. Jonathan Swift, "Cassinus and Peter: A Tragical Elegy," in *Complete Poems*, 463–66, lines 17–18, 117–18.

64. Mary Jacobus, "Madonna: Like a Virgin; or, Freud, Kristeva, and the Case of the Missing Mother," *Oxford Literary Review* 8.1–2 (1986): 45.

1. Misogyny and Literariness

1. Ellen Pollak, *The Poetics of Sexual Myth: Gender and Ideology in the Verse of Swift and Pope* (Chicago, Univ. of Chicago Press, 1985); Mary Poovey, *The Proper Lady and the Woman Writer: Ideology as Style in the Works of Mary Wollstonecraft, Mary Shelley, and Jane Austen* (Chicago: Univ. of Chicago Press, 1984); Margaret Anne Doody, "Swift among the Women," *Yearbook of English Studies* 18 (1988): 68–92.

2. Barbara Johnson, "Gender and Poetry: Charles Baudelaire and Marcelline Debordes-Valmore," in *Displacements: Women, Tradition, Literatures in French*, ed. Joan DeJean and Nancy K. Miller (Baltimore: Johns Hopkins Univ. Press, 1991), 163–81.

3. Nancy J. Vickers, "Diana Described: Scattered Woman and Scattered Rhyme," in *Writing and Sexual Difference*, ed. Elizabeth Abel (Chicago: Univ. of Chicago Press, 1980), 95–110.

4. Poovey, *The Proper Lady*, 1–5; Susan Gubar, "The Female Monster in Augustan Satire," *Signs* 3 (1977): 384; Patricia Meyer Spacks, "Ev'ry Woman Is at Heart a Rake," *Eighteenth-Century Studies* 8 (1974): 27–28, 36–37.

5. Marlene LeGates, "The Cult of Womanhood in Eighteenth-Century Thought," *Eighteenth-Century Studies* 10 (1976): 24; Poovey, *The Proper Lady*, 6; Nussbaum, "Pope's 'To a Lady' and the Eighteenth-Century Woman," *Philological Quarterly* 54 (1975): 446–48, 451.

6. LeGates, "Cult of Womanhood," 21.

7. Nancy Armstrong, *Desire and Domestic Fiction: A Political History of the Novel* (New York: Oxford Univ. Press, 1987), 67.

8. Charlotte Sussman, "'I Wonder Whether Poor Miss Sally Godfrey Be Living or Dead': The Married Woman and the Rise of the Novel," *Diacritics* 20 (1990): 92.

9. Ann Rosalind Jone, "'Nets and Bridles': Early Modern Conduct Books and Sixteenth-Century Women's Lyrics," in *The Ideology of Conduct: Essays on Literature and the History of Sexuality*, ed. Nancy Armstrong and Leonard Tennenhouse (New York: Methuen, 1987), 39–72.

10. Armstrong, *Desire*.

11. Felicity Nussbaum, "Juvenal, Swift, and *The Folly of Love*," *Eighteenth-Century Studies* 9.4 (1976): 550.

12. Gubar, "Female Monster," 382.

13. Felicity Nussbaum, *The Brink of All We Hate: English Satires on Women 1660–1750* (Lexington: Univ. Press of Kentucky, 1984), 15; David Foxon, *Libertine Literature in England, 1660–1745* (New Hyde Park, N.Y.: University Books, 1965), 12–15, 30.

14. It is always seen as an accident of history that Jean de Meung's satiric and antifeminist denunciation of love comprises the second half of Guillaume de Lorris's courtly love poem, the famous *Romance of the Rose*, but I am claiming here that de Lorris needed de Meung's mockery.

Annette H. Tomarken has tracked the emergence of the Lucianic blason (the ironic contre-blason) in Italy and in France at roughly the same time that Petrarch wrote his sonnets and the Pléiade wrote their hymnes-blasons praising parts of women's bodies (1530s and 1540s) ("The Lucianic Blason: A Study of an Edition by Jean de Tournes," in *Literature and the Arts in the Reign of Frances I*, ed. Pauline M. Smith and Ian D. MacFarlane [Lexington, Ky.: French Forum Publishers, 1985]). Even in Tomarken's account, which argues for the centrality of contre-blasons (e.g., encomiums to Gout), parodic blasons are seen as potentially undermining rather than defining the form; yet she notes quizzically that parodies of the blason appeared a year before it was defined by Sebillet (208). Thus, blasons at their inception needed their counter-blasons; parody makes definition possible.

15. Paul Salzman, *English Prose Fiction 1558–1700: A Critical History* (Oxford: Clarendon Univ. Press, 1985), 271–72.

16. Mennipean satire in general has been known, since Burton's *Anatomy of Melancholy*, as an anatomy and thereby relates that satiric, (overly) intellectualized mode of analysis to dissection (Northrup Frye, *Anatomy of Criticism: Four Essays* [Princeton, N.J.: Princeton Univ. Press, 1957], 311). The traditional association of satire and surgery (or worse) upon a female body is still strong in 1729, when *The Art of Knowing Women: or, the Female Sex Dissected* was published (quoted in Felicity Nussbaum, "Juvenal," 543).

17. "Blown" can mean in full bloom, but it also means "ruined," "spoiled," or "rotten," as in "blown meat" (see *OED, The Compact Edition,* s.v. "blow," verb 1, definitions 28 and 30).

18. Sir George Etherege, "To a Very Young Lady," in *Poetry of the Restoration 1653–1700,* ed. Vivian de Sola Pinto (London: Heinemann, 1966), 31–32.

19. Thomas Shipman, "Beauties Periphrasis," in de Sola Pinto, *Poetry of the Restoration,* 39, lines 9–12.

20. In Shipman's parody, the courtly-love poet protests that he does not really rape his lady in his poem: she is "Not here expos'd to [the poet's and readers'] wild desires" because the bright light of her "vertue" scares off "Such thoughts . . . / As rav'nous Beasts retreat from fires" ("Beauties Periphrasis," 41, lines 53–56).

21. Felicity Nussbaum, "Juvenal," 545.

22. Doody points out that, in his *Remarks on the Life and Writings of Dr. Jonathan Swift* (1752), Lord Orrery "elaborates with fascinated hostility on Swift's friendships with women" despite the fact that Swift "lack[ed] the appropriate sexual feelings" (Doody, "Swift among the Women," 68–69). But Orrery's horror contrasts starkly with the popularity of his poems, even among close friends.

23. Sigmund Freud, "A Child is Being Beaten" (1919), in *Sexuality and the Psychology of Love,* ed. Philip Rieff (New York: Collier Books, 1963), 114.

24. See Julia Kristeva, *Powers of Horror: An Essay on Abjection,* trans. Leon S. Roudiez (New York: Columbia Univ. Press, 1982), 38–40.

25. On how satire invites us to identify satiric persona with satiric object, see Alvin Kernan, "A Theory of Satire," in *The Cankered Muse: Satire of the English Renaissance* (New Haven, Conn.: Yale Univ. Press, 1959), esp. 266–69; and Frederic Bogel, "Dulness Unbound: Rhetoric and Pope's *Dunciad," PMLA* 97 (1982): 844–55, who analyzes the problem "that *The Dunciad* seems to weaken certain significant barriers that the critics—like Pope himself—have a powerful stake in maintaining, in particular, barriers between wit and dunce, poet and Dulness, us and them" (844).

26. *Jonathan Swift: The Complete Poems,* ed. Pat Rogers (New Haven, Conn.: Yale Univ. Press, 1983), 463–66, lines 17–22, 118.

27. See Donald Greene, "On Swift's 'Scatological' Poems," *Sewanee Review* 75 (1967): 676.

28. Vickers, "Diana Described"; Cathy Yandell, "*A La Recherche du Corps Perdu*: A Capstone of the Renaissance *Blasons Anatomiques," Romance Notes* 26 (1985): 142.

29. Elizabeth Cropper, "On Beautiful Women, Parmigianino, *Petrarchismo,* and the Vernacular Style," *Art Bulletin* 58 (1976): 385–86.

30. Johnson, "Gender and Poetry," 175.

31. See Kristeva, *Powers,* 38–41.

32. Jean Laplanche, *Life and Death in Psychoanalysis,* trans. Jeffrey Mehlman (Baltimore: Johns Hopkins Univ. Press, 1976), 85–102.

33. "The category 'of literature' names the cultural capital of the old bourgeoisie" (John Guillory, *Cultural Capital: The Problem of Literary Canon Formation* [Chicago: Univ. of Chicago Press, 1993], x, 122–23). "The old bourgeoisie" was newly establishing its cultural hegemony at the end of the eighteenth and beginning of the nineteenth centuries. Some accounts of the emergence of literature as a disciplinary object contradict Guillory's view insofar as they situate its emergence earlier. For instance, Donna Stanton argues "that the modern meaning of literature first emerged in the seventeenth century" (Editor's Column, "What is Literature?—1994," *PMLA* 109.3 [May 1994], 364 n. 1, citing Timothy Reiss, *The Meaning of Literature* [Ithaca, N.Y.: Cornell Univ. Press, 1992]). However, there is much evidence to support a later dating. Three elements of our definition of literature as a concept were not fully in

place until the Romantic period: (1) "literature" had come to designate an object rather than, as it did in John's dictionary, a skill (John Vladimir Price, "The Reading of Philosophical Literature," in *Books and Their Readers in Eighteenth-Century England,* ed. Isabel Rivers [New York: St. Martin's Press, 1982], 173–74); (2) literature had to come to be generically distinguished from philosophical writings, which it was not for Johnson, Hume and Swift (Price 174–76; Alistair Fowler, "Genre and the Literary Canon," *New Literary History* 11 [1979–80], 106–8); (3) and finally, there had to be the modern sense of literary tradition. This sense of a distinctively literary history was first formulated by Thomas Warton's *History of English Literature* and Johnson's *Lives of the Poets* (René Wellek, *The Rise of English Literary History* [Chapel Hill, N.C.: Univ. of North Carolina Press, 1941] 47, 140–41, 166) but was not completed until, from antiquarian researches culminating in the 1780s and 1790s, "there was an actual *history* not of literature *per se,* but of poetry in English" (Stuart Curran, "Romantic Poetry: Why and Wherefore?," in *The Cambridge Companion to British Romanticism,* ed. Stuart Curran [New York: Cambridge Univ. Press, 1993], 225). This chapter examines some of the ideological requirements that form literature into an object; on the cultural work needed to transform literature into canonical objects, see chapter 5.

34. Peter Stallybrass and Allon White, *The Politics and Poetics of Transgression* (Ithaca, N.Y.: Cornell Univ. Press, 1986).

35. [H. Curll, printer], *The Ladies Miscellany* (1718, 1720, 1732); [H. Curll, printer], *The Altar of Love* (1727, 1731); *The Ladies Miscellany: or a Curious Collection of Amorous Poems and Merry Tales* (1730); "Sir Butterfly Maggot, Kt.," *The Gentlemen's Miscellany* (1730, 1731); [A. Moore, printer], *The Beau's Miscellany. Being a new and curious collection of amorous tales, diverting songs, and entertaining poems* (1731, 1736); "T. G.," *The Flowers of Parnassus; or the Ladie's Miscellany,* an annual published two years (1735, 1737); *The School of Venus: or the Lady's Miscellany* (2d ed., 1739); *A New Academy of Compliments* (1748, 1772, 1789); "E. W.," *The Lover's Manual: being a choice collection of poems from modern authors* (1753), reprinted in 1760 as *The Muses Library, and young gentleman [sic] and ladies polite instructor;* "G. Gaylove," *A Select Collection of Original Love Letters, to which are subjoin'd poems by eminent ladies* (1755; perhaps a parody of Colman and Thornton's collection, *Poems by Eminent Ladies,* 2 vols. [London: R. Baldwin, 1755], with the intention of elucidating their motives in gathering their collection?).

36. *Poems for Ladies, selected under the inspection of a lady* (1777); [Oliver Goldsmith, named on the 1770 title page], *Poems for Young Ladies. In three parts. Devotional, Moral, and Entertaining* (1767, 1770, 1785, 1792), "that innocence may read without a blush" (preface, n.p., quoted in Ian Michael, *The Teaching of English from the Sixteenth Century to 1870* [New York: Cambridge Univ. Press, 1987], 180); *The Ladies Poetical Magazine* (an annual, 1781–82, reprinted in 1791); G. Wright, *The Lady's Miscellany: or pleasing essays, poems, stories, and examples* (1793, 1797).

37. John Dryden, "Discourse concerning the Original and Progress of Satire" (1692), in *The Works of John Dryden*, Hugh T. Swedenberg Jr., gen. ed. (Berkeley: Univ. of California Press, 1974), 4: 2–90.

38. Hugh T. Swedenberg Jr., commentary in Dryden, *Works*, 4:526.

39. As evinced most notably by the title of the slightly pornographic sex manual, *Aristotle's Masterpiece*. Romans were associated with homosexuality; I am indebted to Richard Dellamora for the distinction.

40. Dryden, "Discourse," 4:30–31, 44, 32.

41. See W.B. Carnochan, "Some Suppressed Verses in Dryden's Translation of Juvenal VI," *TLS* (21 Jan. 1972), esp. 74, cols. 1 and 2, the bracketed passages that Dryden added to the received text of Juvenal's original.

42. "It was not for a *Clodius* to accuse Adulterers, especially when *Augustus* was of that number" (Dryden, *Progress*, in *Works*, 4:69).

43. Alexander Pope, *Dialogue II* of *Epilogue to the Satires* (1738), in *Poetry and Prose of Alexander Pope*, ed. Aubrey Williams (Boston: Houghton Mifflin, 1969), 286–94, lines 212–19; hereafter quoted by line number in the text.

44. Swift, "Cassinus and Peter: A Tragical Elegy," in *Complete Poems*, 89–90.

45. Doody, "Swift among the Women," 69.

46. Kernan, *The Cankered Muse*, 28.

47. Swift, "Cassinus and Peter," lines 17–18, 21–22.

48. Kernan, *The Cankered Muse*, 28; Maynard Mack, "The Muse of Satire," in *Satire: Modern Essays in Criticism*, ed. Ronald Paulson (Englewood Cliffs, N.J.: Prentice-Hall, 1971), 192.

49. See Mack, "The Muse of Satire," 200.

50. Claude Rawson, "The Character of Swift's Satire: Reflections on Swift, Johnson, and Human Restlessness," in *The Character of Swift's Satire: A Revised Focus*, ed. Claude Rawson (Newark: Univ. of Delaware Press, 1983), 35.

51. On Swift's antirationalism, see Ellen Pollak, *The Poetics of Sexual Myth: Gender and Ideology in the Verse of Swift and Pope* (Chicago: Univ. of Chicago Press, 1985), 136; Robert C. Elliott, *The Power of Satire: Magic, Ritual, Art* (Princeton, N.J.: Princeton Univ. Press, 1960), 109. That Swift was satirizing the Houyhnhnms should be obvious from the fact that they are horses and that we have to whinny like horses to say their names. The phrase "unbridled appetites" appears in *Aristotle's Masterpiece*, quoted in Roy Porter, "'The Secrets of Generation Display'd': *Aristotle's Master-piece* in Eighteenth-Century England," in *Unauthorized Sexual Behavior during the Enlightenment*, ed. Robert P. Maccubbin, special issue of *Eighteenth-Century Life* 9.3 (May 1985): 8. The pornographic passage that Dryden expurgated from Juvenal's Sixth figures one of the participants as a "Panting Stallion" (see Carnochan, cited in note 38 above). In Robert Gould's "The Play-House, A Satyr," the actress's entourage of Fops is called "A Leash of Stallions" and "a Lascivious Herd" (Montague Summers, *The Restoration Theater* [London: Keagan Paul, Trench, Trubner, 1934], appendix 1, 299).

52. Felicity Nussbaum, "Juvenal," 551.

53. Sandra Gilbert and Susan Gubar, *Madwoman in the Attic: The Woman Writer and the Nineteenth-Century Literary Imagination* (New Haven, Conn.: Yale Univ. Press, 1979), 240–43.

54. That is, by claiming that Mary Shelley's male characters, characters condemned by the novel, are "really" females (Victor is really female [ibid., 229–34]; "Victor Frankenstein's male monster may really be a female in disguise" [237], which they subsequently assume by showing his similarity to Eve [239–40]), Gilbert and Gubar manufacture misogyny at least as much as they "find" it. Insofar as they insist, justifiably or not, that Mary Shelley's monster depicts "woman," their own work makes the misogynist move of designating "monstrosity" as female, a move Shelley herself does not make (her monster is explicitly male, and even seeks a female mate). Their work is misogynist insofar as it attributes to "filthy femaleness" (a phrase repeated throughout the chapter, alliteration again pointing to the pleasure of such a repetition) the filthy materiality that the artifact in front of them does not attribute to women.

55. There is no doubt that Freud's theories of sadism are misogynous and perhaps, as some have maintained, they have even added to the oppression of women by justifying the sexual violence they describe; see Kathleen Barry, "On the History of Cultural Sadism," in *Against Sadomasochism: Radical Feminist Analysis*, ed. Robin Ruth Linden, Darlene R. Pagano, Diana E.H. Russell, and Susan Leigh Star (East Palo Alto, Calif.: Frog in the Wall Press, 1982), 51–65. But again, Freud does not describe "natural" desire, only desire as it has been socially constructed. Freud's analyses can be used as long as one is aware of their complicity in propagating those desires that serve the interests of hegemony. I agree with Foucauldian theorists who presume that psychoanalysts do not "discover" true desire underneath repressions, but rather, as agents of their culture, *produce* culturally recognizable forms of desire in the process of ostensibly discovering it (see Armstrong, *Desire,* 13).

56. Jean I. Marsden, "Ideology, Sex, and Satire: The Case of Thomas Shadwell," in *Cutting Edges: Postmodern Critical Essays on Eighteenth-Century Satire*, ed. James E. Gill (Knoxville: Univ. of Tennessee Press, 1995), 43.

57. Rose Zimbardo, "The Semiotics of Restoration Satire," in Gill, *Cutting Edges*, 23–24.

58. Edward Said, "Swift's Tory Anarchy," *Eighteenth-Century Studies* 3.1 (1969): 49, 48–66.

59. In *Jonathan Swift*, ed. Robert A. Greenberg (New York: Norton, 1973).

60. Elliott, *The Power of Satire*, 215.

61. Greenberg, *Jonathan Swift*, 461–62

62. That simile comes from Bernard Mandeville, *A Modest Defence of Publick STEWS* (1724), Augustan Reprint Society no. 162 (Los Angeles: Clark Memorial Library, 1973), xi.

2. Capitalism and Rape

1. This chapter depends on the work of Eve Sedgwick in *Between Men: English Literature and Male Homosocial Desire* (New York: Columbia Univ. Press, 1985), and particularly her chapter on Wycherley. The she-tragedy is, I want to suggest, another version of homosocial exchange, but a failed version. See also Vaska Tumir, "She-Tragedy and Its Men: Conflict and Form in *The Orphan* and *The Fair Penitent*," *Studies in English Literature* 30 (1990): 411–28.

2. Catharine A. MacKinnon, "Feminism, Marxism, Method, and the State: An Agenda for Theory," *Signs* 7.3 (1982): 515–44.

3. Hazel Carby, *Deconstructing Womanhood: The Emergence of the Afro-American Woman Novelist* (New York: Oxford Univ. Press, 1987), 18; quoted in Lynn A. Higgins and Brenda R. Silver, eds., *Rape and Representation* (New York: Columbia Univ. Press, 1991), 9–10.

4. Laura Brown defines the genre of "she-tragedies" as that kind of tragedy which "uses the passive female as its pivot" ("The Defenseless Woman and the Development of English Tragedy," *Studies in English Literature* 22 [1982]: 429–30).

5. Joyce Appleby, "Ideology and Theory: The Tension between Political and Economic Liberalism in Seventeenth-Century England," *American Historical Review* 81 (June 1976): 515, quoted in Neil McKendrick, John Brewer, and J.H. Plumb, *The Birth of a Consumer Society: The Commercialization of Eighteenth-Century England* (Bloomington: Indiana Univ. Press, 1982), 16.

6. R.B. Outhwaite, "Marriage as Business: Opinions on the Rise in Aristocratic Bridal Portions in Early Modern England," in *Business Life and Public Policy: Essays in Honour of D. C. Coleman*, ed. Neil McKendrick and R.B. Outhwaite (New York: Cambridge Univ. Press, 1986), 25.

7. Lisa Jardine, *Still Harping on Daughters: Women and Drama in the Age of Shakespeare* (Sussex, England: Harvester Press, 1983), 78.

8. Property had to "become a right unconditional on the performance of any social function" and "become more generally alienable" or transferable (C.B. Macpherson, "Capitalism and the Changing Concept of Property," in *Feudalism, Capitalism and Beyond*, ed. Eugene Kamenka and Ronald S. Neale [Canberra: Australian National Univ. Press, 1975], 106, 111). Macpherson discusses the difference between a "possessive market society" and "customary or status society" in *The Political Theory of Possessive Individualism: Hobbes to Locke* (New York: Oxford Univ. Press, 1962), 48–50.

9. McKendrick, Brewer, and Plumb, *Consumer Society*, 16.

10. Jardine, *Still Harping on Daughters*, 141–51.

11. Sir Simonds D'Ewes, comp., *Journals of All the Parliaments during the Reign of Queen Elizabeth*, Journal of Lords, 69–70; 5 Elizabeth, c. 6, Stat. L., vol. 6, p. 187; Stat. R, part 1, vol. 4, p. 428. These three sources are quoted in Frances Elizabeth Baldwin, "Sumptuary Legislation and Personal Regulation in England," in *Johns Hopkins University Studies in Historical and Political Sci-*

ence (Baltimore: Johns Hopkins Univ. Press, 1926), 44:208–9. 5 Elizabeth, c.6, Stat. L law states:

> [W]hosoever shall sell or deliver to any person (having not in possession lands or fees to the clear yearly value of 3000 [pounds]) any foreign wares, not first grown or first wrought within the queen's dominions, appertaining to the clothing or adorning of the body, for which wares or the workmanship thereof, the seller shall not have received the whole money or satisfaction in hand, or within eight and twenty days after the making or delivery thereof; the seller, maker, etc. shall be without all remedy by order of any law, custom or de[c]ree, to recover any recompense for such wares or the workmanship, whatsoever assurance he shall have by bond, surety, promise or pain of the party or any other: and all assurances and bonds in that case shall be void.
>
> (vol. 6, p. 187, quoted in Baldwin, 209.)

Thus, this law express paranoia not only about credit but also about foreign imports.

12. Phillip Stubbes, *The Anatomie of Abuses* (London, 1583; reprint, New York: Garland, 1973), 8ff.; quoted in Baldwin, "Sumptuary Legislation," 206.

13. The example given in the *OED* that is dated 1670 may not actually refer to commerce (see meaning no. 22), but the two examples from Steele (1712) and Defoe (*The English Tradesman*, 1727) definitely use "business" to mean financial transactions (see meanings no. 21, 22). The word "business" is used incessantly in Wycherley's *The Country Wife* (1674) and *The Plain-Dealer* (1677), and although it certainly does appear that wealth is at stake in all of these dealings called "business," the word refers primarily to public affairs in general, from which wealth will result. Sir Jasper Fidget habitually contrasts Horner's "business of pleasure" with his own "pleasure in business," but his business always takes place at Whitehall, that is, presumably, with the king and his ministers (*The Country Wife*, in *Restoration and Eighteenth-Century Comedy*, ed. Scott McMillin [New York: W.W. Norton, 1973], 7, 23, 26–27, 36–37). Business could also refer to professional affairs (meaning no. 12), such as the Widow Blackacre's many lawsuits, but again the "business" mentioned is the work of courtiers, flattery, and false promises, carried on at "the Galleries at *Whitehall*" (*The Plain-Dealer*, in *English Plays 1660–1820*, comp. A.E. Morgan [New York: Harper Brothers, 1935], 178). The "business" described in *The Orphan* is explicitly the trade of courtiership and service to the king (Thomas Otway, *The Orphan*, ed. Aline Mackenzie Taylor, Regents Restoration Drama Series [Lincoln, Neb.: Univ. of Nebraska Press, 1976], act 2, lines 15–137; cited hereafter in the text and the notes by act and line number).

14. Otway's play is overtly royalist, dedicated to the Duke of York, the future James II, in the midst of parliamentary attempts to exclude him from the throne (see Philip Harth, "Political Interpretations of *Venice Preserv'd*," *Mod-*

ern Philology 85.4 [May 1988], 372). However, that this play *has* a moral, that it follows out the consequences of aristocrats who rebel or misbehave and punishes them for it, marks it as bourgeois. See Raymond Williams, "Sentimentalism and Social History," in *The Long Revolution* (London: Chatto and Windus, 1961), 256–60, reprinted in McMillin, *Restoration Comedy*, 554–57. *The Orphan* is a pathetic tragedy, a precursor or early incarnation of the bourgeois tragedy that would dominate the stage in the eighteenth century (Laura Brown, *English Dramatic Form, 1660–1760: An Essay in Generic History* [New Haven, Conn.: Yale Univ. Press, 1981] 86–92).

15. René Girard, *Violence and the Sacred,* trans. Patrick Gregory (Baltimore: Johns Hopkins Univ. Press, 1977). In *Restoration Politics and Drama: The Plays of Thomas Otway, 1675–1683* (Newark, Del.: Univ. of Delaware Press, 1995), Jessica Munns presents a similar argument, that Monimia serves as a scapegoat to try to stem the violence of a sacrificial crisis (161–62). But although Munns is concerned with how the play effects changes in "cavalier ideology" (164), she is not concerned to describe the play's relation to specific economic structures, as I am here; nonetheless, she does also see the play as confusedly presenting two modes of (making a) living: "The main characters [in *The Orphan*] are held in suspension between, on the one hand, the complex but fracturing fabric of custom, usage, and habit (as indicated by the brother's botched hunt, the failure to celebrate the royal birthday, the breaking of the incest taboo, and the collapse of the family unit) and, on the other, a universe of personal gratification that functions without the ramification of natural analogy or reference to God, king, or father" (149).

16. Frances Ferguson, "Rape and the Rise of the Novel," in *Misogyny, Misandry, and Misanthropy*, ed. R. Howard Bloch and Frances Ferguson (Berkeley: Univ. of California Press, 1989), 91.

17. Otway, *Orphan*, epilogue, 101, lines 15–19.

18. In "Marriage as Business," Outhwaite provides a table of marriage portions offered by peers from 1300 to 1729 (24). His table compares the data collected by Lawrence Stone (*The Crisis of the Aristocracy 1558–1641* [Oxford: Oxford Univ. Press, 1965], 644–45; 790–91) to that collected by John P. Cooper ("Patterns of Inheritance and Settlement by Great Landowners from the Fifteenth to the Eighteenth Centuries," in *Family and Inheritance: Rural Society in Western Europe 1200–1800*, ed. Jack Goody, Joan Thirsk, and E.P. Thompson [Cambridge: Cambridge Univ. Press, 1976], 307). Cooper contests many of Stone's arguments, but Outhwaite points out that their data basically agrees from the period of 1525–49 onward (23). For the years 1675 to 1729, Stone records an average portion of 9,700 pounds, Cooper one of 9,350 pounds.

19. Compare Polydore with Chamont: when asked if he has "visited the court . . . since [his] return" from the battlefield, he replies, "I have no business there. I have not slavish temperance enough" (2.112–14); in courtship, too,

Serina realizes, he is not the type of man who "[w]ill flatter, feign, and make an art of love" (2.104).

20. Karl Marx, *Capital: A Critique of Political Economy*, vol. 1, trans. Ben Fowkes, with an introduction by Ernest Mandel (New York: Vintage Books, 1977), 874–76.

21. Raymond Williams, *The Country and the City* (New York: Oxford Univ. Press, 1973), 50. On the country and city debate in politics, see H.T. Dickinson, *Liberty and Property: Political Ideology in Eighteenth-Century Britain* (New York: Holmes and Meier, 1977). On the country and city debate in Restoration drama, see Maximillian E. Novak, "Margery Pinchwife's 'London Disease': Restoration Comedy and the Libertine Offensive of the 1670s," *Structure in the Literary Imagination* 10.1 (spring 1977): 1–23.

22. Williams, *Country and City*, 49.

23. Theodor Reik, *Masochism in Sex and Society*, trans. Margaret H. Beigel and Gertrude M. Kurth (New York: Grove Press, 1962), 145, 163, quoted in Gilles Deleuze, *Masochism: An Interpretation of Coldness and Cruelty* (New York: George Braziller, 1971), 78 n. 1; reprinted as Gilles Deleuze, *Coldness and Cruelty*, in *Masochism* (New York: Zone Books, 1991), 137 n. 28.

24. Deleuze, *Masochism: An Interpretation*, 77; *Coldness and Cruelty*, 88.

25. Marcel Mauss, *The Gift: The Form and Reason for Exchange in Archaic Societies*, trans. W.D. Halls, with an introduction by Mary Douglas (London: Routledge, 1990). Mauss's conclusions about the implications of a gift economy for capitalism are colored by a certain kind of nostalgia and thus eliminate the violent implications of giving that are prominent elsewhere in the book.

26. Chamont is right, in fact; Polydore has already tried to extract sexual favors in repayment for Acasto's generosity (1.322–38; 2.346–49).

27. Mauss, *The Gift*, 36–37.

28. It should be noted that there are distinctively homoerotic overtones in the play; see for example the ambiguity of Castalio's speech to Polydore about how he loves Monimia:

> Love reigns a very tyrant in my heart,
> Attended on his throne by all his guards
> Of furious wishes, fears, and nice suspicions.
> I could not bear a rival in my friendship,
> I am so much in love, and fond of thee.
> (1.142–46)

It is not really clear here where Castalio is talking about his love for Monimia and where he refers to his "friendship" for Polydore; ambiguity makes them indistinguishable. However, for the most part, capitalist homosocial relations are not homoeroticized, as they are, for example, in Wycherley's *Country Wife* (Sedgwick, *Between Men*, 49–66).

29. Sedgwick remarks on the relative absence of homophobia in the homosocial desire expressed in the relations of paternalism (*Between Men,* 162). This analysis fits into Sedgwick's program as an attempt to see how and when and where homosocial desire is eroticized.

30. Julia Kristeva, *The Powers of Horror: An Essay on Abjection,* trans. Leon S. Roudiez (New York: Columbia Univ. Press, 1982).

31. René Girard, *Violence and the Sacred.*

32. Mary Douglas, *Purity and Danger: An Analysis of the Concepts of Pollution and Taboo* (London: Ark Press, 1984), 40.

33. Ibid., 35.

34. Ibid., 169–70.

35. Ibid., 171.

36. Girard and Douglas use the term "scapegoat" differently, and I am trying to make sense of that here. For Douglas, scapegoating would instigate the sacrificial crisis; it is always a pejorative term for her, and not the same as sacrifice. For Girard, scapegoating is "incarnating the sacrificial crisis" (*Violence and the Sacred,* 80): it can refer to mimetic violence committed in an act of mimetic rivalry or to sacrifice of the surrogate victim, which thereby ends the crisis (see pp. 49-50 above).

37. Girard, *Violence and the Sacred,* 291.

38. Ibid., 295.

39. Ibid., 50, 51.

40. Stallybrass and White offer a contemporaneous example of violence swelled by indifferentiation once social structure has broken down. With the disintegration of the patronage system, authorship can be envisaged only as "a system of competitive differentiation": "[Pope's] work suggests that even more than Jonson he could envisage authorship only as a system of competitive differentiation which could put him above the Theobalds, the Cibbers and the Grub Street hacks. Indeed Pope could not even imagine the union of knowledge and power, poet and prince which Jonson sometimes believed might stabilize differentiation through its relation to a single, fixed place of authority" (Peter Stallybrass and Allon White, *The Politics and Poetics of Transgression* [Ithaca, N.Y.: Cornell Univ. Press, 1986], 117).

41. Girard, *Violence and the Sacred,* 49–50.

42. Peter Laslett, introduction to John Locke, *Two Treatises of Government,* ed. Peter Laslett (New York: Cambridge Univ. Press, 1960), 45–66.

43. Lois G. Schwoerer, "The Bill of Rights: Epitome of the Revolution of 1688–89," in *Three British Revolutions: 1641, 1688, 1776,* ed. J.G.A. Pocock (Princeton, N.J.: Princeton Univ. Press, 1980), 224–43.

44. Marx, *Capital,* 152.

45. Charles Mackay, *Memoirs of Extraordinary Popular Delusions and the Madness of Crowds,* 2d. ed. (1852).

46. Jonathan Swift, "Upon the South Sea Project," 14 December 1720, in

Jonathan Swift: The Complete Poems, ed. Pat Rogers (New Haven, Conn.: Yale Univ. Press, 1983), pp. 207–14, lines 89–92.

47. Mackay, *Memoirs*, 52.

48. [Edward Ward], "A South-Sea Ballad" [1720], quoted in Mackay, *Memoirs*, 52.

49. J.H. Plumb, *England in the Eighteenth Century* (New York: Penguin, 1950), 14, 17.

50. Mackay, *Memoirs*, 70–71.

51. Plumb, *England in the Eighteenth Century*, 17.

52. Mackay, *Memoirs*, 55, 57, 60–62.

53. Plumb, *England in the Eighteenth Century*, 24–25.

54. Mackay, *Memoirs*, 55–56.

55. Wiliam Maitland, *The History of London: from its Foundation by the Romans to the Present Time* ([S.L.: s.n.], printed by Samuel Richardson, 1739), quoted in ibid., 55.

56. Quoted in ibid., 54.

57. Mackay, *Memoirs*, 54.

58. Thus Pope comments on the crash: "Methinks God has punish'd the avaritious as he often punishes the sinners, in their own way, in the very sin itself" (*The Correspondence of Alexander Pope*, ed. George Sherburn (Oxford: Clarendon Press, 1965), 2:53–54, quoted in Colin Nicholson, *Writing and the Rise of Finance: Capital Satires of the Early Eighteenth Century* (New York: Cambridge Univ. Press, 1994), 66.

59. Quoted in Mackay, *Memoirs*, 86.

60. Mackay, *Memoirs*, 72.

61. Girard, *Violence and the Sacred*, 143, 152.

62. Ibid., 48.

63. Ibid., 37.

64. Ibid., 268

65. It is precisely at the moment of the Exclusion Crisis when those egalitarian notions informing the rise of British liberalism are no longer just making noise but making history. And, as Thomas Laqueur has shown, medical representations of women's bodies as essentially different from men's preserve an absolute (i.e., biological) difference at precisely the moment when a political ideology emerges that threatens to eradicate all difference (*Making Sex: Body and Gender from the Greeks to Freud* [Cambridge, Mass.: Harvard Univ. Press, 1990], 196–97). Katherine Eisaman Maus has argued that it is precisely new notions that women differ *essentially* from men that made it no longer acceptable, in 1660, for men to play women's roles on stage ("'Playhouse Flesh and Blood': Sexual Ideology and the Restoration Actress," *ELH* 46 [1979]: 595–617). For Laqueur, the medical community's discovery that the female body is essentially different from the male justifies not extending new, politically subversive egalitarian notions to them (18). But the new "biology of incommensu-

rability," I would argue, does much more than that: it provides a difference in a world in which all differences are potentially leveled; this essential difference makes it possible for the figure of woman to play the role of scapegoat.

66. Nicholas Rowe, *The Tragedy of Jane Shore*, in *British Dramatists from Dryden to Sheridan*, ed. George Nettleton and Arthur Case (Boston: Houghton Mifflin, 1939), 111–220; the quotation is from act 4, scene 1, lines 159–69.

67. Ian Donaldson, *The Rapes of Lucretia: A Myth and Its Transformations* (Oxford: Clarendon Press, 1982), 17, quoting Michel Lieris, *L'Age d'homme* (Paris, 1939), 142–43.

68. See Ferguson, "Rape and the Rise of the Novel."

3. Engendering Capitalist Desire

1. My account thus fits in with that of "the grotesque body" (Peter Stallybrass and Allon White, *The Politics and Poetics of Transgression* [Ithaca: Cornell Univ. Press, 1986]). Stallybrass and White show how the bourgeoisie "carved out a domain between the realm of kings and the world of the alley-ways and taverns, . . . by forcing together the high and the low as contaminated equivalents, somehow in league with each other and part of a conspiracy of exchange and promiscuity" (109). This process creates "the grotesque body," "a *hybrid* creature trying to straddle the world of popular fairground culture and the 'higher' world of humanistic ethics and ideals" (112). Augustan poetry is simultaneously repelled and fascinated by this body (108–13), which it usually represents as female (109).

2. As to Mandeville's feminism, see Frederick B. Kaye, "The Influence of Bernard Mandeville," *Studies in Philology* 19 (1922): 85, reprinted with original page numbers in *Studies in the Literature of the Augustan Age: Essays Collected in Honor of Arthur Ellicott Case*, ed. Richard C. Boys (New York: Gordion Press, 1966); and Gordon S. Vichert, "Bernard Mandeville's *The Virgin Unmask'd*," in *Mandeville Studies*, ed. Irwin Primer (The Hague: Martinus Nijhoff, 1975), 1–10.

3. Raymond Williams, *The Country and the City* (New York: Oxford Univ. Press, 1973), 30.

4. Laura Brown, "Reading Race and Gender: Jonathan Swift," in *Eighteenth-Century Studies*, 23.4 (summer 1990): 429.

5. The notion that consumerism comes from woman's desire to be fashionably dressed, found everywhere in the early-eighteenth-century works, is in no way supported by historical fact. Swift attacks Irish women for importing silk: "It is to gratify the vanity and pride, and luxury of the women, and of the young fops who admire them, that we owe this insupportable grievance of bringing in the instruments of our ruin," viz. "the importation of all unnecessary commodities," ("A Proposal that All the Ladies and Women of Ireland should appear constantly in Irish Manufactures" [1729], in *Prose Works*, ed. Herbert Davis [Oxford: Oxford Univ. Press, 1951], 12:126, cited and dis-

cussed in Brown, "Reading Race and Gender," 431). Similarly, Addison celebrates trade as a means of adorning women (Laura Brown, *Alexander Pope* [Oxford: Basil Blackwell, 1985], 8–22). Nonetheless, we do not know who the consumers were nor, by any stretch, what kind of desires provoked "the consumer revolution."

In "The New Eighteenth Century," (*New York Review of Books* 31.5 [29 Mar. 1984]: 42–48). Lawrence Stone explores various possible ways of accounting for the birth of the desire to buy, including "the rise of new concepts of individualism and materialism," "the herd instinct to imitate," and the "Veblen model of conspicuous consumption" favored by McKendrick (45; see also Neil McKendrick, John Brewer, and J.H. Plumb, *The Birth of a Consumer Society: The Commercialization of Eighteenth-Century England* [Bloomington: Indiana Univ. Press, 1982]). Stone makes some very Mandevillean conclusions about consumerism: "Fashion drove the market. It altered from year to year, almost from month to month, so that suppliers, Josiah Wedgwood for example, were obsessed with the need to keep up with the fickle winds of change in taste" (45). Stone's comment is indebted to *The Fable of the Bees*; Stone thus quotes Mandeville to back up his ideas about fashion ("Luxury employed a million of the poor, and odious Pride a million more. Envy itself and vanity were ministers of industry" [Bernard Mandeville], *The Fable of the Bees*, ed. F.B. Kaye, 2 vols. (Oxford: Clarendon Press, 1924), 1:25, hereafter cited in the text and the notes by volume and page number]). But Stone does not associate "fashion" or "fickleness" with women and feminine fops, as Mandeville and other eighteenth-century writers do: "We do not know," Stone points out, "exactly who bought or what really impelled them to do so" (45).

6. The poem portion of the *Fable* was first published in 1705 under the title *The Grumbling Hive*. It was republished in 1714 "with a prose commentary of about two hundred pages appended" (Kaye, "Influence," 84) and renamed *The Fable of the Bees: or, Private Vices Publick Benefits*. The *Fable* was reprinted and expanded in 1723, 1724, 1725, 1728, 1729, 1732, and 1733. See Kaye, "Influence," 84–86, and Kaye's introduction to Mandeville, *The Fable of the Bees*, ed. Kaye.

7. Hirschman has written about how the eighteenth century revised Christian categories of sin (avarice, pride, and luxury) into productive social virtues. My account of this scapegoating process fits in well with his discussion of how eighteenth-century writers tried to distinguish between sinful passions and mercantile interests. See Albert O. Hirschman, *The Passions and the Interests: Political Arguments for Capitalism before Its Triumph* (Princeton, N.J.: Princeton Univ. Press, 1977).

8. Adam Smith, *The Theory of Moral Sentiments*, facsimile ed. (New York: Garland Publishing, 1971), 485, quoted in the appendix to Mandeville, *The Fable of the Bees*, ed. Kaye, 2:414.

9. There is considerable debate over whether Mandeville was a mercantilist on the one hand (T.A. Horne, *The Social Thought of Bernard Mandeville: Vir-*

tue and Commerce in Early Eighteenth-Century England, [New York: Columbia Univ. Press, 1978], 66, 70, 106 n. 56, 107 n. 74; Jacob Viner, introduction to Bernard Mandeville, *A Letter to Dion*, Augustan Reprint Society no. 41 [1732; reprint, Los Angeles: Clark Memorial Library, 1953], 11–14), or a proponent of economic liberalism, laissez-faire economics, or economic individualism on the other (Kaye, "Influence," 105–7; Albert Schatz sees Mandeville as the first to formulate economic individualism), or finally whether his ideas exist somewhere in between the two positions (Nathan Rosenberg, "Mandeville and Laissez-Faire," *Journal of the History of Ideas* 24 [1963]: 183–96). See M.M. Goldsmith, *Private Vices, Public Benefits: Bernard Mandeville's Social and Political Thought* (London: Cambridge Univ. Press, 1985), 123–24; Christopher J. Berry, review of *Private Vices*, by Goldsmith, *History of Political Thought* 8.1 (spring 1987): 174–75. Goldsmith views Mandeville as a proponent of "the spirit of capitalism." Everyone agrees that, mercantilist or protocapitalist, Mandeville was in favor of trade, and in favor of the consumerism or "private vice" that stimulated it; it would be possible, however, as Kaye suggests, to see Mandeville as a philosophical "rigorist," a moral absolutist who condemns on moral grounds all worldly commerce ("Influence," 95–98).

10. By "abject," I do mean miserable and degraded. However, I also mean to refer to the work of Julia Kristeva as described in the introduction to this book.

11. René Girard, *Violence and the Sacred*, trans. Patrick Gregory (Baltimore: Johns Hopkins Univ. Press, 1977) [*Le violence et le sacré* (Paris: Bernard Grasset, 1972)]. As against what Girard calls our "'anti-differential' prejudice" (50 [78]), our egalitarian belief that the desire to level distinctions incites people to violence, Girard argues that the leveling of hierarchies is as much the *cause* of violence as its *result*: "it is not [cultural] distinctions but the loss of them that gives birth to fierce rivalries and sets members of the same family or social group at one another's throats" (49 [77]); "perfect equilibrium invariably leads to violence" (51 ["l'équilibre c'est la violence" (80)]). For more information about the sacrificial crisis and the scapegoating event that ends it, see chapter 2.

12. [Bernard Mandeville], *A Modest Defence of Publick STEWS*, Augustan Reprint Society no. 162 (1724; reprint, Los Angeles: Clark Memorial Library, 1973), xii, cited hereafter by page number in the text and the notes. For the attribution of this originally anonymous text to Mandeville, see F.B. Kaye, "The Writings of Bernard Mandeville: A Bibliographical Survey," *Journal of English and Germanic Philology* 20 (1921): 455. In "The Authorship of *A Modest Defence of Publick Stews*, Etc." (*Neophilologus* 18 [1933]: 200–203), J.H. Harder maintains that the *Defence* was written by "Lawrence Le Fever." As Richard I. Cook rightfully points out, "'Lawrence Le Fever' . . . sounds suspiciously like another of the punning pseudonyms ('Luke Ogle, Esq.' is another) which were attributed to the *Modest Defence* in its subsequent editions" ("'The Great Leviathan of Leachery': Mandeville's *Modest Defence of Publick Stews* [1724]," in Primer, *Mandeville Studies*, 23). It is surely the joke of this name, Lawrence Le Fever, to which Defoe refers when he argues against "tolerating Fornica-

tion," a view held, he says, by "several *warm* Gentlemen" ("Some Considerations upon Streetwalkers," University Microfilms, British Museum, Moore no. 485, p. 4, emphasis added; Defoe's treatise was written to answer Mandeville [Richard I. Cook, introduction to Mandeville's *Defence*, viii n. 6]). It is for that reason that R.S. Crane refutes Harder's contention (critical note in Louis I. Bredvold, "English Literature, 1660–1800: A Current Bibliography," *Philological Quarterly* 13 [1934]: 122–23). This history of attribution comes from Cook, "Leviathan," 23 n. 4.

13. Cook translates the name as "Lover of Whores" ("Leviathan," 27). That it is meant to be translated is further suggested by the name appended to Mandeville's 1711 treatise on hypochondria, "Philopirio." Mandeville says in the preface, "In these Dialogues, I have . . . brought my self upon the Stage; . . . I changed [my name] for that of Philopirio, a Lover of Experience, which I shall always profess to be" (*A Treatise of Hypochondriack and Hysterick Passions*, xi; quoted in G.S. Rousseau, "Mandeville and Europe: Medicine and Philosophy," in Primer, *Mandeville Studies*). Notice that even when Mandeville is stating explicitly that his views are identical to those of his persona, he leaves room for ambiguity: he shall "always *profess* to be" a "Lover of Experience," but is he one?

14. "Mandeville is perfectly serious in his mercantilist contention that the government ought to set itself up in the brothel business. But serious though he may be, Mandeville is also perfectly aware of the comic potentialities of writing about a subject like prostitution from within a framework of such typically mercantilist preoccupations as quality controls, cost estimates, and product distribution" (Cook, "Leviathan," 29–30). Kaye agrees with Cook that Mandeville's proposal to legalize and officially govern "stews," to make them public, is "serious," but on different grounds (see Kaye, introduction to Mandeville, *Fable*, 1.lix-lx, lxxv; Cook, "Leviathan," 25).

15. Cook has given the history of Mandeville's *Defence* (introduction to *Defence*, i-iii; "Leviathan," 22–23). The idea of state-regulated prostitution first appears as a comment ("Remark H") in *The Fable of the Bees*: if the state would allow men to consume "Courtezans and Strumpets," England could then preserve the virtue of its "honest Women" (1:95). In 1723 Mandeville appended his infamous "Essay on Charity and Charity-Schools" to *The Fable of the Bees*. Kaye dates 1723 as the beginning of Mandeville's notoriety ("Influence," 87–88): the Grand Jury of Middlesex County condemned *The Fable* as a public nuisance. Mandeville published *A Modest Defence* one year later, in 1724. As Cook points out, Mandeville repeats verbatim in a self-vindicating article in the *London Journal* (10 Aug. 1723; reprinted in *The Fable of the Bees*, 1:385) the grand jury's charge, that he wrote "with a Design to debauch the Nation."

16. See note 9.

17. "The question of Mandeville's sincerity," Irwin Primer notes, "is still a lively issue" (introduction to *Mandeville Studies*, xiii). On the problem of Mandeville's seriousness, see Gordon Vichert, review of *Private Vices*, by M.M. Goldsmith, *Eighteenth-Century Studies* 20.2 (winter 1986–87): 227; Kaye, "In-

fluence," 101; Jacob Viner, introduction to *A Letter to Dion*, 5, 9–11; and Cook, introduction to *Defence*, v. In *A Modest Defence*, Mandeville commends "publick" over "private whoring" because it might deter "[t]he murdering of Bastard Infants . . . which, besides the Barbarity of it, tends very much to dispeople the Country. And since the Prosperity of any Country is allow'd to depend, in a great measure, on the Number of its Inhabitants, the *Government* ought [to intervene]" (4–5). Is he serious—is Mandeville a *real* Modest Proposer? As Cook points out, this treatise precedes "A Modest Proposal" by five years (introduction to *Defence*, v).

18. Henry Abelove, "Some Speculations on the History of Sexual Intercourse during the Long Eighteenth Century in England," *Genders* 6 (fall 1989): 127. Abelove examines inadequate attempts to account for the population explosion of the eighteenth century and shows that the questions we usually ask about fertility are "ideologically determined," partaking of "that essentialism which so disempowers us both as historians and as political beings" (127). Abelove suggests that population growth occurs because "the particular kind of sexual expression which we moderns often name tendentiously 'sexual intercourse' became importantly more popular at that time in England, and so much more popular that by means of that enhanced popularity alone, without any assistance from a decline in mortality, England's population could have doubled in a relatively short span" (126–27). Traditional historians are unable to account for the rise in fertility because they "defensively transform something that ought to be a problem in the history of sexual behavior into a problem in the history of nuptiality," and are consequently unable to correlate it with factors which would enable more people to marry, but "the new popularity of intercourse so-called [i.e., cross-sex genital intercourse for the sake of reproduction] does correlate rather well with a dramatic rise in virtually all indices of production, a rise which the textbooks call the onset of the Industrial Revolution and which as we know distinguished late eighteenth-century England" (128).

19. Abelove, "Speculations," 128.

20. Cook, "Leviathan," 24.

21. Ibid., 3.

22. Chastity is both something used to buy and something to be bought: it is both currency ("Our Business is to contrive a Method how [men] may be gratify'd, with as little Expence of Female Virtue as possible" [62]), and commodity (as when Phil Porney suggests "the Importation of foreign Women" to meet renewed demands [65]).

23. Again, the text overtly argues these things while tropologically undermining them (in more ways than I have had time to discuss here). I have tried to show that this rhetorical undermining could in a crisis situation actually shore up and sustain the text's logical claims (see note 18). Since for us such distinctions (distinctions between a capitalist and sexual pursuits, between innocuous business practices and the alienating effects of commodifying women) have al-

ready been established, such visible undermining serves mostly, it seems to me, to make Mandeville's text unreadable: since we do not know whether to weight the tropological or the logical, since both are too prominent, we do not know what he is trying to argue.

24. William Wycherley, *The Country Wife* (1675), ed. Thomas H. Fujimura (Lincoln: Univ. of Nebraska Press, 1965); George Lillo, *The London Merchant* (1731), ed. William H. McBurney (Lincoln: Univ. of Nebraska Press, 1965). Both plays will be cited in the text by act, scene, and line number.

25. Actually, Diderot's comment is more threatening than that, telling spectators that they truly must feel their emotion augmented by identifying with others in the audience or be seen as harboring "a secret vice": "Celui qui ne sent pas augmenter sa sensation par le grand nombre de ceux qui la partagent, a quelque vice secret; il y a dans son caractère je ne sais quoi de solitaire qui me déplaire." *He who does not feel his emotion intensified by the large number of people who share in it has some secret vice; there is something in his character, some sort of reclusiveness, that displeases me* ("Entretiens sur le fils naturel," *Oeuvres Esthetiques de Diderot,* ed. Paul Vernière [Paris: Garnier Frères, 1965], 122). Diderot's *Entretiens* was published the same year as Edmund Burke's *Philosophical Enquiry into the Origin of Our Ideas of the Sublime and the Beautiful* and David Hume's essay "Of Tragedy" (1757), both of which worry over the degree of "aesthetic distance" that viewers of tragedy have when watching misery befall others.

26. Katharine Eisaman Maus, "'Playhouse Flesh and Blood': Sexual Ideology and the Restoration Actress," *ELH* 46 (1979): 595–617.

27. Thomas Laqueur, "Orgasm, Generation, and the Politics of Reproductive Biology," *Representations* 14 (spring 1986): 1–41.

28. Jonathan Dollimore, "Subjectivity, Sexuality, and Transgression: The Jacobean Connection," in *Renaissance Drama: Renaissance Drama and Cultural Change,* ed. Mary Beth Rose, New Series 17 (Evanston, Ill.: Newberry Library Center for Renaissance Studies, 1986), 53–81.

29. E.P. Thompson, *Whigs and Hunters: The Origin of the Black Act* (New York: Pantheon Books, 1975).

30. Bob Bushaway, *By Rite: Custom, Ceremony, and Community in England 1700–1880* (London: Junction Books, 1982); Stallybrass and White, *Politics and Poetics of Transgression.*

31. Thompson, *Whigs and Hunters,* 256–57.

32. Terry Castle, *Masquerade and Civilization: The Carnivalesque in Eighteenth-Century English Culture and Fiction* (Stanford, Calif.: Stanford Univ. Press, 1986).

33. Kristina Straub, *Sexual Suspects: Eighteenth-Century Players and Sexual Ideology* (Princeton, N.J.: Princeton Univ. Press, 1992), 127.

34. It is probably important to note here that masking was an upper-class phenomena; according to Thompson, blacking among the lower classes devolves

into machine-breaking and rioting as the century progresses and as customary behaviors are more systematically suppressed (by the development of a police force, for instance).

35. Lisa Jardine, *Still Harping on Daughters: Women and Drama in the Age of Shakespeare* (Sussex, England: Harvester Press, 1983), 20–21.

36. Jean Howard, *The Stage and Social Struggle in Early Modern England* (New York: Routledge, 1994), 101.

37. Pat Rogers, "The Breeches Part," in *Sexuality in Eighteenth-Century Britain*, ed. Paul-Gabriel Boucé (Totowa, N.J.: Barnes and Noble Books, 1982).

38. Straub, *Sexual Suspects*, 128–29.

39. Raymond Williams, *Marxism and Literature* (New York: Oxford Univ. Press, 1977), 121–27.

40. In both "The Moral Economy of the English Crowd" (*Past and Present* 50 [Feb. 1971]: 76–136) and *Whigs and Hunters*, E.P. Thompson argues that, during the early 1700s, popular rebellions such as price fixing and blacking directly challenged the new system of laws protecting proprietary rights with customary laws, secured "by Rite," as Bob Bushaway puts it. See also Helen Burke, "*The London Merchant* and Eighteenth-Century British Law," *Philological Quarterly* 73.3 (summer 1994): 348.

41. Karl Kroeber, *British Romantic Art* (Berkeley: Univ. of California Press, 1986), 15.

42. On Millwood as exemplary of rhetoric, see Stephanie Barbe Hammer, "Economy and Extravagance: Criminal Origin and the War of Words in *The London Merchant*," *Essays in Theatre* 8.2 (May 1990).

43. Harry William Pedicord quotes the billings in advertisements ("Masonic Theatre Pieces in London 1730–1780," *Theatre Survey* 25.2 [Nov. 1984]: 158–59). Pedicord says that the play was produced 204 times, Hammer says 230 ("Economy and Extravagance," 99 n. 4).

44. Tejumola Olaniyan, "The Ethics and Poetics of a 'Civilizing Mission': Some Notes on Lillo's *The London Merchant*," *English Language Notes* 29.4 (June 1992): 33–34.

4. Misogyny and Feminism

1. Mary Leapor's poetry appears in *Poems Upon Several Occasions*, [vol. 1] (London: J. Roberts, 1748); *Poems Upon Several Occasions: The Second and Last Volume* (London: J. Roberts, 1751), 2:296–97; her poems will be referred to in the text by volume and page number, as here. A large selection of Leapor's poems appears in George Colman and Bonnell Thornton, eds., *Poems by Eminent Ladies, particularly Mrs. Barber, Mrs. Behn, Miss Carter . . .*, 2 vols. (London: R. Baldwin, 1755); a smaller selection appears in Roger Lonsdale, ed., *Eighteenth Century Women Poets: An Oxford Anthology* (Oxford Univ. Press, 1989).

Leapor was popular enough during the eighteenth century to have her works listed at the Bath lending library forty years after her death (*A Catalogue of Meyler's Circulating Library, in Orange-Grove, Bath; . . .* [Bath, Eng.: Meyler, Printer, 1790?], 38, item 1305). Lately, she has received a great deal of critical attention: see Donna Landry, *The Muses of Resistance: Laboring-Class Women's Poetry in Britain, 1739–1796* (New York: Cambridge Univ. Press, 1990); Richard Greene, *Mary Leapor: A Study in Eighteenth Century Women's Poetry* (Oxford: Oxford Univ. Press, 1993); Betty Rizzo, "Molly Leapor: An Anxiety for Influence," *Age of Johnson* 4 (1991): 313–43; Margaret Anne Doody, "Swift among the Women," *Yearbook of English Studies* 18 (1988): 68–92 (later published in *Critical Essays on Jonathan Swift*, ed. Frank Palmeri [New York: G.K. Hall, 1993], 13–37); and Jocelyn Harris, "Sappho, Souls, and the Salic Law of Wit," in *Anticipations of the Enlightenment in England, France, and Germany*, ed. Alan C. Kors and Paul J. Korshin (Philadelphia: Univ. of Pennsylvania Press, 1987), 232–58. As Martin Wechselblatt has pointed out to me, it is amazing that Leapor has received so much critical attention without a modern edition of her works being available. *The Works of Mary Leapor: A Critical Edition*, edited by Richard Greene and the late Ann Messenger, is forthcoming from Oxford University Press (2000). It is possible to gain access via the World Wide Web to a selection of Leapor's poems, including the full text of *Crumble-Hall*, at http://miavx1.muohio.edu/~leaporm/leapor.htm.

2. Greene, *Mary Leapor*, 152–53.

3. On Duck, see Raymond Williams, *The Country and the City* (New York: Oxford Univ. Press, 1973), 32; on Collier, see Landry, *Muses of Resistance*, 59–60; on the counterpastoral, see John Goodridge, *Rural Life in Eighteenth-Century English Poetry* (New York: Cambridge Univ. Press, 1995); and John Barrell, *The Dark Side of the Landscape: The Rural Poor in English Painting* (New York: Cambridge Univ. Press, 1980).

4. At roughly the same time that Petrarch wrote his sonnets, the Pléiade wrote their hymnes-blasons praising parts of women's bodies. The first collection of blasons, written by Clément Marot, Maurice Scève, Saint Gelais, and others, was called *Blasons anatomiques du corps féminin* (written in 1536, collected in 1543) precisely because each poem described one body part, a foot, a breast, or a tooth, Marot's "Le Beau Tétin" being only the most famous. The French collection of blasons is reprinted by Albert-Marie Schmidt in *Poètes du XVIe Siècle* (Paris: Gallimard, 1953), 291–364. For some reason, Schmidt leaves the word "anatomiques" out of the title.

5. John Locke, *An Essay concerning Human Understanding*, ed. Peter H. Nidditch (1689; reprint, Oxford: Clarendon Press, 1975), 2.1.1, 104. The *Essay* will hereafter be cited in the text by book, chapter, section, and finally page number, as here, or by title of the part of the *Essay* referred to and page number.

6. Locke's *Essay* thus, as Charles Taylor points out, radically redefines "experience," "transpos[ing] first-person experience into an objectified, impersonal mode" (*Sources of the Self: The Making of Modern Identity* [Cambridge, Mass.: Harvard Univ. Press, 1989], 163).

7. Michel Foucault, "What Is Enlightenment?" in *The Foucault Reader*, ed. Paul Rabinow (New York: Pantheon Books, 1984), 38.

8. The term "histories of difference" comes from Joan Scott's analysis of the problematic reliance on "experience" of those historians engaged in identity politics ("Experience," in *Feminists Theorize the Political*, ed. Joan Scott and Judith Butler [New York: Routledge, 1992]: 22–40). My discussion might be seen as examining a less visible, and so perhaps more insidious, reliance—among poststructuralist historians eschewing identity categories—upon "experience" as the ground for performing criticism (see Diana Fuss, *Essentially Speaking: Feminism, Nature, and Difference* [New York: Routledge, 1989], 129 n. 2).

9. Max Horkeheimer and Theodor W. Adorno, *Dialectic of Enlightenment*, trans. John Cumming (New York: Continuum, 1993), 4.

10. Laurence Sterne, *The Life and Opinions of Tristram Shandy*, ed. Ian Campbell Ross (1759–67; reprint, New York: Oxford Univ. Press, 1983), 70.

11. Thomas Sprat, *History of the Royal Society*, ed. Jackson I. Cope and Harold Whitmore Jones (London, 1667; reprint, St. Louis, Mo.: Washington Univ. Studies, 1958), 113.

12. See Jacqueline Rose, *Sexuality in the Field of Vision* (London: Verso, 1986), 105. Naomi Schorr talks about how "femininity [has been] constituted [out] of the refuse of masculine transcendence" ("This Essentialism Which Is Not One," *Differences* 1 [summer 1989]: 40)—and refuse cannot be taken too literally.

13. See Richard Rorty, *Philosophy and the Mirror of Nature* (Princeton, N.J.: Princeton Univ. Press, 1979); Stanley Cavell, *The Claim of Reason: Wittgenstein, Skepticism, Morality, and Tragedy* (New York: Oxford Univ. Press, 1979).

14. Taylor, *Sources of the Self,* ix, 144.

15. Barbara Maria Stafford, *Body Criticism: Imaging the Unseen in Enlightenment Art and Medicine* (Boston: MIT Press, 1991), 362.

16. Ibid., 84.

17. A science that grew up with empiricism, physiognomics so literalizes the rhetoric of the blason tradition as to physically mimic the metaphoric contemplation of body parts in the objectifying practices of phrenology and dissection. This practice, like all empiricisms, has its demystificatory moment, as is obvious from Johann Caspar Lavater's description of the purpose of the art: "To pierce through all these coverings, [the coverings of 'rank, condition, habit, estate, dress'] into [a person's] real character, to discover in these foreign and contingent determinations, solid and fixed principles by which to settle what the Man really is" (Lavater, *Essays on Physiognomy* [1792] I, I, 24–25, quoted in Stafford, *Body Criticism,* 95). Physiognomics is progressive insofar as it posits a universal human essence as disconnected from "rank, condition, habit, estate, dress."

18. Bette London is the only reader of *Frankenstein,* I believe, to have recog-

nized Victor as a mad blasonneur ("Mary Shelley, *Frankenstein*, and the Spectacle of Masculinity," *PMLA* 108.2 [1993]: 261–62).

19. Doody, "Swift among the Women," 68.

20. For an intense debate over the universality of Swift's scatalogical vision, see the Forum in *PMLA* 91 (1976): 464–67.

21. Donald T. Siebert, "Swift's *Fiat Odor*: The Excremental Re-Vision," *Eighteenth-Century Studies* 19 (1985): 21, 24.

22. Laura Brown notices that the female body is absent from the dressing-room poems and convincingly argues that these satires are attacks on cultural corruption, for which women's clothes are a synecdoche ("Reading Race and Gender: Jonathan Swift," *Eighteenth-Century Studies* 23 [1990]: 425–43, later published in Laura Brown, *Ends of Empire: Women and Ideology in Early Eighteenth-Century English Literature* [Ithaca, N.Y.: Cornell Univ. Press, 1993], 170–200). Margaret Doody notices Swift's curiously empowering relations with women friends and writers ("Swift among the Women").

23. *Gentleman's Magazine* 54 (1784): 807, quoted in Greene, *Mary Leapor*, 14–15.

24. Paul de Man, "The Resistance to Theory," in *The Resistance to Theory* (Minneapolis: Univ. of Minnesota Press, 1986), 11.

25. Marjorie Levinson, "The New Historicism: Back to the Future," in *Rethinking Historicism: Critical Readings in Romantic History*, ed. Marjorie Levinson (Oxford: Blackwell, 1989), 20.

26. "Materialism" means simply "the proposition that the origins of all forms of existence, including human activity, can be explained in terms of physical being" (Donna Landry and Gerald MacLean, *Materialist Feminisms* [Cambridge, Mass.: Basil Blackwell, 1993], 3). Competing forms of materialism are proliferating (see David Simpson, introduction to *Subject to History: Ideology, Class, Gender*, ed. David Simpson [Ithaca, N.Y.: Cornell Univ. Press, 1991], esp. 15–18). There is a movement among feminist critics to confine applications of the rubric "materialist" to feminists who are not sympathetic with poststructuralism (see Teresa Ebert, "The Romance of Patriarchy: Ideology, Subjectivity, and Postmodern Feminist Cultural Theory," *Cultural Critique* 10 [fall 1988]: 19–57), but all of the feminist materialists referred to in this chapter are thoroughly postmodern; the designation here thus refers to all of those "feminisms" discussed by Landry and MacLean.

"New historicism" refers only to the group of Renaissance and Romantic scholars customarily designated by that term. On the thorny problem of the differences and similarities between new historicism and cultural criticism, see Patrick Brantlinger, "Cultural Studies versus the New Historicism," in *English Studies/Culture Studies: Institutionalizing Dissent*, ed. Isaiah Smithson and Nancy Ruff (Urbana: Univ. of Illinois Press, 1994), 43–58. The term "historicism" itself is defined below.

27. Carolyn Merchant, *The Death of Nature: Women, Ecology, and the Scientific Revolution*, 2d ed. (New York: Harper and Row, 1989); Evelyn Fox

Keller, *Reflections on Gender and Science* (New Haven, Conn.: Yale Univ. Press, 1985); Sandra Harding, "Feminism, Science, and the Anti-Enlightenment Critiques," in *Feminism/Postmodernism*, ed. Linda Nicholson (New York: Routledge, 1990), 83–106; Sandra Harding, *The Science Question in Feminism* (Ithaca, N.Y.: Cornell Univ. Press, 1986); and Sandra Harding, *Whose Science? Whose Knowledge: Thinking from Women's Lives* (Ithaca, N.Y.: Cornell Univ. Press, 1991).

28. See Adrian M.S. Piper, "Higher-Order Discrimination," in *Identity, Character, and Morality*, ed. Amerlie O. Rorty and Owen Flanagan (Cambridge, Mass.: MIT Press, 1990), 285–309; Adrian M.S. Piper, "Xenophobia and Kantian Rationalism," *Philosophical Forum*, special triple issue: *African-]American Perspectives and Philosophical Traditions*, ed. John Pittman, 24.1–3 (1992–93): 188–232; Susan Bordo, "The Cartesian Masculinization of Thought," *Signs* 11 (spring 1986): 439–56; Susan Bordo, "Feminist Scepticism and the 'Maleness' of Philosophy," *Journal of Philosophy* 85.11 (1988): 619–26; Linda Nicholson, introduction to Nicholson, *Feminism/Postmodernism*, 1–16; Louis M. Antony and Charlotte Witt, eds., *A Mind of One's Own: Feminist Essays on Reason and Objectivity* (Boulder, Colo.: Westview Press, 1993).

29. The kind of "experience" being analyzed here is a rhetorical construct fabricated out of an implicit claim that some state of affairs objectively exists and can be experienced or observed. It is precisely not that personal, subjective experience discussed in relation to identity politics; on that issue, see Joan Scott (note 9 above); Elizabeth J. Bellamy and Artemis Leontis, "A Genealogy of Experience: From Epistemology to Politics," *Yale Journal of Criticism* 6.1 (1993): 163–84.

30. For a summary and a bibliography of views as to the relation of the Scriblerians to the new science, see Douglas Lane Patey, "Swift's Satire on 'Science' and the Structure of *Gulliver's Travels*," *ELH* 58 (1991): 809–40. Swift was of course "an ancient," "hostile to modernity and indifferent to the claims of history" (Joseph M. Levine, *The Battle of the Books: History and Literature in the Augustan Age* [Ithaca, N.Y.: Cornell Univ. Press 1991], 3).

31. Jonathan Swift, "Cassinus and Peter," in *The Complete Poems*, ed. Pat Rogers (New Haven, Conn.: Yale Univ. Press, 1983), line 18. All of Swift's poems will be cited in the text from this edition by line number.

32. Jonathan Swift, *Gulliver's Travels*, in *Gulliver's Travels and Other Writings*, ed. Louis A. Landa (1726; reprint, Boston: Houghton Mifflin, 1960), 23.

33. Ibid., 95.

34. Ibid., 74.

35. Ibid., 90–91.

36. Julia Kristeva, "Freud and Love: Treatment and Its Discontents," in *Tales of Love*, trans. Leon S. Roudiez (New York: Columbia Univ. Press, 1987), 43.

37. Homi Bhabha, "Of Mimicry and Man: The Ambivalence of Colonial Discourse," *October* 28 (spring 1984): 130.

38. Peter Stallybrass and Allon White, *The Politics and Poetics of Transgres-*

sion (Ithaca, N.Y.: Cornell Univ. Press, 1986). Henry Abelove describes resistance to Wesley's claim that "cleanliness is next to Godliness" (*The Evangelist of Desire: John Wesley and the Methodists* [Stanford, Calif.: Stanford Univ. Press, 1990], 101) and demonstrates that Wesley used personal hygiene as one of "the usual counters of genteel conduct" in order to inspire deference among his followers (24, 32).

39. Erica Harth, "The Virtue of Love: Lord Hardwicke's Marriage Act," *Cultural Critique* 9 (1988): 123–54.

40. Gould's poem opens:

> "MADAM! by Heav'n You have an Air so Fine,
> It renders the least thing You do—Divine!
> We dare not say You were Created here,
> But dropt an ANGEL from th'AETHEREAL SPHERE.

> (quoted in full in appendix 1 of Montagu Summers, *The Restoration Theater* [London: Kegan Paul, Trench, Trubner, 1934], 301)

Samuel Butler's *Hudibras* contains a similar parody of fop poetry.

41. For the excremental meaning of "dropping," see *The Compact Edition of the Oxford English Dictionary: Complete Text Reproduced Micrographically* (reproduction of the 13–volume *Oxford English Dictionary* published in 1933) (New York: Oxford Univ. Press, 1971), s.v. "dropping," *vbl. sb.* 6.

42. Williams, *Country and City,* 32.

43. That portion of the poem *Crumble-Hall* which Landry has called "Ursula's Lament" (*Muses of Resistance,* 178) is reprinted in Lonsdale, *Eighteenth Century Women Poets,* 210–11. Landry's chapter on Mary Leapor analyzes *Crumble-Hall* in depth and quotes more of it than is available in Lonsdale. The full text of the poem is available on the World Wide Web at http://miavx1.muohio.edu/~leaporm/leapor.htm.

44. Landry, *Muses of Resistance,* 179.

45. Similarly, Swift's "Phyllis, or the Progress of Love" locates in a Phyllis stupid enough to elope with a servant the new ideology of romantic love that, as described by Harth, "The Virtue of Love," allows for economic transfer between classes.

46. Richard Terdiman describes "what Fredric Jameson has called the 'strategy of containment.' Dominant discourse, when it is fully functional, projects the most airtight strategy of containment of any discourse. Through it a censorship is imposed which brackets any questioning of the very content and form of the dominant; counter-discourses are simply rendered invisible" (*Discourse/Counter-Discourse: The Theory and Practice of Symbolic Resistance in Nineteenth-Century France* [Ithaca, N.Y.: Cornell Univ. Press, 1984], 60 n. 55.

47. Walter Cohen, "Political Criticism of Shakespeare," in *Shakespeare Reproduced: The Text in History and Ideology,* ed. Jean E. Howard and Marion F. O'Connor (New York: Routledge, 1987), 35; Jean E. Howard, "Feminism and

the Question of History: Resituating the Debate," *Women's Studies* 19 (1991): 149–50; and Frederic Jameson, *Postmodernism or, The Cultural Logic of Late Capitalism* (Durham, N.C.: Duke Univ. Press, 1991), 5–6, discussed below.

48. Catherine Gallagher, "Marxism and the New Historicism," in *The New Historicism*, ed. H. Aram Veeser (New York: Routledge, 1989), 42.

49. Ibid., 43. The phrase "hermeneutics of suspicion" comes originally from the work of Paul Ricoeur; see, e.g., *Freud and Philosophy: An Essay on Interpretation*, trans. Denis Savage (New Haven, Conn.: Yale Univ. Press, 1970), 30–36.

50. On the surprisingly self-critical aspect of empiricism, on its status as a critique (in the Kantian sense of the word) as opposed to, as it is often portrayed, precritical thinking, see Cathy Caruth, in *Empirical Truths and Critical Fictions: Locke, Wordsworth, Kant, Freud* (Baltimore: Johns Hopkins Univ. Press, 1991), 4; Jules David Law, *The Rhetoric of Empiricism: Language and Perception from Locke to I.A. Richards* (Ithaca, N.Y.: Cornell Univ. Press, 1993), 1–5. Our critical thinking is entwined with empiricism.

51. Jameson, *Postmodernism*, 5–6.

52. Michel Foucault, *Discipline and Punish* (1975), trans. Alan Sheridan (New York: Vintage Books, 1979), 139; the method here named is "genealogy" (Arnold Davidson, "Archeology, Genealogy, Ethics," in *Foucault: A Critical Reader*, ed. David Couzens Hoy [Cambridge, Mass.: Basil Blackwell, 1986], 224). My implicit argument here is that Foucault's *Discipline and Punish* is fatalistic, produces a vision of power as omnipotent, only insofar as the reader mistakes his method for his conclusion.

53. Gayatri Spivak, "Can the Subaltern Speak?" in *Marxism and the Interpretation of Culture*, ed. Cary Nelson and Lawrence Grossberg (Urbana: Univ. of Illinois Press, 1988), 271.

54. Rey Chow, "Ethics after Idealism," *Diacritics* 23.1 (1993): 8.

55. Homi Bhabha, "Freedom's Basis in the Indeterminate," *October* 61 (summer 1992): 48.

56. David Spurr, *The Rhetoric of Empire: Colonial Discourse in Journalism, Travel Writing, and Imperial Administration* (Durham, N.C.: Duke Univ. Press, 1993), 189.

57. Howard, "Feminism," 151–52 (emphasis added).

58. Spivak, "Can the Subaltern Speak?" 274.

59. Satya P. Mohanty, "Us and Them: On the Philosophical Bases of Political Criticism," *Yale Journal of Criticism* 2.2 (1989): 14; see also Hilary Putnam, "Objectivity and the Science/Ethics Distinction," in *Realism with a Human Face*, by Hilary Putnam, ed. James Conant (Cambridge, Mass.: Harvard Univ. Press, 1990).

60. Howard, "Feminism," 153.

61. Mohanty, "Us and Them," 14.

62. Spivak, "Can the Subaltern Speak?" 275.

63. Figure 2 appears in Thomas P. Roche Jr., *Petrarch and the English Son-*

net Sequences (New York: AMS Press, 1989). See the figure 2 caption for its source.

64. *The extravagant shepherd* is reprinted in Roche, *Petrarch,* appendix B, 523–33.

65. The empirical insistence that language be read as referential, as if it were referring to an extralinguistic reality, is antifeminist, as is suggested by the pictured lady's monstrosity. Shakespeare's sonnet "My Mistress' eyes are nothing like the sun" is not misogynous precisely to the extent that it is an avowedly rhetorical exercise, the deployment of *descriptio* to outdo other sonneteers, rather than an attempt to describe reality.

66. Michael McKeon, "Historicizing Patriarchy: The Emergence of Gender Difference in England, 1660–1760," *Eighteenth-Century Studies* 28.3 (1995): 302.

67. R. Howard Bloch, "Medieval Misogyny," in *Misogyny, Misandry, and Misanthropy,* ed. R. Howard Bloch and Frances Ferguson (Berkeley: Univ. of California Press, 1989), 15.

68. On the murder through neglect of illegitimate children among the poor, see Lawrence Stone, "The New Eighteenth Century," *New York Review of Books* 31.5 (29 March 1984): 46.

69. Bernard Mandeville, *The Fable of the Bees: Or, Private Vices, Publick Benefits,* 2 vols., ed. F.B. Kaye (1714, 1723, 1724, 1725, 1728, 1729, 1732; reprint, Oxford: Clarendon Press, 1924), 75.

70. Mandeville, *A Modest Defence of Publick Stews . . . ,* ed. Richard I. Cook (1724; reprint, Augustan Reprint Society, no. 162. Los Angeles: Clark Memorial Library, 1973), xi.

71. The misogynous basis of McKeon's and Mandeville's "gentlemanly empiricism" is visible only to a partisan criticism, to a feminism that, as Howard says, "acknowledges that the knowledge produced under its banner is linked to a present goal: the amelioration of oppression and exploitation based on gender and sexuality" ("Feminism," 151).

72. Jocelyn Harris and Richard Greene propose that "Man the Monarch" is Leapor's response to reading Locke's *Two Treatises* (Jocelyn Harris, *Samuel Richardson* [Cambridge: Cambridge Univ. Press, 1987], 18, quoted in Greene, *Mary Leapor,* 53). It is not unlikely that Leapor had access to texts by Filmer toward the end of her life, when she had befriended Freemantle, considering the Freemantle family's Jacobite sympathies (Greene, *Mary Leapor,* 20).

73. Sir Robert Filmer, *The Free-holders Grand Inquest, . . . To which are added OBSERVATIONS Upon Forms of Government* (London, 1679; Early English Books, 1641–1700 [Ann Arbor, Mich: Univ. Microfilms International, 1984]), microfilm, wing F913, reel 1383, pp. 59 ff.

74. John Locke, *First Treatise,* in *Two Treatises of Government,* ed. Peter Laslett (New York: Cambridge Univ. Press, 1960, 1987), 60, 184.

75. Sir Robert Filmer, *Patriarcha and Other Political Works,* ed. Peter Laslett (Oxford: Basil Blackwell, 1949), 68–69. This excerpt of *Observations Upon*

Grotius actually appears in the Cambridge manuscript of *Patriarcha* (see Laslett, introduction to *Patriarcha*, 8, 45, 63, 278).

76. For early instances of the word being related to disgust, see the *OED*, s.v. "repugnance," *sb.* 3 (see note 41 above).

77. Mandeville, *The Fable of the Bees*, 65.

78. Marge Piercy, *Small Changes* (Garden City, N.Y.: Doubleday, 1973).

5. Misogyny and the Canon

1. The word "bookseller" often means "publisher" during the eighteenth century (Terry Belanger, "Publishers and Writers in Eighteenth-Century England," in *Books and Their Readers in Eighteenth-Century England*, ed. Isabel Rivers [New York: St. Martin's Press, 1982], 8).

2. Alexander Pope, *The Poems of Alexander Pope*, ed. John Butt (New Haven: Yale Univ. Press, 1963), 279–80.

3. Alexander Pope, "The Author to the Reader," in *The Works of Alexander Pope, Esq.*, 8 vols. (London: B. Lintot, 1736), 2:51, quoted in Barbara Benedict, *Making the Modern Reader: Cultural Mediation in Early Modern Literary Anthologies* (Princeton, N.J.: Princeton Univ. Press, 1996), 140.

4. Pope, *Poems*, 639–40.

5. Ian Watt, "The Ironic Tradition in Augustan Prose from Johnson to Swift," in *The Character of Swift's Satire: A Revised Focus*, ed. Claude Rawson (Newark: Univ. of Delaware Press, 1983), 305–27.

6. Neil Saccamano, "Authority and Publication: The Works of 'Swift,'" *The Eighteenth Century: Theory and Interpretation* 25.3 (1984): 241–62.

7. Pierre Bourdieu, *Distinction: A Social Critique of the Judgment of Taste* (1979), trans. Richard Nice (Cambridge, Mass.: Harvard Univ. Press, 1984), 6.

8. John Guillory, *Cultural Capital: The Problem of Literary Canon Formation* (Chicago: Univ. of Chicago Press, 1993), 333.

9. Bourdieu, *Distinction*, 499, quoted in Guillory, *Cultural Capital*, 333.

10. Pierre Bourdieu, "The Market of Symbolic Goods," *Poetics* 14 (1985): 13–44, 17; see also Peter Stallybrass and Allon White, *The Politics and Poetics of Transgression* (Ithaca, N.Y.: Cornell Univ. Press, 1986).

11. Coterie membership was a form of distinction that persisted into the late seventeenth century. See Ann Baynes Coiro, "Milton and Class Identity: The Publication of *Areopagitica* and the 1645 *Poems*," *Journal of Medieval and Renaissance Studies* 22.2 (1992): 261–89; Arthur F. Marotti, *Manuscript, Print, and the English Renaissance Lyric* (Ithaca, N.Y.: Cornell Univ. Press, 1995), 226–27, 214–15. That form of distinction changes during the eighteenth century with the increased acceptance of printed literature (Richard Helgerson, "Milton Reads the King's Book: Print, Performance, and the Making of a Bourgeois Idol," *Criticism* 23.1 [1987]: 1–25) but has not yet changed for Pope and his circle (Benedict, *Modern Reader*, 129–30).

12. Changes in copyright law during the eighteenth century have been de-

scribed by John Feather (*A History of British Publishing* [New York: Croom Helm, 1988], 73–83). According to Mark Rose, such changes motivate inventing this abstract notion of text ("The Author as Proprietor: *Donaldson v. Becket* and the Genealogy of Modern Authorship," *Representations* 23 [summer 1988]: 51–85, 58–59). But David Saunders and Ian Hunter have shown that arguments about the effect of copyright on authorship such as those posed by Martha Woodmansee and Mark Rose are circular (Saunders and Hunter, "Lessons from the 'Literatory': How to Historicise Authorship," *Critical Inquiry* 17.3 [1991]: 479–509, 491–92; see also Martha Woodmansee, "The Genius and the Copyright: Economic and Legal Conditions of the Emergence of the 'Author,'" *Eighteenth-Century Studies* 17 [1984]: 425–48). In this chapter I offer other reasons why the idea of "the text" in the abstract came into existence, reasons having to do with social conflict, and explain how it was constructed: via misogyny. Margreta De Grazia and Peter Stallybrass analyze the mystificatory effects of the abstract, immaterial notion of "text" (in their essay, the "work") upon editing and criticism in the field of Shakespeare studies ("The Materiality of the Shakespearean Text," *Shakespeare Quarterly* 44.3 [fall 1993]: 255–83, 256ff).

13. Steven Knapp, *Literary Interest: The Limits of Anti-Formalism* (Cambridge, Mass.: Harvard Univ. Press, 1993), 65.

14. The dictum that loose women do not write great literature is interesting when set next to the early-eighteenth-century notion, analyzed by Mary Poovey, that women writers were lascivious (*The Proper Lady and the Woman Writer: Ideology as Style in the Works of Mary Wollstonecraft, Mary Shelley, and Jane Austen* [Chicago: Univ. of Chicago Press, 1984]; see also Roger Lonsdale, introduction to *Eighteenth-Century Women Poets: An Oxford Anthology*, ed. Roger Lonsdale [New York: Oxford Univ. Press, 1989], xxiii). Women who write are necessarily immoral, and immoral women cannot write great works—it is an interesting double bind.

15. Harold Bloom, *The Western Canon: The Books and School of Ages* (New York: Harcourt Brace, 1994), 24; Guillory, *Cultural Capital*, 20, 327; Knapp, *Literary Interest*, 129.

16. Donna Landry, *The Muses of Resistance: Laboring-Class Women's Poetry in Britain, 1739–1796* (New York: Cambridge Univ. Press, 1990), 76.

17. Margaret Ezell, *Writing Women's Literary History* (Baltimore: Johns Hopkins Univ. Press, 1993), 28–38, 47.

18. Douglas Lane Patey, "The Eighteenth-Century Invents the Canon," *Modern Language Studies* 18.1 (1988), 18. On the word "literature," see Wlad Godzich, *The Culture of Literacy* (Cambridge, Mass.: Harvard Univ. Press, 1994), 7; Michael McKeon, "Cultural Crisis and Dialectical Method: Destabilizing Augustan Literature," in *The Profession of Eighteenth-Century Literature: Reflections on an Institution*, ed. Leo Damrosch (Madison: Univ. of Wisconsin Press, 1992), 52–53; and Timothy J. Reiss, *The Meaning of Literature* (Ithaca, N.Y.: Cornell Univ. Press, 1992). See also chapter 1, note 31.

19. Patey, "The Eighteenth-Century Invents the Canon," 19.

20. Thomas Vogler, "Romanticism and Literary Periods: The Future of the Past," *New German Critique* 38 (summer 1986): 132. On the functioning of the concept of period, see René Wellek, "Periodization in Literary History," in *Dictionary of the History of Ideas: Studies of Selected Pivotal Ideas*, Philip P. Wiener, gen. ed., 5 vols. (New York: Scribner's, 1973), 3:481–86; Marlon Ross, "Breaking the Period: Romanticism, Historical Representation, and the Prospect of Genre," *ANQ*, n.s., 6.2–3 (1993): 128; John Reider, "Wordsworth and Romanticism in the Academy," in *At the Limits of Romanticism: Essays in Cultural, Feminist, and Materialist Criticism*, ed. Mary A. Favret and Nicola J. Watson (Bloomington: Indiana Univ. Press, 1994), 26. On the Romantics as the first poets to have a sense of themselves as writing within a tradition of English poetic history, see Stuart Curran, "Romantic Poetry: Why and Wherefore?" in *The Cambridge Companion to British Romanticism*, ed. Stuart Curran (New York: Cambridge Univ. Press, 1993), 225.

21. Trevor Ross, "The Emergence of 'Literature': Making and Reading the English Canon in the Eighteenth Century," *ELH* 63.2 (1996): 397.

22. Patey, "The Eighteenth-Century Invents the Canon," 25; Andrew Ashfield, introduction to *Romantic Women Poets, 1770–1838*, ed. Andrew Ashfield (New York: St. Martin's Press, 1995), xvi n. 3.

23. Frank Kermode, "Strange, Sublime, Uncanny," review of *The Western Canon*, by Harold Bloom, *London Review of Books*, 22 Dec. 1994, 9.

24. Matthew Arnold, general introduction to *The English Poets; Selections with Critical Introductions by Various Writers and a General Introduction by Matthew Arnold* (1885), comp. Thomas Humphrey Ward (Freeport, N.Y.: Books for Libraries Press, 1971), xxxiv.

25. Thomas F. Bonnell, "Bookselling and Canon-Making: The Trade Rivalry over the English Poets, 1776–1783," *Studies in Eighteenth-Century Culture* 19 (1989): 53.

26. Guillory, *Cultural Capital*, 30.

27. Benedict argues that anthologies and miscellanies are not distinct (*Modern Reader*, 4).

28. Among the early-eighteenth-century miscellanies in which women's works are interspersed are Gildon's *New Collection of Poems, On Several Occasions* (London: Peter Buck, George Strahan, 1701), which contains thirty pages of Anne Finch's poetry anonymously printed, as well as a poem by Mrs. Wharton; [Jacob Tonson's and/or Nicholas Rowe's] *Poetical Miscellanies, The Sixth Part* (London: Jacob Tonson, 1709), which contains Anne Finch (Lonsdale, notes to *Eighteenth-Century Women Poets*, 516); *Divine Hymns and Poems . . . by the E. of Roscommon, Mr. Dryden, Mr. Dennis, Mr. Norris, Mrs. Katherine Phillips, Philomela [Elizabeth Rowe], and others. Most of them never before printed* (London: J. Baker, 1704, 1709, 1719); J. Greenwood's *The Virgin Muse* (1717, 1722, 1731), which opens with "The Virgin, by Mrs. Philips"; A. Hammond's *The New Miscellany of Original Poems, Translations, and Imitations. By the most Eminent Hands, viz. Mr. Prior, Mr. Pope, Mr. Hughes, Mr. Harcourt, Lady*

_M. W. M._————, _Mrs. Manley, etc._ (London: T. Jauncy, 1720), which contains in addition to the women mentioned on the title page Susanna Centlivre and Martha Samson (Lonsdale, notes to _Eighteenth-Century Women Poets,_ 518); Richard Savage's _Miscellaneous Poems_ (London: David Lewis, 1726), containing Martha Samson (Lonsdale, notes to _Eighteenth-Century Women Poets,_ 520); _A New Miscellany . . . from Bath_ [1726?] (_New Cambridge Bibliography of English Literature,_ ed. George Watson, 5 vols [Cambridge, England: Cambridge Univ. Press, 1968] 2:356), containing a poem by Arabella Morton (Lonsdale, notes to _Eighteenth-Century Women Poets,_ 539); [Matthew Concanen's] _The Flower-Piece: A Collection of Miscellany Poems by Several Hands_ (London: J. Walthoe, 1731), containing Judith Madan's _The Progress of Poetry,_ which also appears in Fawkes and Woty's _Poetical Calender._ Numerous women poets appear in the other volumes of the Dodsley group in addition to Fawkes and Woty (see note 49 for full references to those collections and works analyzing their contents).

29. At one point in her argument, Ezell says that canonical anthologies edited by male authors have been less exclusive than those edited by women (_Writing Women's Literary History,_ 60–61). My work below will call that particular part of her argument into question, but not the main point of her critique of contemporary feminist anthologizers, whom she rightly sees as relying too heavily on an evolutionary model of feminism (18) and on a modern valuation of professionalism (47) to do anything other than replicate "the male tradition" (59).

30. Catherine Gallagher, _Nobody's Story: The Vanishing Acts of Women Writers in the Marketplace 1670–1820_ (Berkeley: Univ. of California Press, 1994).

31. Edward P. Thompson has written convincingly that class struggle during the eighteenth century is not the same as nineteenth-century struggles that depended on a self-conscious sense of class identity ("Eighteenth-Century English Society: Class Struggle without Class?" _Journal of Social History_ [May 1978]: 148). In fact, I think that the rise of the anthology form constitutes one instance of forging this identity and consciousness.

32. Stallybrass and White originally formulated the notion central to this chapter, that high and low artistic realms are separated by abjection (_Politics and Poetics of Transgression_).

33. Alexander Dyce, _Specimens of British Poetesses_ (London: T. Rodd, 1827), iii–iv.

34. Curran, "Romantic Poetry," 220; Lonsdale, introduction to _Eighteenth-Century Women Poets,_ xlii; Bonnell, "Bookselling and Canon-Making," 60–61. Paradoxically, at the very moment when women poets are being excluded from late-eighteenth- and early-nineteenth-century collections of poetry, they are publishing like mad (Lonsdale, introduction to _Eighteenth-Century Women Poets,_ xxi; Stuart Curran, "Women Readers, Women Writers," in Curran, _Cambridge Companion,_ 177–96; Greg Kucich, "Gendering the Canons of Romanticism: Past and Present," _Wordsworth Circle_ 27.2 [1996]: 100; see also Ezell,

Writing Women's Literary History, 4–7, 53–63). However, as can be seen by the suppression of Hazlitt's 1824 collection, which contained his contemporaries, booksellers had difficulties over copyright if they included living poets in collections of British poetry (Percival P. Howe, *The Life of William Hazlitt* [New York: George Doran, 1922], 369). And yet the eighteenth-century poet Mary Leapor was still popular at the moment when these collections were being produced. In 1790 Leapor's two-volume collection of poems was featured in the Bath lending library (*A Catalogue of Meyler's Circulating Library, in Orange-Grove, Bath* . . . [Bath, Eng.: Meyler, printer, 1790?] 38, item 1305). In 1779 *The Ladies Magazine* proclaimed Leapor "one of the most extraordinary women that ever appeared in the poetic world" (*Ladies Magazine* [1779]: 1640, quoted in Ezell, *Writing Women's Literary History,* 116–17). But even those still-popular, deceased women poets were absented from these multivolume collections that claim to contain, as John Bell puts it, *"all* the British Poets from the time of Chaucer to Churchill" (advertisement for Bell's series, *The Poets of Great Britain,* quoted in Bonnell, "Bookselling and Canon-Making," 57–58). Churchill died in 1764, Leapor in 1748—she should have been equally a contender for inclusion. What I am going to show below is this: it is not that booksellers such as Bell said "all" and hoped that people would not notice that women were missing. Rather, saying "all" and excluding women makes the "all" into the complete, imaginary, ideal totality that it is.

35. Ian Michael, *The Teaching of English from the Sixteenth Century to 1870* (New York: Cambridge Univ. Press, 1987), 196–97.

36. William Hazlitt's collection is meant to succeed Knox's volumes, as can be seen by the subtitle of the 1824 suppressed edition: *New Elegant Extracts from Chaucer to the Present Time* (see note 39).

37. Vicessimus Knox, *The Poetical Epitome; or Elegant Extracts Abridged from the Larger Volume, for the Improvement of Scholars at Classical and Other Schools, in the Art of Speaking, Reading, Thinking, Composing; and in the Conduct of Life* (London: C. Dilly, 1792, 1807), iii. "Youth" in the title of a collection is often a sort of code word for the uneducated who would like to raise their status. See M.L. Stretch, *The Beauties of History; or, Pictures of Virtue and Vice, Drawn from Real Life; Designed for the Instruction and Enterntainment of Youth,* 6th ed., 2 vols. (London: Charles Dilly, 1785), 1:xi, xiii.

38. *Select Collection of Poems, From Admired Authors, and Scarce Miscellanies* (North Shields, Eng.: W. Kelley, 1790); Sidney Melmouth, comp., *Beauties of British Poetry,* 2d ed. (Huddersfield, Eng.: Brook and Lancashire, 1803); *The Monitor; A Select Collection of Poems on the Most Important Subjects* (London: S. Rousseau, 1808); *Poetical Selections Consisting of the Most Approved Pieces of our Best Poets* . . . (Birmingham: Thomson and Wrightson, 1811); Elizabeth Mant's *The Parent's Poetical Anthology: Being a Selection of English Poems Primarily Designed to Assist in Forming the Taste and the Sentiments of Young Readers* (London: J. Rivington et al., 1814); and *Choice Selections and Original Effusions; or Pen and Ink Well Employed. By the Daughter*

of a Clergyman (London: Longman, Rees, Orme, Brown, and Green, 1828) are all examples of miscellanies that contain numerous women poets.

39. William Hazlitt, *Select British Poets, or New Elegant Extracts from Chaucer to the Present Time* (London: William C. Hall, 1824)—suppressed; William Hazlitt, *Select Poets of Great Britain* (London: Thomas Tegg; Glasgow: R. Griffen; Dublin: R. Milliken; Paris: M. Baudry, 1825).

40. *The British Anthology; or, Poetical Library*, 8 vols. (London: John Sharpe, 1824).

41. John Aikin, *Select Works of the British Poets with Biographical and Critical Prefaces* (1820) (Philadelphia: Thomas Wardle, 1831).

42. Thomas Campbell's *Specimens of the British Poets*, 7 vols. (London: John Murray, 1819), contains 238 male poets, most of them complete unknowns, and three women poets. In the 1809 anthology *Specimens of the British Poets from Lord Surrey to Cowper*, 2 vols. (London: W. Suttaby, B. Crosby, Seateherd and Letterman, 1809), three poems by only two women are included within the huge panorama of British literary history. Some examples of twentieth-century collections of this sort are Russell Noyes, ed., *English Romantic Poetry and Prose* (New York: Oxford Univ. Press, 1956), containing 50 male writers to 2 women; James Stephens, Edwin Beck, and Royall Snow, eds., *English Romantic Poets* (New York: American Book Co., 1935), containing 25 men to 1 woman; Cecil A. Moore, ed., *English Poetry of the Eighteenth Century* (New York: Henry Holt, 1935), 52 to 1; and finally, Thomas Ward's collection, in which volumes 3 (the eighteenth century) and 4 (the nineteenth century) contain 2 and 4 women, respectively, out of upwards of 50 poets per volume.

43. John Bullar, comp., *Selections from the British Poets* (London: Thomas Baker, 1822). Joseph Ritson's *English Anthology*, 3 vols. (London: T. and J. Egerton, 1793), is not fully organized in the anthological format that sustains canonical literary history, despite the claims of Ritson's title and preface; it is half miscellany and half anthology, a hybrid form that does indeed include women. Like Bullar's, the 1969 collection edited by Geoffrey Tillotson, Paul Fussell, and Marshall Waingrow, *Eighteenth-Century English Literature* (New York: Harcourt Brace, 1969), includes women writers (albeit only three) but confines them to one specific section of the text called "A Miscellany of Poems."

44. I am quoting S.C. Hall's headnote to Mary Tighe, *The Book of Gems. The [Modern] Poets and Artists of Great Britain*, 3 vols. (London: Saunders and Otley, 1836, 1837, 1838; London: Fisher, 1838, 1845; London: Whittaker and Co., 1838; London: H.G. Bohn, 1844, 1846, 1848, 1853), 2 vols. (London: Bell and Dandy, 1866; London and Paris: Fisher and Son, 1840, 1844). See also George Croly, *The Beauties of the British Poets* (London: R.B. Seeley, W. Burnside, 1828); [John Frost, ed.], *Select Works of the British Poets in a Chronological Series from Falconer to Sir Walter Scott* (Philadelphia: Thomas Wardle, 1838).

45. There are throughout the period collections of women's poetry: [George Colman and Bonnell Thornton, eds.], *Poems by Eminent Ladies*, 2 vols. (Lon-

don: R. Baldwin, 1755); Dyce, *Specimens of British Poetesses*; Frederic Rowton, *The Female Poets of Great Britain* (1853), facsimile ed., ed. Marilyn Williamson (Detroit: Wayne State Univ. Press, 1981). However, Colman and Thornton, Rowton, and Dyce are presenting the history of *women* writers, not British literary history itself.

46. Coiro, "Milton and Class Identity," 184; Marotti, *Manuscript, Print*, 214–15. The *Academy of Compliments* volumes published throughout the late seventeenth and early eighteenth centuries function like rhyming dictionaries and are similarly laden with "errors." On seeing multiple material versions as not erroneous but something else, see Donald F. McKenzie, *Bibliography and the Sociology of Texts*, The Panizzi Lectures (London: British Library, 1985); De Grazia and Stallybrass, "The Materiality of the Shakespearean Text."

47. John Aikin, prefatory essay, *The Spleen and Other Poems*, by Matthew Green, ed. John Aikin (London: T. Cadell Jr. and W. Davies, 1796), vii.

48. Oldys, William, "Preface, Containing an Historical and Critical Review of all the Collections of this Kind that were ever published," in *The British Muse, or A Collection of Thoughts, Moral, Natural, and Sublime of our English Poets: Who Flourished in the Sixteenth and Seventeenth Centuries*, comp. Thomas Hayward (London: F. Cogan and J. Nourse, 1738), vii-ix.

49. [Robert Dodsley, comp.], *A Collection of Poems. By Several Hands. In Three Volumes* (1748)—extended to four volumes in 1755 and to six volumes in 1758 (reprinted in various forms in 1748–49, 1751, 1760, 1763, 1765, 1766, 1770, 1775, and [a new ed.] 1782)—and then "supplemented" by Francis Fawkes and William Woty's *Poetical Calender* (1763), 12 vols., (reprint, 1764); Richardson and Urquhart's single-volume *Collection of the Most Esteemed Pieces of Poetry that have appeared for several years, with variety of originals, By the late Moses Mendez, Esq., and other contributors to Dodsley's collection* (1767, 1770); George Pearch's *Collection of Poems in Two Volumes* (1768)—extended to 4 volumes in 1770 (1775, 1783); and finally John Nichols's eight-volume *Select Collections of Poems* (1780–82; 1784). My view here of the connection among these collections differs slightly from that of Harold Foster, who does not see Nichols as a supplement to Dodsley (*Supplements to Dodsley's Collections of Poems* [Oxford: Oxford Bibliographical Society, 1980], vii). On the contents of the many versions of Dodsley, see Robert Chapman, "Dodsley's Collection of Poems by Several Hands," *Oxford Bibliographic Society Publications*, vol.1, pt. 3 (1933): 269–316. The imitations of Dodsley's format extend beyond the works listed here through piracy: the notorious Alexander Donaldson, over whose publications the court battle for perpetual copyright was eventually lost (Rose, "Author as Proprietor"), printed in 1768 and 1772 *A Select Collection of Poems, from the most Approved Authors*. Volume 1 virtually duplicates volume 1 of Dodsley (second edition, 1748) and Pearch (1783). Thus, when Donaldson writes in the advertisement, "The Publisher takes this opportunity for returning his thanks to the Gentlemen who favoured him by selecting the Materials for this Collection," he is actually thanking Dodsley for "allowing"

Donaldson's piracy, satirically goading "the Executors" of Dodsley and Pearch's copyright estate to stop him from using their material.

50. [Robert Dodsley], "Advertisement to the Former Editions," in *A Collection of Poems in Four Volumes. By Several Hands* (London: G. Pearch, 1783), 1.

51. Michael F. Suarez, S.J., "Trafficking in the Muse: Dodsley's *Collection of Poems* and the Question of Canon," in *Tradition in Transition: Women Writers, Marginal Texts, and the Eighteenth-Century Canon*, ed. Alvaro Ribeiro, S.J., and James G. Basker (Oxford: Clarendon Press, 1996), 306. See also Benedict, *Modern Reader*, 160.

52. While Michael Suarez posits that most purchasers of the Dodsley collection were aristocrats ("Trafficking in the Muse," 306–7), it is important to realize that such a fact made the book marketable to emulators of aristocrats as well: it was recommended, Suarez tells us, in *Directions for a Proper Choice of Authors to Form a Library* (1766), a pamphlet surely not addressed to peers and established gentlemen who already had a library and who could gain knowledge about the most important works of high culture recently produced through their acquaintances; this pamphlet is addressed to class climbers. That Dodsley's collection was purchased by would-be aristocrats, or even those who wish to vicariously experience a rise in status, is borne out by comments such as Chatterton's (in a letter) that the collection could be found "'in every library'" (Suarez, "Trafficking in the Muse," 298).

53. This list actually appears in the title of another miscellany compiled by Matthew Concanen in 1728, a collection of those who wish to respond to the "Miscellanies [written and compiled] by Pope and Company" because of having been "abused in those volumes," *A Compleat Collection . . . .* (London: A. Moore, 1728).

54. Green is so identified in vol. 1, first edition (1748), table of contents; in vol. 1 (1782), p. 128; and in vol. 5 (1782), table of contents and p. 171.

55. See the note in the 1782 edition of Dodsley, *Collection of Poems*, 2:275.

56. James Boswell, *The Life of Johnson* (New York: Alfred A. Knopf, 1992), 653.

57. Quoted in Suarez, "Trafficking in the Muse," 300.

58. William Mason, *The Poems of Mr. Gray. To Which are Prefixed Memoires of his Life and Writings by W. Mason, M.A.* (York: A Ward, 1775), 335, quoted in Suvir Kaul, *Thomas Gray and Literary Authority: A Study in Ideology and Poetics* (Stanford, Calif.: Stanford Univ. Press, 1992), 40; see also 47 n. 20.

59. Courtney Craig Smith has analyzed miscellaneous collections known as "drolleries"—often having that word in their titles—published between 1655 and 1682. Politically threatening to the Interregnum and the Protectorate, and prosecuted as such, these lewd volumes were produced, Arthur Marotti points out, by "a Royalist cosmopolitan coterie"; their audience was, according to Smith, "'those who were not regularly accepted into the inner circles of the court but considered themselves the social superiors of the city merchants and tradesmen'" (Smith, "The Seventeenth-Century Drolleries," *Harvard Library*

Bulletin 6 [1952]: 48–49; quoted in Marotti, *Manuscript, Print,* 268 n. 122). *Choyce Drollery* and *Sportive Wit,* published in 1656, were "burned by order of the authorities" (Marotti, *Manuscript, Print,* 268); other drolleries published that year were *Parnassus Biceps* and *Wit and Drollery,* and two years later, *Wit Restor'd.* Courtney Smith says of these collections that they were "compiled by the Cavaliers for the sake of registering protest against the Puritans. . . . Until the Restoration brought relief, they were the 'subversive propaganda' of an 'occupied' people who had lost out in the field, yet were unwilling to submit to the rule (or the preaching) of the 'Saints.' Even with the Restoration, the character of the drolleries did not change, except that the protest became more social than political" (Smith, "Drolleries," 45, quoted in Marotti, *Manuscript, Print,* 271).

60. It is precisely the contrast between high, serious and low, vulgar, fun poetry that prompts the title "Pills to purge melancholy" for collections of songs. H[enry] P[layford], *Wit and Mirth: an antidote against melancholy compounded of ballads, songs, and catches,* 3d. enlarged ed. (1682); [Henry Playford], *Wit and Mirth: or Pills to Purge Melancholy* (1699); part 2 (1700); 2d ed. (1705); vol. 4 (1706); 3d ed. (1706–7); vol. 4, 2d ed. (1709); vols. 2–4, 3d ed. (1712); vol. 1, 4th ed., vol. 5 (1714); vol. 6 (1720); Thomas D'Urfey, *Wit and Mirth; or Pills to Purge Melancholy* (1719, 1720); *Wit and Mirth; or, Tom D'Urfey's Pills to Purge Melancholy* (1791); *Buck's Delight, or Pills to Purge Melancholy (for 1799)* (1798, 1799).

61. Benedict, *Modern Reader,* 160; Suarez, "Trafficking in the Muse," 306.

62. Although only a small percentage of poems in the collection are devoted to melancholy or are about it, are poems on death (monodies, elegies, and inscriptions) or pensive odes (e.g., to fancy, night, indifference), Eleanor Sickels has rightly suggested that Dodsley somehow grants melancholy poetry prominence (*The Gloomy Egoist* [New York: Columbia Univ. Press, 1932], 7): the third poem in the first edition of the first volume is Matthew Green's long poem *The Spleen,* and Dodsley himself considered that poem to be a sort of centerpiece (Boswell, *Life of Johnson,* 653); the first poem in the 1755 edition of volume 4 is Gray's "Elegy Written in a Country Churchyard"; and the poems that close Dodsley's collection, appearing just before his final postscript in the sixth volume of 1758, are William Mason's "Ode. On Melancholy"—which features Gray in it—and two more odes by Gray. Others include Thomas Warton's "The Pleasures of Melancholy" (Dodsley, *Collection of Poems,* 1755, vol. 4), "Ode to Melancholy" by Elizabeth Carter (Pearch, *Collection of Poems,* 1768, vol. 1), "Ode to Melancholy" by Richard Shepherd (Pearch, *Collection of Poems,* 1768, vol. 1), "Ode to Melancholy" by John Oglivie (Pearch, *Collection of Poems,* 1768, vol. 2), and two imitations of Milton's pair ("L'Allegro" and "Il Penseroso") by John Gilbert Cooper (Dodsley, *Collection of Poems,* 1748, vol. 3) and Frances Greville (Pearch, *Collection of Poems,* 1768, vol. 1), as well as numerous elegies, inscriptions, and pensive poems.

63. Elizabeth Carter is the most frequently represented woman poet in the

collection of "school anthologies" analyzed by Ian Michael (*Teaching of English*, 198); many of the items that Michael calls "anthologies" I would term "miscellanies" based on the distinctions made below.

64. That William Collins's poetry is central to these collections is shown by the fact that all of his works (except a sonnet written as a child, a "Song" of dubious attribution, and "An Ode on the Popular Superstitions of the Highlands of Scotland," written in 1750 but not published until 1788) appeared first in these volumes before—and after—an edition of his works was published by John Langhorne in 1765. Dodsley's second and all subsequent editions of vol. 1, from 1748 on, contain three of Collins's odes, which are printed *again* in the 1749 volume called "volume IV" (which subsequent volume 4s do not resemble), and the 1755 vol. 4 contains his "Epistle to Hanmer" and "Song from *Cymbeline*"; the Pearch collection prints every known poem by Collins not in Dodsley; Fawkes and Woty's *Poetical Calender* prints all of Collins's works, including those poems found in Dodsley.

65. Dodsley, *Collection of Poems*, 1758, 6:376.

66. [Elizabeth Cooper, comp.], *The Muses [sic] Library; Or a Series of English Poetry, from the SAXONS, to the Reign of CHARLES II* (London: J. Wilcox, T. Green, J. Brindley, and T. Osborn, 1737; reissued by T.J. Wilcox, 1738); 2d ed. with new title, *The Historical and Poetical Medley: or the Muses [sic] Library* (London: T. Davies, 1738; reissued 1741), viii; Elizabeth L. Eisenstein, *The Printing Revolution in Early Modern Europe* (New York: Cambridge Univ. Press, 1983), 115.

67. George Pearch, *A Collection of Poems in Four Volumes*, 1775, 1:5.

68. Every once in a while, a dead poet will appear in one of these collections. The rule changes, however, with Nichols's later collection: in order to find works not yet published, Nichols is forced to go back to poets publishing before Dodsley began collecting in 1748.

69. Bourdieu, *Distinction*, 72.

70. Henry Headley, comp., *Select Beauties of Ancient English Poetry* 2 vols. (London: T. Cadell, 1787), 1:xi.

71. Robert Folkenflik pointed out to me that Headley quotes here from Horace's *Satires*, book 1, satire 4 (*Horace: Satires, Epistles, and Ars Poetica*, trans. H. Rushton Fairclough, Loeb Classics, rev. ed. [Cambridge, Mass.: Harvard Univ. Press, 1929], 1.4.62, pp. 52–53). Horace is here alluding, of course, to the story of Orpheus.

72. Headley, *Ancient English Poetry*, 2:160–61

73. Ibid., 1:ix.

74. Lonsdale considers 1757 a major moment in the process of reconceiving borrowing as plagiarism, the date when Bishop Hurd's "Letter to Mr. Mason on the Marks of Imitation" was published ("Gray and 'Allusion': The Poet as Debtor," in *Studies in the Eighteenth Century IV*, ed. R.F. Brissenden and J.C. Eade [Canberra: Australian National Univ. Press, 1979], 42, 44). Lonsdale wonders whether "Gray's virtual creative silence after this date" (44) might

indicate that he himself was aware of "his apparently compulsive acquisitiveness" (53).

75. Guillory, *Cultural Capital*, 87–88.

76. *The Spleen* originally appeared in an earlier edition of Dodsley, vol. 1 of the first edition (1748), and in every edition thereafter.

77. Rose, "Author as Proprietor"; and Woodmansee, "The Genius and the Copyright" (see note 12). Both articles appear in their books: Mark Rose, *Authors and Owners: The Invention of Copyright* (Cambridge, Mass.: Harvard Univ. Press, 1993); Martha Woodmansee, *The Author, Art, and the Market: Rereading the History of Aesthetics* (New York: Columbia Univ. Press, 1994).

78. Egerton Brydges, *Censura Literaria*, 10 vols. (London: Longman Hurst, Rees, and Orme, 1805–9), 7:317–18, quoted in Lonsdale, "Gray and 'Allusion,'" 47.

79. Lonsdale, "Gray and 'Allusion,'" 48.

80. Aikin, prefatory essay to *The Spleen*, v-vii.

81. On the discussion surrounding them, see Guillory, *Cultural Capital*, 91–96.

82. *The Poems of Thomas Gray, William Collins, Oliver Goldsmith*, ed. Roger Lonsdale (New York: Norton, 1972), 127, lines 53–56.

83. Lines 155–58, quoted in Kaul, *Thomas Gray*, 125.

84. Samuel Johnson, *A Dictionary of the English Language* (1755), 5th ed., corrected (London: Strahan et al., 1773). Lonsdale's notes to Gray's "Elegy" cite the passage from "The Rape of the Lock," but not the passage from Cowley. Since the "Elegy" was published in 1751, Gray would not have gotten his "memory" of Cowley's poem from reading Johnson's *Dictionary* (1755), but rather from reading the same things Johnson read.

85. Bourdieu, *Distinction*, 71–72.

86. Aikin, prefatory essay to *The Spleen*, iv.

87. Headley, *Ancient English Poetry*, 1:xxxii.

88. Nicholas Garnham and Raymond Williams, "Bourdieu and the Sociology of Culture," in *Media, Culture, and Society: A Critical Reader*, ed. Richard Collins, James Curran, Nicholas Garnham, Paddy Scannell, Philip Schlesinger, and Colin Sparks (Beverly Hills: Sage Publications, 1986), 124–55, 126; Bourdieu, *Distinction*, 282.

89. Guillory, *Cultural Capital*, 45–46; John Guillory, "Literary Critics as Intellectuals: Class Analysis and the Crisis of the Humanities," in *Rethinking Class: Literary Studies and Social Formations*, ed. Wai Chee Dimock and Michael T. Gilmore (New York: Columbia Univ. Press, 1994), 137–38.

90. Guillory, *Cultural Capital*, 335.

91. Benedict Anderson, *Imagined Communities: Reflections on the Origin and Spread of Nationalism*, rev. ed. (New York: Verso, 1991).

92. [William Oldys, comp.], *The Harleian Miscellany: or a Collection of Scarce, Curious, and Entertaining Pamphlets and Tracts*, with an introduction by Samuel Johnson (London: T. Osbourne, 1744); Thomas Percy, *Reliques of*

Ancient English Poetry (1765), 5th ed. (London: Rivington, Longman, Hurst, Rees, Orme, Brown, 1812); [George Ellis, comp.], *Specimens of the Early English Poets* (London: printed for Edwards, 1790); Robert Southey, *Specimens of the Later English Poets*, 3 vols. (London: Longman, Hurst, Rees and Orme, 1807).

93. [Samuel Johnson], "Origin and Importance of Small Tracts and Fugitive Pieces," in *Miscellaneous and Fugitive Pieces*, [ed. Thomas Davies], 2 vols., 2d ed., corrected (London: T. Davies, 1774), 9 (a reprint of the introduction to [Oldys], *Harleian Miscellany*).

94. Volumes 1 and 2 of the *Harleian Miscellany* were published in 1744, vols. 3–6 in 1745, and vols. 7–8 in 1746; vol. 1 was reprinted in 1753; a reprint of the whole collection in twelve volumes was produced between 1808 and 1811, and a reprint in ten volumes between 1808 and 1813.

95. Southey, *Specimens*, iv.

96. Percy, *Reliques*, vii.

97. Sigmund Freud, *Three Essays on the Theory of Sexuality* (1905), in *Standard Edition of the Works of Sigmund Freud*, James Strachey, gen. ed., 24 vols. (London: Hogarth Press, 1953–66), 7:123–245. According to Nicholas Thomas, who has analyzed the desire in eighteenth-century explorers, the eighteenth-century curiosity of collectors is infantile in structure (Nicholas Thomas, "Curiosity: Colonialism in its Infancy," in his *Entangled Objects: Exchange, Material Culture, and Colonialism in the Pacific* [Cambridge, Mass.: Harvard Univ. Press, 1991], 127). For a detailed description of eighteenth-century curiosity, see Barbara Benedict, "The 'Curious Attitude' in Eighteenth-Century Britain: Observing and Owning," *Eighteenth-Century Life* 14.3 (Nov. 1990): 59–98.

98. Headley, *Ancient English Poetry*, 2:161.

99. Matthew Arnold, "The Function of Criticism at the Present Time," in *Essays in Criticism: First Series*, ed. Sister Thomas Marion Hoctor (Chicago: Univ. of Chicago Press, 1968), 17.

100. Freud, "On the Sexual Theories of Children" (1908), in *Standard Edition*, 9:205–6.

101. Patey, "The Eighteenth Century Invents the Canon," 26.

102. Hazlitt, *Select Poets*, i (emphasis added).

103. Thus, Collins's poems appear in volumes 1 and 4 of Dodsley's 1748–49 collection, and Samuel Johnson's works, listed anonymously, are spread out in volumes 1, 4, and 9 of Fawkes and Woty's *Poetical Calender* (Foster, *Supplements*, 55).

104. Ellis, *Early English Poets*, iii.

105. Karl Marx, *Capital: A Critique of Political Economy*, vol. 1, trans. Ben Fowkes (New York: Vintage Books, 1977), 249; for a more complex discussion of the relation between *Capital* and canonical literature, see Reider, "Wordsworth and Romanticism in the Academy."

106. Southey, *Specimens*, iv.

107. Hazlitt, *Select British Poets*, ii.

108. Ernst Kantorowicz, *The King's Two Bodies: A Study in Medieval Political Theology* (Princeton, N.J.: Princeton Univ. Press, 1957). That Kantorowicz's model of the king's two bodies is relevant here was suggested to me by John Stevenson. See also Bourdieu, *Distinction*, 72.

109. Headley, *Ancient English Poetry*, i.

110. Bloom, *Western Canon*, 4, 23; Knapp, *Literary Interest*, 40–41.

111. See [John Dryden], *The Annual Miscellany: For the Year 1694. Being the Fourth Part of Miscellany Poems* (London: Jacob Tonson, 1694): "The Enjoyment" (164–71); "Apollo's Grief: For having kill'd Hyacinth by Accident. . . By my Lord R." and "Song [Where is he gone whom I Adore,] by my Lord R." (192–94).

112. *Deliciae Poeticae; or, Parnassus Display'd* (London: John Nutt, 1706).

113. *A New Academy of Complements* [*sic*]: *or the Lover's Secretary* was published throughout the century: 1715 (4th ed.), 1721, 1726, 1741, 1743, 1750, 1754 (14th ed.), 1766 (18th ed.), 1784 (17th ed.), 1788 (*New Cambridge Bibliography of English Literature*, vol. 2 (1660–1800), ed. George Watson [New York: Cambridge Univ. Press, 1971], 349).

114. [H. Curll, printer], *The Ladies Miscellany* (1718, 1720, 1732); [H. Curll, printer], *The Altar of Love* (1727, 1731); *The Ladies Miscellany: or a Curious Collection of Amorous Poems and Merry Tales* (1730); "Sir Butterfly Maggot, Kt.," in *The Gentlemen's Miscellany* (1730, 1731); [A. Moore, printer], *The Beau's Miscellany. Being a new and curious collection of amorous tales, diverting songs, and entertaining poems* (1731, 1736); "T. G.," *The Flowers of Parnassus; or the Ladie's Miscellany*, an annual published two years (1735, 1737); *The School of Venus: or the Lady's Miscellany*, 2d ed. (1739); *A New Academy of Compliments* (1748, 1772, 1789); "E. W.," *The Lover's Manual: being a choice collection of poems from modern authors* (1753), reprinted as *The Muses Library, and young gentleman* [*sic*] *and ladies polite instructor* (1760); "G. Gaylove," *A Select Collection of Original Love Letters, to which are subjoin'd poems by eminent ladies* (1755) (perhaps a parody of Colman and Thornton's collection, intent to elucidate their motives in gathering their collection?). All of this information comes from the *NCBEL*, 2:356ff.

115. *Poems for Ladies, selected under the inspection of a lady* (1777); [Oliver Goldsmith, named on the 1770 title page], *Poems for Young Ladies. In three parts. Devotional, Moral, and Entertaining* (1767, 1770, 1785, 1792), "that innocence may read without a blush"; *The Ladies Poetical Magazine* (an annual (1781–82; reprint, 1791); G. Wright, *The Lady's Miscellany: or pleasing essays, poems, stories, and examples* (1793, 1797) (*NCBEL*, 2:387ff).

116. Benedict, *Modern Reader*, 112.

117. Headley, *Ancient English Poetry*, 2:160–61.

118. Hazlitt, *Select British Poets*, ii.

119. Colman and Thornton, *Poems by Eminent Ladies*, iii.

120. Frank Kermode, *An Appetite for Poetry* (Cambridge, Mass.: Harvard Univ. Press, 1989), 192.

121. The sixth edition of the Norton claims to be opening up the canon through its changes, and many more women authors are included. But in fact, except for those few authors already canonized, such as Mary Shelley, women are still excluded from those parts of the Norton that are organized anthologically. Instead of intermingling with canonical authors, women and writers who were not members of the literary elite appear in sections separate from the sections containing "great authors." These sections are called "Literary Modes of the Early Seventeenth Century," "Poetry: Augustan Modes," "Romantic Lyric Poets" (as if Wordsworth, whose works appear in the main Romantic literature section were not a Lyric poet???), and "Victorian Issues." M.H. Abrams, gen. ed., *The Norton Anthology of Poetry*, 2 vols., 6th ed. (New York: W.W. Norton, 1993), vol. 2.

122. Introduction to *Cultural Studies*, ed. Lawrence Grossberg, Cary Nelson, and Paula A. Treichler (New York: Routledge, 1992), 12–13.

123. Alan Liu, "Program Introduction," in *The Canon and the Web: Reconfiguring Romanticism in the Information Age*, current web site http://humanitas.ucsb.edu/liu/canonweb.html.

124. Guillory, "Literary Critics."

125. Stephen Greenblatt, "Resonance and Wonder," in *Learning to Curse: Essays in Early Modern Culture* (New York: Routledge, 1990), reprinted in *Literary Theory Today*, ed. Peter Collier and Helga Geyer-Ryan (Ithaca, N.Y.: Cornell Univ. Press, 1990), 79.

126. De Grazia and Stallybrass, "The Materiality of the Shakespearean Text," 283.

127. Cheryl Walker, "Feminist Literary Criticism and the Author," *Critical Inquiry* 16 (1990): 551–71.

6. Transcending Misogyny

1. For the absence of Barbauld and other Romantic women poets from twentieth-century anthologies, see their tables of contents, available through two web sites: Laura Mandell, "Twentieth-Century Anthologies," http://miavx1.muohio.edu/~update/20thc.htm; Harriet Kramer Linkin, Laura Mandell, and Rita Raley, "The Anthologies Page," *The Romantic Circles Project*, http://www.muohio.edu/anthologies. See also Alan Richardson, "British Romanticism as a Cognitive Category," *Romanticism on the Net* 8 (1997), http://www-sul.stanford.edu/mirrors/romnet/. In 1993 three of Barbauld's poems made it into the sixth edition of the *Norton Anthology*, M.H. Abrams, gen. ed. (New York: Norton, 1993), 863–65, in a section not of major but rather of minor Romantic poets. In 1994 Barbauld was first featured as a major Romantic writer on her own in Duncan Wu's *Romanticism: An Anthology* (Cambridge, Mass.: Blackwell, 1994), 17–24; she was then presented in the same way in 1995 in David Perkins's second edition of *English Romantic Writers* (Fort Worth: Harcourt Brace, 1995), 29–43, and in 1996, most substantially, in Anne Mellor

and Richard Matlak's *British Literature 1780–1830* (Fort Worth: Harcourt Brace, 1996), 165–91.

2. David Perkins, *English Romantic Writers* (New York: Harcourt Brace Jovanovich, 1967), 404–5 (interpolation is by Perkins), quoting Samuel Taylor Coleridge, *Table Talk*, ed. Carl Woodring, vol. 14, pt. 1 of *The Collected Works of Samuel Taylor Coleridge*, Bollingen Series LXXV (Princeton, N.J.: Princeton Univ. Press, 1990), 272–73.

3. See for instance Paul de Man, "Wordsworth and the Victorians," *The Rhetoric of Romanticism* (New York: Columbia Univ. Press, 1984).

4. Charles Lamb, *Works*, ed. E.V. Lucas (London, 1905), 6:252–53, quoted in P.M. Zall, "The Cool World of Samuel Taylor Coleridge: Mrs. Barbauld's Crew & the building of a Mass Reading Class," *Wordsworth Circle* 2 (1971): 74–79, 74.

5. Henry Crabb Robinson, *Henry Crabb Robinson on Books and Their Writers*, ed. Edith J. Morley (London: J.M. Dent and Sons, 1938), 79, 12 May 1812.

6. On Coleridge's progressive disenchantment with Unitarian dissent and its effect on his relationship to Anna Barbauld, see Deirdre Coleman, "The Unitarian Rationalist and the 'Winged Spider': Anna Letitia Barbauld and Samuel Taylor Coleridge," in *Imperfect Apprehensions: Essays in Honour of G.A. Wilkes*, ed. Geoffrey Little (Sydney, Australia: Challis Press, 1996).

7. "The reverential attitude, a legacy of romantic aestheticism, is the one most natural in literary interpretation as we have practiced it" (Robert Scholes, *Textual Power: Literary Theory, and the Teaching of English* [New Haven, Conn.: Yale Univ. Press, 1985], 16, quoted in Charles Altieri, *Canons and Consequences: Reflections on the Ethical Force of Imaginative Ideals* [Evanston, Ill.: Northwestern Univ. Press, 1990], 5). On the connections among Romanticism, aestheticism, and canons, see also Peter Jaszi and Martha Woodmansee, "The Ethical Reaches of Authorship," *SAQ* 95.4 (fall 1996): 947–77.

8. See Cora Kaplan, "Language and Gender," *Sea Changes: Culture and Feminism* (London: Verso, 1986), 71, quoted in Philip Cox, "Samuel Taylor Coleridge and Anna Laetitia Barbauld: Gender, Genre, and Pastoral," *Gender, Genre, and the Romantic Poets* (New York: Manchester Univ. Press, 1996), 34. On the prevalence of abjection during the late eighteenth century, see Susan Green, "A Cultural Reading of Charlotte Lennox's *Shakespear Illustrated*," in *Cultural Readings of Restoration and Eighteenth-Century English Theater*, ed. J. Douglas Canfield and Deborah C. Payne (Athens: Univ. of Georgia Press, 1995), 228–57. The classical work on the problem of being embodied as a woman writer is Mary Poovey, *The Proper Lady and the Woman Writer: Ideology as Style in the Works of Mary Wollstonecraft, Mary Shelley, and Jane Austen* (Chicago: Univ. of Chicago Press, 1984).

9. Susan Wolfson, "Gendering the Soul," in *Romantic Women Writers: Voices and Countervoices*, ed. Paula R. Feldman and Theresa M. Kelley (Hanover, N.H.: Univ. Press of New England, 1995), 36.

10. I am speaking here about a fantasy discernibly informing Barbauld's writing without wishing to argue that Barbauld *consciously* believed in the materiality of the soul. Priestley certainly advocated a materialist philosophy, and Barbauld came in contact with it through him. She may have rejected materialist theology consciously, however, while making use of it unconsciously.

11. See M.H. Abrams, *Natural Supernaturalism: Tradition and Revolution in Romantic Literature* (New York: Norton, 1971); Philippe Lacoue-Labarthe and Jean-Luc Nancy, *The Literary Absolute: The Theory of Literature in German Romanticism*, trans. Philip Barnard and Cheryl Lester (Albany: State Univ. of New York Press, 1988).

12. See Marlon Ross, "Configurations of Feminine Reform: The Woman Writer and the Tradition of Dissent," in *Re-Visioning Romanticism: British Women Writers, 1776–1837*, ed. Carol Shiner Wilson and Joel Haefner (Philadelphia: Univ. of Pennsylvania Press, 1994), 91–110, esp. 107.

13. *Joseph Priestley: Selections from His Writings*, ed. Ira V. Brown (University Park: Pennsylvania State Univ. Press, 1962), 31, cited hereafter in the text as "Brown."

14. Joseph Priestley, "An History of the Corruptions of Christianity" (Birmingham, 1782), in *The Theological and Miscellaneous Works of Joseph Priestley*, ed. John T. Rutt, 25 vols. (London, 1817–1832), vol. 5, quoted in Brown, 279.

15. Priestley, preface to *Experiments and Observations on Different Branches of Air*, 6 vols. (1774), quoted in Basil Willey, *The Eighteenth-Century Background* (New York: Columbia Univ. Press, 1940), 171.

16. John Aikin, *Essay on the Application of Natural History to Poetry* (1777), 25, quoted in M.H. Abrams, *The Mirror and the Lamp: Romantic Theory and the Critical Tradition* (New York: Oxford Univ. Press, 1953), 304, 387.

17. Lamb, *Works*, 6:252–53, quoted in Zall, "World of Coleridge," 74.

18. Willey, *Eighteenth-Century Background*, 171.

19. Priestley, "Corruptions," quoted in Brown, 280.

20. Samuel T. Coleridge, *Table Talk and the Omniana of Samuel Taylor Coleridge*, (London: Oxford Univ. Press, 1917), 311, quoted in Willey, *Eighteenth-Century Background*, 183.

21. The *Dictionary of National Biography* says of John Aikin, Barbauld's father, that he believed in "that system of Low Arianism, as it was then called, which afterward became the distinguishing feature of the Warrington Academy" (Rpt. 1937–38, s.v. Aikin, John [1713–1780]). And in *The Arian Movement in England*, J. Hay Colligan says, "Priestley has left it on record, that at Warrington they were all Arians, the only subject upon which there was a difference of opinion being that of Atonement, regarding which Aikin had some obscure notions" ([Manchester: Univ. of Manchester Press, 1913], 73). The terms "Socinian" and "Unitarian" are often used as synonyms, but both are distinct from Arianism. However, Deirdre Coleman calls Barbauld a Unitarian in "The Unitarian Rationalist and the 'Winged Spider': Anna Letitia Barbauld

and Samuel Taylor Coleridge," in *Imperfect Apprehensions: Essays on English Literature in Honour of G. A. Wilkes*, ed. Geoffrey Little (Sydney: Challis, 1996), 148–63.

22. *The Works of Anna Lætitia Barbauld. With a Memoir*, ed. Lucy Aikin, 2 vols. (London: Longman, Hurst, Rees, Orme, Brown, and Green, 1825), 2:432, cited hereafter parenthetically in the text and the notes. Barbauld's essay is available on the World Wide Web at http://miavx1.muohio.edu/~leaporm/barbauld2.htm.

23. Lucy Aikin, quoted in Betsy Rodgers, *Georgian Chronicle: Mrs. Barbauld and Her Family* (London: Methuen, 1958), 52–53. Elsewhere, Lucy Aikin remembers that there was less agreement about manners, as is suggested by the occasion of Barbauld's poem "To Wisdom." According to McCarthy and Kraft, Lucy Aikin describes the occasion in a letter to Henry Bright: "Somebody [at Warrington Academy] was bold enough to talk of getting up private theatricals. This was dreadful business! All the wise and grave, the whole tutorhood, cried out, it must not be! The students, the Rigbys, and, I must add, my aunt, took the prohibition very sulkily; and my aunt's Ode to Wisdom was the result" (*The Poems of Anna Letitia Barbauld*, ed. William McCarthy and Elizabeth Kraft [Athens: Univ. of Georgia Press, 1994], 253).

24. *Experience of Several Eminent Methodist Preachers, with an Account of Their Call to, and Success in The Ministry. In a Series of Letters, Written by Themselves, To John Wesley* (Barnard, Vt.: Joseph Dix, 1812).

25. *Poems of Anna Letitia Barbauld*, ed. McCarthy and Kraft, 132, lines 18–19, 21. All poems will be quoted from this volume and cited in the text and the notes by page and line number.

26. Adam Phillips, "Getting Ready to Exist," *London Review of Books*, 17 July 1997. Although I find Phillips's formulation an accurate and useful expression of the high Romantic aesthetic as it has been constructed by readers, I am not sure that Wordsworth's poetry, for instance, is quite as melancholically antisocial as it seems. See Laura Mandell, "Rehistoricizing Romantic Ideology: New Perspectives on Gender and Class Conflict, 1730–1800," *Blake* 27.2 (fall 1993): 46–63.

27. In response to Wakefield's assertion that Christ did not lead public prayer, Barbauld responds with: "But his whole life was a prayer" (2:433). As noted above, Barbauld seems to see Christ as not differing materially from any man or woman. Thus she believes that actions are prayers.

28. For an important analysis as to how Barbauld sees her writings in relation to the public sphere, see Dan White, "The 'Joineriana': Anna Barbauld's Prose, the Aikin Family Circle, and the Collaborative Production of the Dissenting Public Sphere," *Eighteenth-Century Studies* 33.1(forthcoming).

29. Jonathan Brody Kramnick, "The Cultural Logic of Late Feudalism: Placing Spenser in the Eighteenth Century," *ELH* 63.4 (winter 1996): 873. In a forthcoming chapter entitled, "Print Capitalism and the Cultural Past: The Emergence of English Literary History," Kramnick says that Hurd compares

Spenser's *Faerie Queene* to "a fallen aristocrat. . . . less to suggest that the aristocracy is Spenser's modern audience, however, than to aestheticize an extinct feudal hierarchy as the literary canon" (Kramnick, *The Making of the English Canon: Print-Capitalism and the Cultural Past, 1700–1770* [New York: Cambridge Univ. Press, forthcoming, 1998]).

30. Stuart Curran, "Romantic Poetry: Why and Wherefore?" in *The Cambridge Companion to British Poetry*, ed. Stuart Curran (New York: Cambridge Univ. Press, 1993), 225.

31. Barbauld is indeed critiquing high Romantic poetry for instilling in readers an appetite for self-debasement that might carry over into their political relations. Lisa Vargo has pointed out to me that her argument demystifies the alleged egalitarianism of *Lyrical Ballads*.

32. Marlon Ross, *The Contours of Masculine Desire: Romanticism and the Rise of Women's Poetry* (New York: Oxford Univ. Press, 1989); Stuart Curran, "Romantic Poetry: The I Altered," in *Romanticism and Feminism*, ed. Anne Mellor (Bloomington: Indiana Univ. Press, 1988), 185–207.

33. McCarthy and Kraft, introduction to *Poems of Anna Letitia Barbauld*, xxxii.

34. Vicessimus Knox, *Elegant Extracts, or Useful and Entertaining Pieces of Poetry, Selected for the Improvement of Young Persons* (1784) (London: Luke Hansard, Printer, 1801); William Hazlitt, *Select Poets of Great Britain* (London: Tegg, Griffen, Milliken, Baudry, 1825).

35. [Anna Letitia Barbauld], *Devotional Pieces Compiled from the Psalms and the Book of Job: To Which Are Prefixed, Thoughts on the Devotional Taste, on Sects and on Establishments* (London, 1775), 23, quoted in Margaret Maison, "'Thine, Only Thine!' Women Hymn Writers in Britain, 1760–1835," in *Religion in the Lives of English Women, 1760–1930*, ed. Gail Malmgreen (Bloomington: Indiana Univ. Press, 1986), 49.

36. See her poem "On Wisdom," expressing her disappointment with the Calvinistic bias at Warrington Academy, which led the tutors there to prohibit the production of a play (McCarthy and Kraft, *Poems of Anna Letitia Barbauld*, 52–53).

37. Willey, *Eighteenth-Century Background*, 179.

38. Priestley, "Illustrations of Philosophical Necessity," in *Works*, 3:482.

39. Willey, *Eighteenth-Century Background*, 179.

40. McCarthy and Kraft, *Poems of Anna Letitia Barbauld*, 223.

41. Priestley, "A Discourse on Habitual Devotion," in *Works*, 15:105–6, quoted in McCarthy and Kraft, *Poems of Anna Letitia Barbauld*, 221.

42. Barbauld, "Hymn VI," in *Hymns in Prose for Children*, 4th ed. (London: J. Johnson, 1787), 20. See also "Hymn I" and "Hymn IV," for instance, in which each object that the child sees is connected to God.

43. Priestley, "Disquisitions Relating to Matter and Spirit," *Works*, 3:233.

44. Barbauld, "A Summer Evening's Meditation," 81, lines 37, 49.

45. William Enfield, *The Speaker: or, Miscellaneous Pieces, selected from*

the Best English Writers, and Disposed Under Proper Heads, with a View to Facilitate the Improvement of Youth in Reading and Speaking. To Which is Prefixed an Essay on Elocution (London: Joseph Johnson, 1774); Knox, *Elegant Extracts,* contains poems by women poets such as Barbauld, Carter, Williams, Smith, and Thrale, as well as by male poets who are canonical (Milton, Johnson, Collins, Cowper) and noncanonical (Otway, Rowe, Savage).

46. R.L. Edgeworth says in the preface to *Moral Tales for Young People* (1801), written jointly with Maria, "[T]hose [children] who have tasted with the keenest relish the beauties of Berquin, Day, and Barbauld, pursue of demonstration of Euclid, or a logical deduction, with as much eagerness, and with more rational curiosity, than is usually shown by students who are nourished with the hardest fare, and chained to unceasing labour" (R[obert] L[ovell] Edgeworth, preface to Maria Edgeworth, *Moral Tales for Young People*, 3 vols. [London: J. Johnson, 1801], 1.vii-viii, rpt. [New York: Garland Press, 1974]. Quoted in Ian Michael, *The Teaching of English: From the Sixteenth Century to 1870* [New York: Cambridge Univ. Press, 1987], 208). Michael claims that Enfield disagreed with the Edgeworths in seeing "instruction and enjoyment [as] separate tasks" (208).

47. Barbauld, *Hymns in Prose for Children,* 23d ed. (London, 1820), v-vi, quoted in Maison, "'Thine, Only Thine!'" 22.

48. Barbauld, "On Female Studies," in Perkins, *English Romantic Writers,* (1995), 41, cited hereafter in the text by page number.

49. Mary Wollstonecraft, *Mary, A Fiction* (1788), in Mary Wollstonecraft, *Mary and The Wrongs of Woman,* ed. Gary Kelly (New York: Oxford Univ. Press, 1976), 55.

50. I do not see Barbauld as primarily a feminist, but for another point of view, see William McCarthy, "'We Hoped the *Woman* Was Going to Appear': Repression, Desire, and Gender in Anna Letitia Barbauld's Early Poems," in *Romantic Women Writers: Voices and Countervoices,* ed. Paula R. Feldman and Theresa M. Kelley (Hanover, N.H.: Univ. Press of New England, 1995), 113–37.

51. Charles Lamb, "On the Tragedies of Shakespeare," in *The Romantics on Shakespeare,* ed. Jonathan Bate (New York: Penguin, 1992), 113.

52. On abjection as a process that accompanies the collapse of distinctions, as well as their erection, see chapter 2, pp. 52-53.

53. Lisa Vargo, "The Case of Anna Laetitia Barbauld's 'To Mr C[olerid]ge," *Charles Lamb Bulletin,* n.s., 102 (April 1998): 56. Lamb's essay "On the Tragedies of Shakespeare" first appeared in 1811, long after the incident over *John Woodvil.* But Coleridge was still calling Barbauld "Mistress Bare and Bald" in a notebook entry of 1810; Coleridge's own public attack, promised to Lamb via Southey in 1804, occurred in an 1812 lecture on Milton. I do not want to claim that this particular disconcerting textual ambiguity directly caused Lamb to attack Barbauld; I do want to claim that the anxieties about textual production revealed in this ambiguous passage invited male writers to launch misogynous

attacks and perhaps stimulated paranoia about being attacked by a woman writer.

54. This passage is discussed by Vargo, "Barbauld's 'To Mr C[olerid]ge,'" 59, and by Cox, "Coleridge and Barbauld," 34–36.

55. Cox, "Coleridge and Barbauld," 36.

56. John Guillory, "Literary Capital: Gray's 'Elegy,' Anna Laetitia Barbauld, and the Vernacular Canon," in *Early Modern Conceptions of Property*, ed. John Brewer and Susan Staves (New York: Routledge, 1995), 402, 403.

57. On the contents of teaching anthologies, see Michael, *Teaching of English* (see note 43 above).

58. Aikin died four years before Barbauld, and it was customary, as we can see from Hazlitt's canceled 1824 edition of *Select Poets*, to include only dead authors in the new medium, the anthology. But Aikin included no women in his collection, and he listed them all by last name alone; so whether he would have included his sister, despite his high regard for her work, is open to question. John Frost added two volumes to Aikin's collection, beginning in 1838; fifteen poems by Barbauld are included in the 1843 edition of the set, in volume 5, edited by Frost. That Barbauld occurs in this volume, along with Joanna Baillie, as a token woman writer rather than a canonical poet, is evinced by the biographical preface: "she is an amiable example to her sex that it is possible to combine, without danger to its morals or religious principles, a manly understanding with a feminine and susceptible heart" ([John Frost, comp.], *Select Works of the British Poets, in a Chronological Series from Falconer to Sir Walter Scott . . . Designed as a Continuation of Dr. Aikin's British Poets* [Philadelphia: A. Hart, 1850], 35).

59. Arthur Symons, *The Romantic Movement in English Poetry* (New York: E.P. Dutton and Co., 1909), 30.

60. Eleanor M. Sickels, *The Gloomy Egoist: Moods and Themes of Melancholy from Gray to Keats* (New York: Columbia Univ. Press, 1932); Laura Quinney, *Literary Power and the Criteria of Truth* (Gainesville: Univ. Press of Florida, 1995).

61. Terry Eagleton, *The Ideology of the Aesthetic* (Cambridge, Mass.: Basil Blackwell, 1990), 44.

Conclusion

1. Jonathan Swift, *Gulliver's Travels*, in *Gulliver's Travels and Other Writings*, ed. Louis A. Landa (Boston: Houghton Mifflin, 1960), 150–51.

Index

23; intellectual class and, 119–20; miscellanies and, 162 n. 26; misogyny and, 110; moralism and, 124; presentation of authors' names in, 122–23; valuation of literature and, 10. *See also* literature, canonical

antiblasons, 8; *Essay concerning Human Understanding* as, 91; *Gulliver's Travels* and, 91, 92; history of, 85; Mary Leapor and, 84–86, 87–88; misogyny and, 87, 88–89; objectivity and, 86–87; as progressivist literary history, 88–90

antihero, 52

antiquarian miscellanies, 121–22, 154

Argument against Abolishing Christianity, An (Swift), 33–34

Arianism, 134, 207n. 21

Arnold, Matthew, 109, 122

Baldwin, Frances, 39

Barbauld, Anna Letitia: abjection of, 151, 210n. 53; in Aikin's poetry collection, 211 n. 58; ambiguity and, 151–53; community and, 137–41; contemporary critics of, 129–30; dissent against Romantic aestheticism, 130–37, 151–53; exclusion from canonical literature, 11, 154–55; feminism and, 147–50; Joseph Priestley and, 131, 133, 153, 154; literary value and, 10–11; materialism and, 207 n. 10; opposition to melancholia, 134–37; transcendence and, 141–50; Unitarianism and, 207 n. 21; views of Christ, 208n. 27. Works: *An Address to the Deity,* 138–39, 142, 144, 145; *Answer to Wakefield,* 134–36, 137, 139; *Corsica,* 138, 139–40;

Eighteen Hundred and Eleven, 154; *Hymns for Children,* 129; *Hymns in Prose,* 145, 147; *Life,* 11, 154; *On a Lady's Writing,* 149; *On Female Education,* 148, 149; *On Female Studies,* 147; *Origin of Song-Writing, The,* 142, 143; *Pious Friendship,* 143; *Summer Evening's Meditation,* 144–45, 146, 151, 152–53; *To a Lady, with some painted Flowers,* 148, 149; *To Lord Byron,* 131; *To Mr. S.T. Coleridge,* 131, 136, 151–52; *To the Salt of the Earth,* 153; *To Wisdom,* 208 n. 23

bawdiness: satiric personae and, 21, 31

Beauties Periphrasis (Shipman), 24

Beautiful Young Nymph, A (Swift), 1

Bell, John, 111

Benedict, Barbara, 124, 162 n. 26

Berkeley, George, 136

Bhabha, Homi, 93, 98

Black Act, 75

blacking, 75–76, 79, 81, 183–84 n. 34, 184 n. 40

Blason du miroir (La Tour), 26

blasons: Barbauld and, 141–44; first collection of, 185 n. 4; male masochism and, 26; misogyny and idealization of women in, 22–24; mobility of identification in, 26; physiognomics and, 186 n. 17; sadomasochistic structure and, 21–22. *See also* antiblasons

Blasons anatomiques du corps féminin (Marot and Scève), 23, 85, 91, 185 n. 4

Bloom, Harold, 109

Blount, Martha, 107

body metaphor: anthologies and, 115–16, 119, 120; canonical literature and, 116–17, 120; miscellanies and, 114, 115–16,

121; rhyming dictionaries and, 112–13; sublime misquoting and, 117–19. *See also* female body

Bonnell, Thomas, 109

borderline personality, 161 n. 21

Boswell, James, 14

bourgeois: conceptions of personality, 164 n. 49; opposition to mobility of identification, 15–16; poetic miscellanies and, 114–15

bourgeois tragedy, 40, 81, 174 n. 14

British Anthology, The, 112

British Muse, The (Hayward), 112, 114

Brothers, The (Wordsworth), 130, 141

Brown, Ira, 134

Brown, Laura, 65, 159 n. 4, 172 n. 4

Brydges, Egerton, 117

bubbles. *See* joint-stock companies

Bushaway, Bob, 76

business: meanings of, 40, 173 n. 13. *See also* business relations; capitalism; mercantilism

businessmen: idealization of, misogyny and, 7–8; in *Modest Defence of Publick STEWS,* 69, 72, 73; in *The Orphan,* 40–41

businessmen poets: compared to canonical poets, 117, 118, 119–20; miscellanies and, 114–15; use of rhyming dictionaries and, 117, 118

business relations: consumer revolution and, 39–40; in feudal society, 38–39; figured as courtship and marriage, 42–43; in *The Orphan,* 40–41, 47–48; represented as rape, 38; as sadistic desire, 40; sadistic pleasure of dispossession and, 45, 48. *See also* capitalism

Butler, Judith, 12, 13, 17

Byron, Lord (George Gordon), 137, 138

Calvinism: Barbauld's opposition to, 134–35, 136–37; predestination and, 144

canon reform, 128

capital, cultural: canonical literature as, 122

capitalism: abjection and, 35; civic humanism and, 160 n. 12; development of, 39–40; dispossession and, 45, 48; engendering, 64–65; equality and labor in, 53; homophobia and, 47; idealization of, 80–81, 82; misogyny and, 3, 7–8; mobility of identification and, 15–16; noncanonical, propagandist literature and, 82–83; in *The Orphan,* sadomasochistic pleasure of, 47–48; power relations in, rape and, 37–38; reconceptions of literature and, 2–3; as sadistic desire, 40; scapegoating of female consumerism and, 66–67; structural crisis and, 53. *See also* business relations; consumerism; mercantilism

Carter, Elizabeth, 114, 200–201 n. 63

Cassinus and Peter: A Tragical Elegy (Swift), 25–26, 29, 30, 88

Castle, Terry, 76

castration, 26

Chalmers, Alexander, 111

character: aesthetic, 107; Pope on, 107; women writers and, 107, 108, 128

chastity, 69, 70, 182 n. 22

Chaucer, 109

Child Is Being Beaten, A (Freud), 14, 34

children: women writers and, 146–47

Christian ritual: scapegoating as, 7

civic humanism, 160n. 12

class consciousness, 164 n. 49;

anthologies and, 120; miscellanies and, 113–14

class mobility. *See* social mobility

class oppression: Swift on, 157–58

class struggle, 195 n. 31

clothing: development of consumerism and, 39–40; status and, 2; sumptuary laws and, 2

clothing imagery, 1

Coleman, Deirdre, 207 n. 21

Coleridge, Samuel, 129, 130, 134, 136, 138, 151, 152, 210 n. 53

Collection of Poems (Dodsley), 111, 113, 114, 116, 123

Collins, William, 114, 120, 201 n. 64

commodity: canonical literature as, 122; poetry as, 110, 111; raped women figured as, 41

community: Barbauld and, 132, 137–41; sacrificial crises and, 49–50, 58–59

competition: dispossession and, 45, 47–48; rape and, 44

Congreve, William, 77

consumables: noncanonical literature as, 122

consumerism, 178–79 n. 5; development of, 39–40; *Fable of the Bees* and, 65–67; as female desire, 65; as sadomasochistic desire, 40; scapegoating of women for, 66–67

containment, 189 n. 46

contaminated protest, 96–97

contre-blasons, 23, 167 n. 14. *See also* antiblasons

conversion narratives, 135

Cook, Richard, 68

Cooper, Elizabeth, 114, 121

copyrights, 192–93 n. 12

Corsica (Barbauld), 138, 139–40

coteries, 108, 192 n. 11

Country and the City, The (Williams), 94

country-house poems: parody of, 94–96

Country Husband, The (Sedgwick), 48

Country Wife, The (Wycherley), 74–75, 78–79

courtship: business relations figured as, 42–43

Cowley, Abraham, 119

Cropper, Elizabeth, 26

cross-dressing, 75–78, 165 n. 54

Crumble-Hall (Leapor), 94–96, 97

cultural artifacts: engendering, 11–12

cultural studies: canonical knowledge and, 128

curiosity, 121–22, 203 n. 97

Curran, Stuart, 141

D'Assigny, Fifield, 126

death: Barbauld on, 146; satire of empiricism and, 93

decay: satire of empiricism and, 92–93

Deleuze, Gilles, 46, 99

Deliciae Poeticae, 124

demystification: misogyny and, 100–106

desire to consume. *See* consumerism

Dialogue II (Pope), 29, 30

Dictionary of the English Language (Johnson), 125 fig. 4

Diderot, Denis, 75

differentiation, 176 n. 40; sacrificial crises and, 52–53

dirt: of society, 50–51

Discipline and Punish (Foucault), 96

Discourse concerning the Original and Progress of Satire (Dryden), 27–28

disidentification: abjection and, 5, 31; empiricism and, 93; in sacrificial crises, 52; in scapegoating, 50; in she-tragedy, 35, 36, 63, 64, 156

dismemberment: empiricism and, 91,
92; love poetry and, 23
dispossession: capitalism and, 45, 48;
rape and, 45, 48
Disquistions on Matter and Spirit
(Priestley), 145–46
dissenting aesthetic: Barbauld and,
130–33, 151–53
Dodsley's poetry collection, 111,
113, 114, 123; imitators of, 198–
99n. 49; melancholy poetry in,
200n. 62; purchasers of, 199 n.
52; William Collins in, 201 n. 64
Dollimore, Jonathan, 75
Donaldson, Alexander, 198–99 n. 49
Doody, Margaret, 22
doting, 44–45, 46
Douglas, Mary, 1, 48, 50, 51
dress. *See* clothing
drolleries, 199–200n. 59
Dryden, John, 21, 27–28, 123, 124
fig. 3
dualism, 145–46
Dunciad, The (Pope), 29, 90, 108
Dyce, Alexander, 111–12

Eagleton, Terry, 9, 155
Edgeworth, Richard, 147
ego, 5–6
Eighteen Hundred and Eleven
(Barbauld), 154
Elegant Extracts (Knox), 126, 141,
146, 154
Elegy in a Country Churchyard
(Gray), 116–17, 118–19
Elizabeth, Queen, 115, 121, 126
Ellis, George, 121, 122
empiricism: feminist literary history
and, 89–90; misogyny and, 93; in
parodies of upper-class poetry,
93–96; in progressive histories,
86; referential nature of language
and, 191n. 65; representational

epistemology and, 86–87; satire
and, 90–93. *See also* objectivity
Enfield, William, 146, 150–51
English theater: cross-dressing and,
76–78
Entretiens sur Le Fils naturel
(Diderot), 75
Epilogue to the Satires (Pope), 28
Epistle to a Lady (Pope), 107
equality: capitalism and, 53
*Essay concerning Human Under-
standing* (Locke), 86, 91
*Essay on Charity and Charity-
Schools* (Mandeville), 68
Essay on Criticism, An (Pope), 108
*Essay on the Application of Natural
History to Poetry* (Aikin), 133
Etherege, George, 23–24
excerpts: body metaphor and, 116, 119;
in rhyming dictionaries, 112–13
Exchange Alley, 54, 55
Exclusion Crisis, 53
excrement: in satire of empiricism,
90–91. *See also* scatological
imagery
extravagant shepherd, The (Sorel),
100, 101 fig. 2
Ezell, Margaret, 109, 195n. 29

Fable of the Bees (Mandeville), 64,
65–67, 102, 104–5
fantasy: in conceptualizations of
literariness, 12–13
female body: abjected by anthologies, 126–27; abjection and, 5;
Barbauld on, 149; biomedical
representations of, 75, 177–78 n.
65; inherent violence of love
poetry and, 23–24; Swift and,
159 n. 1, 187 n. 22. *See also*
misogyny
feminism: Barbauld and, 147–50;
contaminated protest and, 96–97;

in *Fable of the Bees,* 67; materialism and, 187 n. 26; in misogynous works engendering capitalism, 64; misogyny and, 18–19; in *Modest Defence of Publick STEWS,* 67, 74, 82–83; in noncanonical, propagandist literature, 82–83; partisanship and, 99–100, 106; on rape, 37–38; sadomasochistic reading economy and, 18; scapegoating and, 67; in she-tragedy, purpose of, 35; subjectivity and, 97, 98–99. *See also* feminist literary history

feminist anthologies, 195 n. 29

feminist literary history: antiblason tradition, 87; awareness of rhetorical strategies and, 89–90; empiricism and, 89–90; misogynous representation and, 87–88, 90; partisanship and, 99–100, 106. *See also* feminism; literary history

Filmer, Robert, 103

flame imagery: Barbauld and, 133, 143

flattery, 43, 44–45

footnotes, 123

Foucault, Michel, 96, 99

Francus, Marilyn, 165 n. 58

"Free Dissenters," 134

Freemantle, Bridget, 85

Freud, Sigmund, 34, 93, 122; misogyny and, 171 n. 55; repression and, 4, 5–6; sadomasochistic fantasy and, 14

frontispieces: of anthologies, 123, 124 fig. 3, 125 fig. 4

Frost, John, 211 n. 58

Frost at Midnight (Coleridge), 152

Fuseli, Henry, 126

Fuss, Diana, 13, 16

Gallagher, Catherine, 90, 96–97

gender ambiguity: Barbauld and, 151–53; cross-dressing and, 76–78, 165 n. 54; misogyny and, 17; scapegoating of, 81

gender distinction: abjection of women and, 5, 19–20, 151; canonical literature and, 108; cross-dressing and, 75; emergence of, 78; in *London Merchant,* 79–80, 81; misogyny of empiricism and, 93; sadistic reading economy and, 17; scapegoating and, 59–60

Gentleman's Magazine, 88, 89

Georgian Chronicle, The (Rodgers), 134

Gibbon, Edward, 57

Gift, The (Mauss), 46–47

gift economy: total self-expenditure and, 46–47

Gilbert, Sandra, 32

Girard, René, 6, 7, 41, 48, 49–50, 51–53, 66, 67, 180 n. 11

Glorious Revolution, 53

Goody Two Shoes (Newbery), 129

Gould, Robert, 94

Gray, Thomas, 113, 114, 116–17, 118–20, 201–2 n. 74

Great Britain: Exclusion Crisis and, 53; poetic history, exclusion of women from, 112; South Sea Bubble crisis and, 53–58

Greek satire: Dryden on, 27

Green, Matthew, 113, 114, 116, 117–18, 119

Greenblatt, Stephen, 128

Grossberg, Lawrence, 128

"grotesque body, the," 178 n. 1

Grumbling Hive, The (Mandeville), 179 n. 6

Gubar, Susan, 32

Guillory, John, 9, 27, 110, 116, 120, 154, 163 n. 37

Gulliver's Travels (Swift), 31, 90–93, 157–58

Habermas, Jürgen, 164 n. 49
Hall, Samuel, 127
Harleian Miscellany (Oldys), 121
Harley, Robert, 121
Hartley, David, 144
Hayward, Thomas, 112, 114, 116, 121
Hazlitt, William, 112, 122, 123, 126
Headley, Henry, 115, 116, 119, 123, 126
headnotes, 123
Hebrew Melodies (Byron), 137
hero(es): sacrificial crises and, 52; scapegoated victim as, 50
hierarchies: leveling of, Girard on, 180n. 11
"high literature." *See* literature, canonical
Hirschman, Albert, 2, 8, 65
historicism: positivist, 89. *See also* new historicism
histories of difference, 86, 98, 186 n. 8
History of the Royal Society (Sprat), 86–87
Hobsbawm, Eric J., 164 n. 49
homoeroticisim, 47
homophobia: capitalism and, 47; paternalism and, 176 n. 29
Horace, 27
horses: as sexual image, 31
Howard, Jean, 77, 98, 99
Hume, David, 136
Hymns for Children (Barbauld), 129
Hymns in Prose (Barbauld), 145, 147

idealization: of capitalism, 80–81, 82; dialectic with abjection, 3–5; parody and, 23; of women, misogyny and, 22–24
identification: abjection and, 5; empiricism and, 93; scapegoating ritual and, 41

identification, mobility of: abjection and, 19–20; Barbauld and, 151–53; capitalism's opposition to, 15–16; literariness and, 13, 14; in satire, 25–34
"Ideology, Sex, and Satire" (Marsden), 32–33
Il Penseroso (Milton), 130, 138
immorality: women writers and, 193 n. 14
indeterminacy: literariness and, 156
indifferentiation: capitalist social mobility and, 55; distinguished from indeterminacy, 82; in *The Orphan*, 58; sacrificial crises and, 52, 53, 58; in she-tragedy, 74; South Sea Bubble crisis and, 56
inferior poets. *See* poets, inferior
intellectual class, 120
Intellectuals and Power (Foucault and Deleuze), 99
ironic space, 105

Jacobus, Mary, 20
Jameson, Frederic, 97–98
Jane Shore (Rowe), 38, 59, 74
Jardine, Lisa, 39, 77
Johnson, Barbara, 22, 26
Johnson, Esther, 126
Johnson, Samuel, 109, 111, 119, 121, 123, 125 fig. 4
John Woodvil (Lamb), 151
joint-stock companies: South Sea Bubble crisis and, 54, 55–57
Jones, Ann Rosalind, 159n. 4, 165 n. 58
Jonson, Ben, 65
joy: Barbauld on, 139
Juvenal: Dryden on, 27, 28

Kaplan, Cora, 10
Kaul, Suvir, 118
Kermode, Frank, 109, 127
Kernan, Alvin, 29, 30, 33
Killigrew, Thomas, 77

Knapp, Steven, 163–64 n. 44
Knox, Vicessimus, 111, 141; *Elegant Extracts,* 126, 141, 146, 154
Kristeva, Julia, 4–6, 19
Kroeber, Karl, 808
kudos, 58

labor, 3, 160–61 n. 14; in capitalism, 53; portrayed in *Crumble-Hall,* 95
Ladies Miscellany, The, 27, 124, 125
Lady's Dressing Room, The (Swift), 90–91
Lamb, Charles, 129, 130, 133, 150–51, 153, 210–11 n. 53
Lancashire Witches, The (Shadwell), 32–33
Landau, Norma, 160 n. 12
language: as referential, 191 n. 65; rhetorical power and, Swift on, 157–58
Laqueur, Thomas, 75, 177 n. 65
La Tour, Béranger de, 26
Lavater, Johann Caspar, 186 n. 17
Leapor, Mary, 157; anthologies and, 127; antiblasons, 84–86, 87–88, 88–89; literary criticism and, 97, 105–6; literary value and, 10; misogyny and, 8; parodies of upper-class poetry, 93–96; on patriarchy, 103–6; popularity of, 184–85 n. 1, 196 n. 34. Works: *Crumble-Hall,* 94–96, 97; *Man the Monarch,* 103, 104, 105; *Mira's Picture,* 84–85, 87–89, 105; *Strephon to Celia,* 93–94; *The Visit,* 88
Le berger extravagant (Sorel), 100, 101 fig. 2
LeGates, Marlene, 22
Lele people, 51
Levinson, Marjorie, 89
Life (Barbauld), 11, 154
Life of Samuel Johnson, The (Boswell), 14

Lillo, George, 35, 63. *See also* London Merchant
Lintot, Bernard, 107
literariness: aesthetic value and, 12; capitalism's opposition to, 15–16; feminist aesthetics and, 10–11; indeterminacy and, 156; literary conceptualization of, 13; as literary value, 10; misogyny and, 157; mobility of identification and, 13, 14; objectification of literature and, 14–15; psychoanalytic conceptualization of, 12–13; role of misogyny in, 17; sadomasochistic reading economy and, 14, 16, 18; of satire, mobility of identification and, 25–34; valuation of women writers and, 10–12
literary criticism: confusing rhetoric and reality in, 97, 100; ironic space and, 105; misogyny and, 93–96; parody as, 93–96; partisanship and, 99–100, 106; power concepts and, 97–98; subjectivity and, 97, 98–99; unknowability of the Other and, 99
literary history: antiblasons as, 86, 88–90; British, exclusion of women from, 112; canonical literature and, 108–10; concept of, 169n. 33; exclusion of Barbauld from, 154–55; misogyny and, 90; naive view of subjectivity and, 98–99; objectivity and, 86; oppositional, 97, 105–6; partisanship and, 99–100, 106; positivist, 89; power concepts and, 97–98; representational epistemology and, 86–87; unknowability of the Other and, 99. *See also* feminist literary history
"literary interest," 163–64 n. 44
literary value, 10. *See also* literariness

literature: bourgeoisification of, 27; capitalism and, 2–3; as discipline, 163 n. 37, 168–69 n. 33; distinguished from propaganda, 82; interrelationship with misogyny, 157; objectification of, 14–15. *See also* literature, canonical

literature, canonical: abjection of women and, 8–9, 35; anthologies and, 108, 110, 119–20; body metaphor and, 116–17; emergence of, 107–8, 109–10; exclusion of women from, 8–9, 11, 108–9, 110, 154–55; literary value and, 10; quality of indeterminacy in, 82; reform and, 128; sadist reading economy and, 17; satire and, 31, 32; sexism and, 11. *See also* anthologies

Locke, John, 86, 103

London Merchant (Lillo), 63; abjection in, 74–75; emergent gender distinctions and, 78, 79–80, 81; engendering capitalist desire and, 64; idealization of capitalism in, 8; popularity of, 81–82; as propaganda, 82, 83; sadistic reading economy and, 16, 35–36, 156

Lonsdale, Roger, 116

Love for Love (Congreve), 77

love poetry: Barbauld and, 141–44; bourgeoisification of, 27; Leapor's parody of, 93–94; misogyny and idealization of women in, 22–24; mobility of identification in, 26; sadomasochistic structure and, 21–22. *See also* blasons

Lukács, George, 18

lyric poetry: male masochism and, 26

Mack, Maynard, 30, 31

Mackay, Charles, 53–55, 56–57

MacKinnon, Catherine, 37

Macpherson, C.B., 39

madness: Swift and, 33, 161 n. 21

Madwoman in the Attic (Gilbert and Gubar), 32

Maitland, William, 56

Mandeville, Bernard, 35, 63; on consumerism, 65–67; economics and, 179–80 n. 9; feminist statements and, 36; misogynous demystification and, 102, 104–5; typing of women, 71. Works: *Essay on Charity and Charity-Schools*, 68; *Fable of the Bees*, 64, 65–67, 102, 104–5; *The Grumbling Hive*, 179 n. 6; *Philopirio*, 181 n. 13. *See also* Modest Defence of Publick STEWS

Man the Monarch (Leapor), 103, 104, 105

market society. *See* business relations; capitalism

Marot, Clément, 23, 26, 184 n. 4

marriage: business relations figured as, 42; financial interest and sexual desire in, 71

marriage portions, 174 n. 18

Marsden, Jean, 32–33

Marx, Karl, 3, 45, 53

masking, 76, 183–84 n. 34

masochism: Barbauld and, 148–49; as total self-expenditure, 46–47

Mason, William, 113

masquerades, 76

materialism: Barbauld and, 141–50, 151–53, 20 n. 10; meaning of, 187 n. 26

Maus, Katherine, 75, 177 n. 65

Mauss, Marcel, 46–47

McKendrick, Neil, 3, 39

McKeon, Michael, 90, 102

melancholia: Barbauld and, 131, 132, 134–37, 139, 140, 141, 152; Romantic poets and, 131, 138

melancholy poetry, 114, 200 n. 62

Memoirs (Priestley), 133, 135
Memoirs of Extraordinary Popular
Delusions and the Madness of
Crowds (Mackay), 53–55, 56–57
Mennipean satire, 167 n. 16
mercantilism: London Merchant on,
79–81; Modest Defence of
Publick STEWS and, 68
Michael, Ian, 201 n. 63
middle class. See bourgeois
millenialism, 51
mimetic violence, 6; sacrificial crises
and, 49–50, 58; scapegoating
ritual and, 41
Mira's Picture (Leapor), 84–85, 87–
89, 105
misandry, 32
miscellanies, 27; abjection of women
and, 150; anthologies and, 110,
162n. 26; antiquarian, 121–22;
body metaphor and, 114, 115–16;
class consciousness and, 113–14;
drolleries, 199–200 n. 59; Hazlitt
on, 123; history of, 112–13;
middle class and, 114–15;
presentation of authors' names in,
122; prurient poetry and, 124,
125; women writers and, 8–9,
111–12, 154
Miscellanies (Dryden), 124
Miscellanies (Pope and Swift), 107
misogyny: abjection and, 5, 31;
anthologies and, 110; antiblasons
and, 88–89; canonical literature
and, 128; capitalism and, 3, 7–8;
consequences of, 18–19;
demystification and, 100–106;
empiricism and, 93; failure to
maintain literariness and, 63;
feminism and, 18–19; feminist
literary history and, 87–88; Freud
and, 171 n. 55; gender ambiguity
and, 17; idealization of men and,
7–8; interrelationship with

literature, 157; in Lamb's disem-
bodying of text, 151, 153;
literariness and, 17, 157; in love
poetry, idealization of women
and, 22–24; modern readings of,
18, 159n. 4; as "natural," 165 n.
58; new historicism and, 90;
objectivity and, 87; in parody as
critique, 93–96; patriarchy and,
100–106; political theory, 103–4;
religious ritual and, 7; representational epistemology and, 87;
sadistic reading economy and,
156; sadomasochistic reading
economy and, 31–32, 156; satire
and, 22, 25–27, 31–32; socioeconomic anxiety and, 1–2; Swift on,
157–58. See also abjection
misquoting, 117. See also plagiarism;
sublime misquoting
mob, 107, 108
mobility of identification. See
identification, mobility of
Modest Defence of Publick STEWS
(Mandeville), 63, 102; abjection
of women in, 73, 74; engendering
capitalist desire and, 64; feminist
arguments in, 67, 74, 82–83;
idealization of capitalism in, 8; as
noncanonical literature, 82–83; on
profiteering as sexual activity, 67–
73; purpose of feminism in, 36;
sadistic structure and, 35–36, 156
modesty: misogynous demystification
of, 102
money: sex figured as, 42
moralism: in anthologies, 124
Munns, Jessica, 174 n. 15
My Mistress' Eyes are Nothing like
the Sun (Shakespeare), 85, 191n.
65

narcissism, 4
national poetry, 116, 120, 123

nature: Barbauld on, 144–45
necessitarianism, 144
negative pregnant, 103–4, 105, 106
Newbery, John, 129
new historicism: awareness of
  rhetorical strategies and, 89–90;
  contaminated protest and, 96–97;
  empiricism and, 89–90; meaning
  of, 187 n. 26; misogyny and, 90;
  positivist and, 89
Nichols, John: *Select Collection of
  Poems, A,* 123, 124 fig. 3, 201 n.
  68
noncanonical literature, 9, 82–83
Norton Anthology, 154, 205 n. 121

objectivity: antiblasons and, 85; John
  Locke on, 86; misogynous
  demystification and, 100–105;
  misogyny and, 87; representational epistemology and, 86–87.
  See also empiricism
Observations (Hartley), 144
*Observations Concerning the
  Original Government* (Filmer),
  103–4
oeuvre: body metaphor and, 115,
  116; commodification of, 122;
  emergence of anthologies and,
  115, 120
Olaniyan, Tejumola, 82
Oldys, William, 112–13, 116, 121
On a Lady's Writing (Barbauld), 149
On Female Education (Barbauld),
  148, 149
On Female Studies (Barbauld), 147
oppositional history, 97, 105–6
oppression: Swift on, 157–58
Origin of Song-Writing, The (Barbauld), 142, 143
Orphan, The (Otway), 6; as bourgeois tragedy, 174 n. 14; capitalist
  business relations and, 40–41, 42–
  43, 45, 47–48; competition and,

44; exaggerated pathos and, 62–
63, 64; figuring of courtly love in,
42–43; figuring of sex in, 42;
flattery and, 43, 44; homoeroticism and, 175 n. 28;
indifferentiation in, 74; James II
and, 173 n. 14; meaning of
"business" in, 173 n. 13; as
noncanonical literature, 82, 83;
popularity of, 35; problem of
disidentification in, 35, 63, 64;
rape in, 37, 38, 43–44, 47–48;
sadistic pleasure of dispossession
in, 45, 48; sadomasochistic
pleasure and, 46–47, 48, 62–63;
scapegoating and, 41, 59–60, 62;
total self-expenditure and, 46–47;
woman's superiority and, 59
Otway, Thomas, 35, 63. *See also*
  Orphan, The
oxen: as sexual image, 31

pangolin ritual, 51
Parnassus Biceps, 200 n. 59
Parnassus Display'd, 124
parody: idealization and, 23; as
  literary critique, misogyny in, 93–
  96. *See also* satire
Parson's Wedding (Killigrew), 77
partisanship: in literary criticism, 99–
  100, 106
Passions and the Interests
  (Hirschman), 8
paternalism, 43, 44, 45–46; homophobia and, 176 n. 29; masochistic self-expenditure and, 46–47
Patriarcha (Filmer), 103
patriarchy: misogyny and, 100–106
Pearch, George, 114, 115–16, 123
penis, 72
Percy, Thomas, 121
Persius, 27
personality: bourgeois conception of,
  164 n. 49

Phillips, Adam, 138
Philopirio (Mandeville), 181 n. 13
Phyllis, or the Progress of Love (Swift), 189 n. 45
physiognomics, 186 n. 17
Piercy, Marge, 106
Pious Friendship (Barbauld), 143
plagiarism, 116, 201–2 n. 74
Playhouse, The (Gould), 94
Plumb, J.H., 3, 54, 56
Pocock, J.G.A., 2, 160 n. 12
Poems by Eminent Ladies (Colman and Thornton), 126–27
Poetical Library, 112
poetry: as commodity, 110, 111; national, 116, 120, 123; poet's identity and, 110. *See also* literature; literature, canonical; oeuvre
poetry collections. *See* anthologies; miscellanies
poets: commodification of, 122; disembodiment of, 110, 111, 127; idealization of, misogyny and, 7–8; immortalization of, 122–23; inferior, 122; melancholy poetry and, 114; separation of canonical and noncanonical, 116–20. *See also* businessmen poets; oeuvre; Romantics; women writers
political theory: misogyny and, 103–4
Pollak, Ellen, 22
pollution rituals, 50–51
Poovey, Mary, 22, 193 n. 14
Pope, Alexander: abjection and, 20; canonical reading (sadistic structure) of, 35; on character, 107; criticism of, 28–29; emergence of canonical literature and, 107–8; exaggeration of satiric personae, 29–30; Gray's use of, 118–19; moralistic model of satire and, 33; sadomasochistic structure

and, 34; scatological imagery, 29; sexual imagery, 28, 31. Works: *Dialogue II*, 29, 30; *The Dunciad*, 29, 90, 108; *Epilogue to the Satires*, 28; *Epistle to a Lady*, 107; *An Essay on Criticism*, 108; *Miscellanies*, 107; *The Rape of the Lock*, 118–19; *To Augustus*, 107, 108, 119
positivism, 89
potential space, 12–13
potlatch, 46–47
power: literary criticism and, 97–98
power relations: in capitalism, represented as rape, 37–38
Powers of Horror, The (Kristeva), 4
prayer: as public action, Barbauld on, 140
predestination, 144
pregnant negative, 105
Priestley, Joseph: Barbauld and, 131, 133, 153, 154; conversion narratives and, 135; dualism and, 145–46; materialism and, 207 n. 10; necessitarianism and, 144; religious views of, 133, 134, 144, 145–46; Unitarianism and, 134
"primary masochism," 26
primary narcissism, 4
primary repression, 4, 5–6
printing: emergence of canonical literature and, 109–10
profiteering: as sexual activity, 69–73
propaganda, 82, 83; noncanonical literature and, 9
property: development of capitalism and, 39
prostitution: in *Modest Defence of Publick STEWS*, 68–69, 70, 72–74
protest: contaminated, 96–97
psychoanalysts: discovery of desire and, 171 n. 55
psychoanalytic theory, 3–6

public worship: Barbauld and, 135–36, 137–38, 139
publishing: emergence of canonical literature and, 109–10
Purity and Danger (Douglas), 50–51

race: empiricism and, 93
rape: capitalist power relations and, 37–38, 40, 48; competition and, 44; feminism on, 37–38; in love poetry, 24; in *The Orphan*, 37, 38, 40, 43–44, 47–48; sadistic pleasure of dispossession and, 45, 48; scapegoating ritual and, 41. *See also* women, raped
Rape of the Lock, The (Pope), 118–19
rapists: sadistic pleasure of dispossession and, 48
Rawson, Claude, 31
realism: misogyny and, 96. *See also* empiricism
Reform Movement, 68–69
reform societies: satirization of, 68
Reik, Theodore, 46
religion: Barbauld and, 131, 132, 135–36, 137–38, 139, 141–50; Priestley's views of, 133, 134, 144, 145–46. *See also* Calvinism
religious ritual: scapegoating as, 7
Religues of Ancient English Poetry (Percy), 121
representational epistemology: feminist literary history and, 87–88; new historicism and, 89–90; rhetoric of empiricism and, 86–87
repression, 4, 5–6
Repression (Freud), 4
rhyming dictionaries, 112, 113, 116, 117, 118, 119
Rime of the Ancient Mariner (Coleridge), 129
Robinson, Henry Crabb, 129, 130
Rodgers, Betsy, 134
Rogers, Pat, 77, 78

Romantics: abjection of Barbauld, 151, 210 n. 53; Barbauld's dissent against, 130–33; melancholia and, 131, 138
Rose, Jacqueline, 87
Rose, Mary Beth, 164 n. 49
Ross, Marlon, 141
Ross, Trevor, 109
Rowe, Nicholas, 63; *Jane Shore,* 38, 59, 74

sacrificial crisis: dynamics of, 6, 49–53; in *The Orphan,* 59–60; resolution of, 58–59; self-murder and, 59–60; South Sea Bubble crisis as, 53–58
sadism: capitalist business relations and, 40; Freud and, 171 n. 55; pleasure in dispossession, 48
sadistic reading economy: canonical literature and, 17; in *London Merchant,* 16, 35–36, 156; misogyny and, 156
sadomasochistic desire: consumerism as, 40
sadomasochistic reading economy: abjection and, 19; concept of, 14; feminism and, 18; Freud and, 34; literariness and, 14, 16, 18; love poetry and, 21–24; misogyny and, 31–32, 156; *The Orphan* and, 46–47, 48, 62–63; satire and, 21–22, 31–32, 34, 156
Said, Edward, 33
Saint Gelais, Mellin de, 23, 185 n. 4
salvation: Barbauld and, 131
Salzman, Paul, 23
satire: abjection and, 20, 31, 34–35; association with surgery, 167 n. 16; canonizing of, 32; disidentification and abjection in, 31; misogyny and, 22, 25–27, 31–32; mobility of identification and, 25–34; modern reading of, 18;

women, raped: figured as commodity, 41; self-murder and, 59–60, 61 fig. 1, 62

women's labor: portrayed in *Crumble-Hall,* 95

Women's Labour (Collier), 85

women writers: antiquarian miscellanies and, 122; character and, 107, 108, 128; Dyce's anthology of, 111; exclusion from anthologies, 111–12, 126, 141, 154–55; exclusion from canonical literature, 8–9, 11, 108–9, 110, 154–55; as immoral, 193 n. 14; literary value and, 10–11; miscellanies and, 8–9, 111–12, 154; in the Norton anthology, 205 n. 121;

popularity of, 195–96 n. 34; as representing physical body, 126–27; teaching anthologies and, 146–47, 154

Wordsworth, William, 129, 130, 141, 154

Works of the English Poets, The, 119

worship: public *vs.* private, Barbauld on, 135–36, 137

Wycherley, William: *The Country Wife,* 74–75, 78–79

Yandell, Cathy, 26

Zall, P.M., 129

Zimbardo, Rose, 33